Husband,
SOCIOPATH

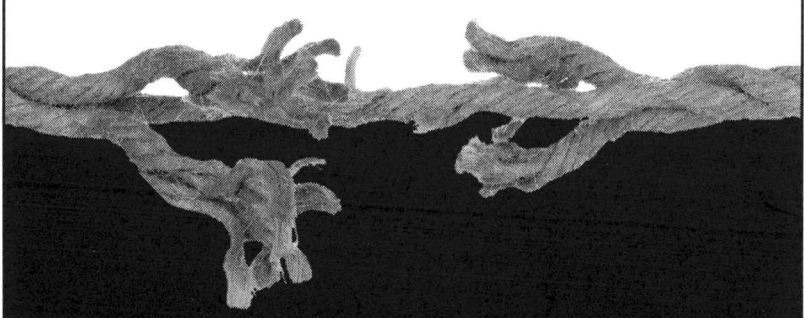

How He Lied, Why I Fell For It
& The Painful Lessons Learned

O.N. WARD

HUSBAND, LIAR, SOCIOPATH
How He Lied, Why I Fell For It & The Painful Lessons Learned
is a work of nonfiction. All names and many identifying details along with chronology have been changed. Any resemblance to persons living or dead is entirely unintentional and coincidental.

Copyright © 2015 by O.N.WARD All Rights Reserved

ISBN-13: 978-1508737681

ISBN-10: 1508737681

Acknowledgments

This book is dedicated to
my children, who gave me purpose,
my friends and family, who offered light in the darkness,
my therapist, who helped me understand the agenda
and legacy of abusive people, and
my faithful dog, who offered unconditional love and
the inspiration of a fierce, determined spirit.

Thanks to everyone who helped me bring this book to fruition:
my friends, who read and commented on the manuscript,
my family, who offered support,
my editors, for their helpful guidance, and
my designer, for working magic.

Author's Note

When I refer to sociopaths throughout this book, I typically use the pronoun "he." By doing this, I do not mean to dismiss the fact that many sociopaths are women and that these women inflict considerable damage on others. My sole reason for using the pronoun "he" is because this book is based on my personal experience with a male sociopath—my ex-husband.

"Sociopath" is not a medical term or an official diagnosis. Others refer to such individuals as psychopaths, suffering from narcissistic personality disorder or antisocial personality disorder.

If you would like to contact me to share your story or share how this book has impacted you, please email me at OnwardAftSociopath@gmail.com.

Husband, Liar, Sociopath

I'm free of him. At last. At last.
The future's mine. The past is past.

A vulture masked that preys on doves,
He baited me with care and love,

Then tried to steal my very soul.
He came so close; my life's the toll.

It seemed at first like hearts entwined,
A soul mate I was blessed to find.

But it was false, a trap, ensnared,
Just illusion that he cared.

In public, princely, caring, kind.
This grand performance kept me blind

To his assault of subtle lies,
Perceptions challenged, truths denied.

His velvet voice, so deftly used,
Allured, seduced, disarmed, confused.

He groomed me as possession, pawn,
And if I failed to yield or fawn,

Then I was clearly "selfish," "cold,"
"Controlling," "ingrate," often told.

He muddled and he numbed my mind.
To live depleted, I resigned.

Convinced I could do nothing right,
Upon his star, *I* was the blight,

An awful mom, ungrateful wife.
Potential squandered ... wasted life.

My strength was drained, I was mere dust,
So dim were faith and hope and trust.

Just lucky that he cared for me,
For I was "nothing." All could see.

"Wake up!" my faded embers cried.
It's ALL an orchestrated lie.

The truth? He's evil, void, and dark.
There's no compassion. Not a spark.

No conscience, just a puppeteer.
I called him husband ... twenty years.

Husband Liar Sociopath

Introduction

I am writing this book to protect you. Twenty years ago, I married my soul mate—a kind, charming, smart classmate from a top MBA program. But it was all a lie. He was a brilliantly camouflaged sociopath—a master manipulator disguised as caring, honest, and ethical so he could exploit with impunity. The experience of being deceived and nefariously influenced for almost two decades by this puppeteer was psychologically toxic, emotionally numbing, and financially devastating. Like a tsunami, the destructive force my husband unleashed upon me was life-altering and, very nearly, life-destroying.

SOCIOPATHS—THE TSUNAMIS OF OUR LIVES

Prior to the devastating 2004 Christmas tsunami in the Indian Ocean, few of us understood that the rapid retreat of water from the shoreline signals approaching disaster. Yet, this odd behavior of the ocean may be the only warning those in the most danger—those on the water's edge—get. If you understand this sign and run to higher ground, you will probably live to see the next dawn. If, however, you do not recognize this innocuous indicator for what it is and linger at the shoreline wondering, "Wow, how odd," your demise is all but guaranteed. Fortunately, as a result of the newscasts following that deadly 2004 disaster, more of us recognize this peculiar behavior of the sea for what it is—a harbinger of doom. No matter how beautiful the day, how blue the sky, how pristine the beach, or how much money you have invested in your vacation, the moment you observe the water receding suddenly from the beach, the only thing you should do is to run.

What's true of tsunamis is also true of sociopaths. Just as we are drawn to the sparkling ocean and soft sand under an azure sky, sociopaths pull us toward them with promises of love and fulfillment. They are accomplished actors, often masquerading as Prince Charming to our Cinderella, Romeo to our Juliet, Tony to our *West Side Story*'s Maria. So certain he loves you and offers a bright future together, you fall deeply in love with him, marry him, and have children with him. Over time, however, his manipulation is so masterful, and the control he gains is so profound, that, drop-by-drop, your soul, self-confidence, and strength are sapped. Then, even when you see a deadly wall of water racing toward you, you may be too depleted to run. Behavior that suggests your new romantic interest may be a sociopath is subtle but evident if you know what to look for. And if you fail to heed the signs, the consequences of your ignorance or inaction can be catastrophic.

Many helpful books, websites, articles, and checklists about sociopaths exist. I found these resources immensely helpful as I looked back on my situation. Yet, it took me almost twenty years to realize that the man I married was, and is, a sociopath. How could I have known to consider this possibility and correctly label what was happening to me sooner? How could I have known that my "Prince Charming" was a fake designed specifically to lure and exploit me? Understanding the following five facts would have made a huge difference:

1. Sociopaths are common and, therefore, present much more of a threat to everyday people than most of us realize.

2. These wolves in sheep's clothing are so good at what they do that they can fool *anyone*, even for a long period of time.

3. Signs that someone might be a sociopath are subtle at first and even for years.

4. Sociopaths have specific verbal and other tools that they use to manipulate and obfuscate. Most of us do not know what these tools are. We need to change that. This book will help.

5. Nonsociopaths have characteristics that enable sociopaths to deceive and manipulate us. By learning what these characteristics are, you can become more aware of occasions when your own humanity is being used against you and then take the steps necessary to protect yourself.

WHO ARE THESE "PEOPLE"?

As psychologists and sociopath experts Dr. Martha Stout, Dr. Robert Hare, and Dr. George Simon have documented in their must-read books *The Sociopath Next Door*[1], *Without Conscience: The Disturbing World of Psychopaths Among Us*[2], and *Character Disturbance: The Phenomenon of Our Age*,[3] sociopaths are skilled at faking it, even for long periods of time, and appearing as not just nice guys but great guys. Two carefully veiled characteristics, however, are the deep, hidden well from which the rest of a sociopath's behavior springs:

1. Sociopaths have no empathy. They simply do not feel any positive emotional connection with other human beings, not even their own children. Unable to care for other people, they care about only three things:

POWER – as a means to their second and third goals,
PREVAILING – the "rush" of winning and dominating,
PLEASURE – excitement, stimulation, sex, and so forth.

2. **Sociopaths have no conscience.** Obeying the law or being ethical or moral is of no consequence to sociopaths. They understand the concept of right and wrong as others apply it to their lives, but they lack an internal moral compass. They think the rules of society do not apply to them, but they don't hesitate to use those rules to exploit others.

These core characteristics are often invisible, because sociopaths are so good at hiding them and at making us think we do not see these qualities in them even when we do. Without empathy or a moral code, sociopaths are chronic liars.[4] Many are such skilled liars that we may not discover their lies or, more likely, their web of lies for a long time, if ever. Most of us think we know when someone is lying, but typically, we do not have a clue.[5] Think of Bernie Madoff, the investment manager who perpetrated the biggest Ponzi scheme in US history, bilking his clients out of billions. His deceit went undetected for years, even by his family. It is important to know not only that sociopaths lie but also to become aware of the specific ways they craft sentences to deceive and obfuscate and to take these and other subtle red flags seriously.

If you can be useful to a sociopath in attaining his goals (unwittingly, of course), you may have what seems like a fairytale relationship with him as a spouse, parent, mentor, business partner, and so on. In the context of a strong bond that you believe is based on mutual love, respect, and trust, you will automatically and unconsciously gloss over small suspicions. Indeed, the sociopath has ways of encouraging you to do this.

Although you may think there is a shared and lasting bond, once you are of no more use to the sociopath, he will discard you as quickly as turning off a light switch, leaving you heartbroken, betrayed, and confused. Even worse, he may transform you from friend to foe and wage a seemingly endless war against you. Why? Sociopaths value winning and prevailing over other people, not relating to and connecting with them, and the more you are diminished or destroyed, the bigger and more satisfying the sociopath's victory. For a sociopath, the best way to prevail is to weaken his victim emotionally, physically, professionally, financially, and in any other way he can. This manifests itself in as many ways as there are human relationships: divorces from hell, exploding business partnerships, parents turning on their children, and countless others.

With no empathy and no conscience, only profoundly negative consequences to the sociopath may limit his destructive and hurtful behavior. The consequences have to be almost certain and highly significant, because sociopaths do not have a strongly developed sense of fear.[6] Because sociopaths have inflated, grandiose opinions of themselves,[7] they underestimate the possibility of getting caught. In addition, sociopaths are confident that if they are caught, they can lie or charm their way out of any ramifications of their behavior—often by sweet-talking a decision-maker, continuing to claim their innocence and the rightness of their actions and views to the bitter end. Ironically, a sociopath's acumen at lying and manipulating is so great that his confidence in his ability to talk his way out of things is grounded in a successful track record of doing just that.

The boldness of their lies over both trivial and crucial matters, often built around a sliver of truth, is beyond what a normal person can imagine. A divorced sociopath I know promised to pay for his teenage daughter, Linda, to go on a trip with friends on a weekend for which he was legally and financially responsible for her. He gave Linda permission to go (verbally, not in writing) and a check to cover expenses, but in the memo section of the check he wrote "for child support." Due to the memo, Linda returned the check to her father, but he refused to give Linda a new check with a blank memo section. Linda's mom was willing to pay for the trip but could not. When she had paid for something similar in the past, her ex-husband took her to court for "custodial interference," using the check she had written for Linda's activity as documentation of how she had "interfered" with Linda's time with her father.

Soon after the trip, the father was heard raging, "I gave Linda money for the trip, but her mother wouldn't let her use it. Linda had to use her own money. What a bitch!" Of course, everything in the first two sentences is true, but the statement omits and spins critical information, leaving the listener with an understanding that is the opposite of what actually transpired. Even though the check was returned, the father reduced the child support by the amount of the check anyway.

With no internal moral code, concern for others, or fear of consequences, anything goes for sociopaths—lying, manipulating, cheating, stealing, threatening, stalking, physically harming, and many other forms of interpersonal violence—behavior from which most nonsociopaths would recoil.

Knowing that "winning" motivates the sociopath, you may think you can cut your losses and get on with your life. This may not work though, because the sociopath is unlikely to simply let you escape and may keep toying with you for his amusement, like a cat with an injured mouse. Your destruction is his satisfaction, so sometimes there is no obvious way out.

Since such behavior is anathema to the rest of us, sociopaths stay camouflaged most of the time. Perhaps only when they accumulate enough power that they can play by their own rules (which are often the opposite of those by which the rest of the world plays) does their true nature become apparent to *some* of us. Since their behavior often appears normal, even saint-like, around others, those of us who cry foul are often labeled as crazy, weak, resentful, paranoid, damaged, hurtful, vengeful, or vindictive. Why else would we accuse such a wonderful person of such heinous, totally out-of-character (to the point of being clearly impossible) behavior?

INTRODUCTION

Ironically, the fact that a person is charming, well educated, and successful may increase the odds of him being a sociopath. Charm is a characteristic of sociopaths.[8] Recent research suggests that CEOs are up to four times more likely than the general population to be sociopaths.[9] Why? Intelligent sociopaths tend to use their talents to become outwardly successful and reach positions of great influence, because sociopaths crave power, control, and winning. They will do whatever is necessary, even if it is unethical or illegal, to accomplish their goals.

Unfortunately, popular films, television programs, and books that identify sociopaths largely as serial killers have distracted us from understanding the destructive role sociopaths play in everyday people's everyday lives. It is unlikely that you or I will ever cross paths with a serial killer. Yet, we conduct our daily lives, making key personal decision after key personal decision, oblivious to the statistical reality that these predators walk among us. If like me, the sociopath who enters your life is brilliantly disguised as your soul mate, as they commonly are, the experience will end badly—very badly. If you become involved with a sociopath, the only questions are how long it will take for your personal tsunami to crash ashore and how devastating it will be to you and the people you love.

SOCIOPATH INVISIBILITY

As Yogi Berra famously said, "You can see a lot just by looking." Experts believe that up to four percent of the population in this country are sociopaths.[10] This is alarmingly high, especially given how destructive sociopaths can be. This statistic means it is more likely that you will encounter a sociopath today than you will encounter someone with naturally blond hair and blue eyes. Women need to be particularly aware of the signs that a romantic interest might be a sociopath, because studies indicate that men are considerably more likely than women to be sociopaths.

If sociopaths are so common and destructive, why don't we already know about them and how to spot them? One reason may be that, just like victims of other forms of intimate partner abuse (two groups that, not surprisingly, overlap considerably[11]), many of the people sociopaths target do not sound the alarm. Victims may feel ashamed and responsible for their lives being derailed. I certainly did. Victims of sociopaths may also be scared of the consequences they will face from the sociopath if they speak out. Remember, sociopaths do not play by the rules and shamelessly disregard laws, so their victims have good reason to be afraid. That's why I am still afraid of my ex-husband.

Adding insult to injury, if a victim finally works up the courage to tell someone what is going on, the sociopath's behavior may sound so bizarre and out of character that people refuse to believe it. Victims are afraid they may be discounted or blamed somehow, just as rape victims are often blamed for being assaulted. If I hear, "There are always two sides to every story," or "The victim was clearly too trusting and naïve," another time, I will scream. This is just plain wrong when it comes to dealing with sociopaths. If someone were secretly poisoning you, would you be responsible for being poisoned?

Lastly, victims of sociopaths are often so emotionally, psychologically, financially, professionally, and even physically battered that they need to focus almost exclusively on regaining their own, and often their children's, mental and physical health. The lives of women who become involved in long-term relationships with sociopaths are not just derailed for a short period of time; often, their futures are altered permanently. Becoming unwittingly entangled with a sociopath is so "crazy making" and toxic that more than 90% of women involved in extended relationships with sociopaths become depressed or anxious, 77% become ill due to stress, 65% experience post-traumatic stress disorder, 38% consider or attempt suicide, 27% lose their homes, 19% have lawsuits filed against them, 12% have criminal charges filed against them, and the list goes on. This makes it practically impossible for these women to just "get on with their lives."[12] I experienced all of the above, except for suicidal thoughts (at times, I felt like I wanted to die, but I never wanted to take my life) and criminal charges.

SUFFER THE CHILDREN

If having your life derailed does not scare you enough so that you become educated about the wolf in sheep's clothing to whom you might be married or engaged, then think about this: The flaw of having no capacity for empathy and no conscience is believed to have a genetic component and cannot be remedied with drugs, life experience, 12-step programs, or any other known therapy.[13] There is evidence that sociopaths are simply hardwired differently.[14] Does this different hardwiring mean we should excuse their behavior as being beyond their control? No—sociopaths are well aware of the damage and pain they inflict, as evidenced by the fact they are more than capable of conforming to societal norms when it suits them. So, although sociopaths may face an "empathy deficit," they are not slaves to their genes and are fully responsible for the choices they make.

Women who are nurturing, invest in relationships, and who are compassionate and empathetic (all wonderful qualities) are favorite targets of sociopathic men, especially for long-term relationships.[15] As a caring, altruistic woman who has children with someone masquerading as your soul mate, but who is really a sociopath, you are increasing the odds immeasurably that your children will be sociopaths. Even if they do not turn out to be sociopaths, if their father is a sociopath, his true but initially disguised nature may cause him to abandon his children. Other than the financial consequences, having the sociopath get out of your life and your children's lives is a gift.

INTRODUCTION

The worst, but all too common, scenario is that a sociopathic parent will use his children—your children—as pawns to hurt and control you by hurting and controlling them. This happened to me. The emotional pain of seeing my daughter, "Jessica," and my son, "Daniel,"[1] manipulated and hurt was almost unbearable. Jessica, who valued her father's sudden, new-found wealth, became a puppet to her puppet-master father and accepted expensive gifts, including a car, under the condition that she not see me.

My wealthy ex-husband tried to extract money from me in exchange for allowing our son to continue to participate in a sport he loved and in which he excelled. (When one parent controls every other weekend of a child's time and half of the child's vacations, it is easy to use the child as a pawn to blackmail the caring parent. Think about it: What team wants to take a player who can only attend half of the practices and games?) But this is trivial compared to what happened to one woman I know. Her sociopathic ex-husband got one of their teenage children to manufacture sexual abuse charges against her. Ultimately, she was cleared, but the resulting emotional and financial toll was immense. Stories like this abound.

Don't make the mistake of thinking the courts will come to your rescue either, because they are part of the problem. All too often, courts view shared custody as the gold standard and fail to understand how physically and psychologically harmful this can be to children who have a narcissistic or sociopathic parent. Tina Swithin chronicles the nightmare of battling a narcissistic ex-husband for custody of her children in *Divorcing a Narcissist: Advice from the Battlefield*[16] and *Divorcing a Narcissist: One Mom's Battle*[17]. Within a four-year span, her battle for the custody of her two daughters included more than thirty court dates, two full custody evaluations, twelve police reports, and three child welfare investigations. The fact that her ex-husband left her two-year-old daughter sleeping alone in a car for thirty to forty-five minutes and that he left both children unsupervised in a swimming pool (involving a near drowning) were dismissed after child welfare representatives gave him a pamphlet on pool safety and after her ex-husband assured them he would not leave their child alone in a car again. Although Tina is admirable in her love for her children and her unyielding efforts to protect them, do you really want to risk walking in her shoes?

FORWARD IN DISGUISE

Since ending what turned into a toxic marriage, suffering through a divorce from hell, and enduring severe post-divorce emotional, legal, and financial aftershocks, I have educated myself about sociopaths. Armed with this knowledge, it is clear to me now that my ex-husband and the father of my children is a sociopath. By sharing my story and painfully gained wis-

---

[1] Their names and other characteristics have been changed to protect their identity.

dom, I hope to help you identify some of the markers that indicate someone in your life might be a sociopath.

In addition, I hope to help you recognize and offset the qualities in you—as in all of us—that encourage you to give these all-too-commonly disguised predators a "pass," giving them access to your trust, your life, and your family until it is too late. Like knowing that a receding shoreline signals the destructive power of a tsunami, knowing the subtle signs that someone is a sociopath can save you and those you love.

This book is a memoir. I wrote it under a pseudonym and modified names, places, and specifics (even the examples in this introduction), but not the dynamics. I had to write my story this way out of concern for my children and fear for my safety. My ex-husband's anger is triggered when I do *anything* contrary to his desires, no matter how trivial. And because I no longer ask "How high?" when he demands that I jump, he is angry with me all the time.

Although most experts recommend that you have absolutely no contact with a sociopath, this option is not available to me. The laws of the state in which we were divorced require that we share legal custody of our minor child. Therefore, I cannot sever contact with him—yet. The law requires that he know where I live, how to contact me, and that I do my best to make joint decisions with him about our son. I am required to do this with a man who has broken into my house, tapped my phone, violated my privacy, threatened me, lied repeatedly to judges and lawyers, hidden marital assets, stolen my property, failed to split our remaining marital assets as specified in our mediation agreement, scarred our son emotionally, used what is in the best interest of our son to try to extort money from me, bribed and manipulated our daughter, engaged in chronic groundless litigation against me, all while maintaining the facade of a saint for his family, mother, and new wife. His mantra is "I'll do whatever I want!" I believe him. I believe he would even hire a hit man.

So, my name is not Onna, and my ex-husband's name is not Paul. I do not have a daughter named Jessica or a son named Daniel. I am not from Vermont, and I do not have an undergraduate degree from Harvard or an MBA from Yale. Yet, just as I do have more than one child and I do have multiple degrees from top colleges and universities, the essence of everything in this story is true—based on actual events, including conversations and bizarre behavior as best as I remember them or, later on, recorded in my journal. Twenty years after marrying Paul, I stumbled through a train-wrecked life, tried to salvage what I could, abandoned what I couldn't, and searched to understand what had happened and the best way to move beyond the trauma, depression, and ongoing emotional battering and legal

INTRODUCTION

and financial harassment in which Paul still engages for sport.

I had to write this book. I have to derive purpose from my pain. I have to share the knowledge that I paid such a high price to gain. I have to try to prevent as many people as possible from becoming me.

Husband Liar Sociopath

He Deserves Me

During my first few months in Yale's MBA program, I hardly noticed Paul. Although we shared many courses, he rarely participated in class discussions, and our friends and study groups did not overlap.

That changed in January when Paul and I were assigned to the same team in a school-wide simulated business competition. When I learned who else was in my group, I felt both lucky and cursed. My team comprised some of the smartest but also the most egotistical students in the program—a potentially noxious combination if it led to head butting instead of problem-solving. If we could not figure out how to work together, I was in for two days of frustration and disaster rather than intellectual challenge and success. Ironically, Paul was not one of the students who concerned me. Like me, he was one of the older students in the program. Other than that, I knew little about him.

Each business school team was put in charge of a hypothetical company. We started with the same resources, but forty-eight hours later, after making a series of interdependent business decisions, only one would emerge the winner—the one with the most profit. After all, this was business school.

My fears about my team materialized immediately. After two hours, we had no assigned responsibilities or overall strategy. We were deadlocked, and the clock was ticking. While others postured like competing peacocks and engaged in unproductive discussions, Paul sat quietly, reviewing the materials provided and the interactions among our teammates. Then, in a moment of exasperation, he stood up and took control.

I don't know how Paul did it, but it happened seamlessly, with everyone suddenly willing to take on the roles and responsibilities Paul suggested. We worked hard, long hours, laughed a lot, and ate way too much junk food. Other than returning home to grab a few hours' sleep, the team spent most of the forty-eight hours together. With the clock down to zero, and with Paul still at the helm, we emerged victorious.

Over that weekend, I came to see Paul in a whole new light. In fact, I was smitten. When we were not crunching numbers or reviewing the moves our competition had made and how our pseudo company should respond, Paul and I opened up to each other. I told him that I was from Burlington, Vermont, where my dad was a professor of education at the university and my mom was a high school librarian. I had one brother, and my small family

Husband Liar Sociopath   1

CHAPTER 1

was athletic, shared a love of the outdoors, and was intellectually vibrant and emotionally close. I had considered an academic career in psychology, my undergraduate major, but I loved the immediacy and challenge of the business world. Prior to returning to school to get an MBA, I had worked in the nonprofit sector and then, for about five years, in a small regional advertising company. It was more important for me to believe in what I was doing and to work with people I respected and enjoyed than to become wealthy. I still played squash, a sport in which I had competed nationally in my youth and as the top player at Harvard as an undergraduate. Hiking and cross-country skiing were other passions of mine. The outdoors, especially in winter, filled me with a sense of magic and wonder.

Paul seemed so modest that, at first, it was hard to get a lot out of him. Yet, after I opened up about myself, it seemed to break the ice, and he started telling me about himself. Paul joked about being picked last for teams throughout grade school and middle school and not even attempting to participate in organized sports in high school or college. As a late bloomer, he was now making up for lost time. Paul was an avid downhill skier and loved to work out and hike. He also enjoyed the outdoors, especially in winter. Like me, he said he was pursuing an MBA not because he wanted to pave a road to considerable financial and material wealth but because he valued having a challenging, rewarding career. Being intellectually alive was paramount to him. As Paul told me about himself, I felt an immediate connection. We were so much alike.

That weekend, Paul mentioned that he wanted to work hard for about ten years and then retire to a university town where he could teach and have an outdoors-oriented life, similar to the lifestyle I had known growing up and that my parents still enjoyed. From spending time skiing in Vermont, he adored the place and could see himself retiring there or to a similar location with mountains and snow. Paul also said he had volunteered with underprivileged kids prior to business school and could not wait to have more free time to do so again. I admired Paul for his leadership and for being helpful to others as well as for being unruffled in a high-powered academic environment that most people, including me, found taxing.

Like me, Paul had also been married before and had decided to go to business school as a fresh start after his divorce. His short marriage to Jenny, a fellow undergraduate at Stanford, ended when he discovered she was cheating. Paul was crushed. Trust and honesty were paramount to Paul, so he could not live with a wife who lied. He had made no attempt to mend the relationship.

Paul seemed shaken as he talked about Jenny's betrayal—his eyes glassy, his words deliberate, and his voice tight. Sometimes he stopped to regain his composure so he could continue his story of deep love and devastating heartbreak. I warmed to Paul. How could such a nice person be so mistreated by the woman he loved? Paul deserved so much better—he deserved me.

Pay No Attention To The Man Behind The Curtain

This probably sounds like the beginning of a love story, a second chance for two people moving on after unsuccessful first marriages. That is how I viewed it at the time, but I was wrong. I would not figure it out for twenty years, but the man to whom I was so attracted was, and is, a sociopath. Already, he was using techniques predators have used throughout time to get their victims to trust and fall in love with them, paving the way for future erosion and exploitation.

Although anyone can become the target of a sociopath, those of us who are empathetic, kind, and trusting are especially good targets, because we are less likely to understand that evil people exist aside from malevolent historical figures and violent criminals. In a sea of competitive MBA students, I was the one always wanting to help and to play nice. I tutored struggling classmates for free and ran study sessions in my areas of expertise—marketing and advertising. If someone was bullied by another student, I offered a shoulder to cry on and a sympathetic ear. Everyone knew I was happy to lend others my notes. To a well-camouflaged sociopath like Paul, it must have been as if I was screaming, "Pick me!"

In his bestseller, *The Gift of Fear and Other Survival Signals that Protect Us From Violence,*[18] fear, danger, and risk expert Gavin de Becker describes how "forced teaming" creates vulnerability, because it manufactures the view that "we're in this together." Forced teaming (acting as if two or more people are part of a team, when, in fact, they are not) produces the illusion of common goals where none really exist, weakens interpersonal barriers, and facilitates unwarranted trust. Conmen and others who would do harm use forced teaming to get potential victims to lower their defenses. If forced teaming is effective, any self-respecting sociopath knows how to take advantage of an actual team that requires shared time, experiences, and objectives, such as the simulated business team to which Paul and I were assigned. Is it any surprise that groups such as AA report that some individuals join their organization simply to prey on vulnerable members?

Once the opportunity arises, Paul and fellow sociopaths are skilled at fabricating personal qualities and details of their past and present as well as aspirations for their future to lure potential victims by pretending to be "just like them." Hence, as I did, those targeted by sociopaths often feel an immediate and strong attraction to the sociopath and believe they have found their soul mate.[19] Be warned: A sense of instant compatibility and attraction may be a sign you have met your soul mate, but it may also be a sign you are being targeted by a sociopath. Damn those romantic novels and movies that make us believe an immediate spark heralds true love! Maybe it does, but maybe it is a harbinger of something far more nefarious.

The more a sociopath already knows about you (and he will gather information for this purpose, whether from you, your friends, your family, the Internet, or anywhere else he can find it), the better a sociopath can craft a personality, history, and personal goals tailored to entrap you. Before I knew who Paul really was, he used the information I had divulged so willingly and trustfully to morph into my perfect boyfriend— altruistic, athletic, grounded, and intellectually vibrant.

The best lies take root from seeds of truth. Paul had been married briefly to Jenny, and his description of his marriage and divorce were heartbreaking. Eliciting sympathy and pity is another common tactic sociopaths use to ensnare their victims—a horrible ex-spouse or ex-partner (a favorite ploy), a profound betrayal, a painful childhood, a boss who never appreciated him, or other personal hurts (e.g., always being picked last for teams in grade school). They do this because, if you feel sorry for a person and if you feel he has revealed something personal to you, you are more likely to connect with him emotionally, reveal your own personal hurts and sensitivities (which can be used to exploit and manipulate you later on), and do things for that person that you would not do if your feelings were not as strong.

According to Dr. Martha Stout, author of *The Sociopath Next Door*,[20] pity is a key weapon in the sociopath's arsenal, one that is particularly effective on compassionate people who have great empathy for others. If the storyteller is a sociopath, the sad tale being spun is laced with purposeful emphases and embellishments to get you to lower your guard, to offer information that can be used against you, and to develop a strong affinity for the sociopath. Sociopaths use this tactic because it works.

While Paul's story about Jenny's betrayal brought me close to tears, the real story was, and is, truly heartbreaking—for Jenny, that is. Two decades later, while purging old files in preparation to downsize after my divorce from Paul, I stumbled across a file on Paul's divorce from Jenny. That, combined with the family lore about this relationship, put their marriage into an entirely different light.

When Jenny was just eighteen years old and a freshman at Stanford University, she fell so head over heels in love with Paul (then a senior) that they got engaged. She left Stanford to follow Paul to his first job in Connecticut. Her grandfather, who was funding her Stanford education, disapproved of Jenny getting married so young and refused to continue paying for college

CHAPTER 2

if Jenny left Stanford to marry Paul. *Poof!* There went Jenny's funding from her grandfather. *Poof!* There went her Stanford education! Before starting her sophomore year in a nearby, convenient university, nineteen-year-old Jenny married Paul. Both she and Paul signed for the sizeable loans she needed now to complete her education.

To pave the way for success, Paul logged long hours at work and traveled extensively for "business" (or so the story went), and so he was rarely home. Jenny had sacrificed everything for Paul but was getting almost nothing positive back, not even her new husband's company. Now, away from her family and married, while most students her age were single, she was isolated and alone. It must have been emotionally devastating. Not that I am justifying her *alleged* affair, but I can understand how a young, vulnerable, lonely teenager, separated from family and friends, would turn to another human being for the warmth and companionship she expected but was not getting from her husband. When Paul discovered her alleged affair, they separated.

In Connecticut, far away from her family, who were on the west coast, Jenny was alone—a college student with no money to hire a lawyer. In many states, it is customary to split all of the marital debt and assets between both parties. Jenny's student loans were acquired as Paul's wife, so it was their debt, not hers alone. Yet, the documents I discovered showed that Jenny agreed to be solely responsible for *all* of her student debt. That was her repayment for giving up her Stanford education and family funding!

Paul walked away from the marriage with their fancy sports car (that he alone would be able to afford after the divorce), their dog, no student debt, and the beginning of a fruitful career that he would leverage into a successful application to Yale's MBA program. Jenny left the divorce a financial and emotional wreck. I'm not sure the real story warrants a lot of sympathy for Paul. In fact, it is even possible that Paul is the one who had the affair and that Jenny left him. I know now that Paul is an adulterer and a chronic liar who accuses others of his own unsavory behavior. Either way, Paul emerged unscathed with a story of heartbreak he could leverage into attracting his next target—me.

Sociopath Math

I can almost hear the collective cacophony. "Onna! That can't be the whole story. There has to be something more to it. There are always two sides."

In an attempt to be fair and to give everyone involved the benefit of the doubt, we tend to discount and dismiss malicious, destructive behavior. Sociopaths count on this. Contrary to the popular saying, there are *not* always two valid sides to any story (and it would not surprise me if it was a sociopath who first planted this idea in our collective unconscious). Are there two sides to the story of Bernie Madoff's multi-billion dollar Ponzi scheme? Does the heart-breaking story of Laci Peterson and her unborn son's 2002 Christmas-time murder at the hands of her philandering husband Scott have two sides? What about the conviction of ex-policeman Drew Peterson for murdering his third wife—are there two sides to that story? (His fourth wife has been missing since 2007.) It is critical to realize that there does not have to be more to the story of Paul and Jenny—not if Paul is a sociopath.

Since *we* have empathy and a conscience, it is almost impossible for us to imagine that there are people, like Paul, who are devoid of both. Yet, there are—lots of them. To help silence those voices in your head that want to give Paul a legitimate side to the story, I would like to give you a crash course in what I call *sociopath math*.

Although simplistic, I'm guessing we make tradeoffs and choices when we balance our needs against the needs of others by some implicit mental math: We compare the importance of a person to us and the importance of their needs to the importance of our needs. As a result, sometimes we will compromise our needs in favor of someone else's, and at other times we will allow our needs to trump those of another person. But a sociopath does not and cannot care about other people, so the importance of any other person to the sociopath is always *zero* (unless the sociopath is valuing the other person as part of a long-term manipulation). Let that simmer in your mind for a moment. Since a sociopath always values every other person at zero, the sociopath's need, no matter how small, *always* trumps the other person's need, no matter how big. It does not matter if that other person is the sociopath's child, parent, spouse, sibling, or a total stranger. Of course, a sociopath does not act like this at first, because his initial priority is to lure you into developing a relationship—one that can be leveraged for his gain.

CHAPTER 3

For Paul, his need for a wife to be a built-in maid, cook, errand runner, dog watcher, and source of sex trumped Jenny's need to lay a solid educational and financial foundation for her future. As a sociopath, Paul never gave her needs or her future a second thought. It was always only about how Paul could use Jenny to serve his needs. End of story. There are no two-sides to this story, no footnotes needed. No happy ending possible for Jenny, me, Paul's new wife, or any of his future targets.

Speaking of footnotes, the sports car Paul took from his first marriage is likely also a manifestation of sociopath math. I am not suggesting that the purchase of a hot sports car is a sign that someone might be a sociopath. However, for Paul to have purchased a sports car at that point in his life suggests warped priorities, the kind associated with a selfish, stimulation-seeking, status-hungry sociopath. Why on earth would a man with no savings, an entry-level job, and a wife in college with prohibitive student loans choose an expensive sports car as the family car? Wouldn't the money saved on a more practical car have been better spent on the education of the woman he "loved," who gave up her free Stanford education and relocated across the country to be his wife?

It would have been helpful if I had investigated and determined the truth about Paul and Jenny's relationship earlier, because it contained multiple early warning signs. Why did Paul get Jenny to marry so young? Why did he get her to give up so much (a free Stanford education) to become his wife? If they were destined to be together, why not wait to get married after Jenny graduated? Why did Paul not make any tradeoffs so he and Jenny could be together? Who really suffered disproportionately by their short marriage?

Unfortunately, what I did not have was the knowledge that *every* woman needs to be vigilant for signs the man with whom she is falling in love might be a sociopath. Paul exhibited many signs that only now do I realize are relevant: a sense of instant compatibility; someone clearly interested in being in charge or being in control; a life-story that elicited "pity"; emotional isolation of a partner even, ostensibly, for valid reasons (i.e., Jenny's emotional isolation as Paul's wife); short relationships; lack of fear or strain in situations most others find stressful (e.g., a rigorous graduate program that did not faze Paul); and selfish behavior (the sports car, getting Jenny to give up her Stanford education). A dangerous constellation was already starting to form, but I didn't know about sociopaths. The water was receding from the beach, but I certainly did not know the warning signs. It never occurred to me that a feeling of instant compatibility with an attractive, smart fellow Yale MBA candidate who was comfortable taking the lead and who seemed calm when others were stressed could be warning signs of anything dark and malevolent. It seemed more like a dream come true.

Love At First Sight Is Possible …
Just Be Sure You're Seeing Clearly

Paul was romantic, caring, and attentive. He took me to plays, cooked dinner with me, and shared hikes and long walks. When our relationship evolved to physical intimacy, he was an amorous but gentle lover. I felt so lucky to have found him.

By the time we started dating, Paul already had a contract to live in a graduate dorm during his second year in business school. There, he would have one small bedroom with a desk, share a bathroom with others on his hall, and everyone in his building would share a common room with one TV. In contrast, I had rented a small, comfortable, conveniently located apartment. He moved in.

I did not charge him rent. I convinced myself he could not get out of his rooming contract, and I had planned to pay the full rent myself anyway. He had sold his sports car to raise money for business school, so I gave him full access to my car. Perhaps giving more than I was getting financially was my way of proving what a nice, gracious, empathetic person I was and what a great wife and mother I would be.

Time passed quickly. My days with Paul were filled with shared classes, shared studying, shared dinners, shared trips to the gym, proofing each other's resumes and cover letters, and helping each other prepare for job interviews. I admired Paul for his relaxed approach to business school compared to my more intense, stressed-out approach. I also respected his intelligence, ability to make quick decisions, and his natural, easy leadership style. He balanced me. I loved him, and I was sure he loved me. He told me so often.

We got away on a weekend to visit his family and then on another weekend for Paul to meet my parents and brother. Paul was reserved and tired when he met my family. He attributed his lethargy to exhaustion due to the grueling business school schedule. Later, Paul told me that he sought solitude because he did not enjoy my intellectual brother who kept trying to engage Paul in conversations about topics Paul cared little about.

Paul's mother and father had divorced during Paul's high school years. His alcoholic father had fallen on difficult times and not contributed financially to Paul and his two siblings, forcing Paul's mother, Ruth, to resurrect her career as a paralegal to support the family. Ultimately, she married a successful lawyer. Although her second husband died only a few years after they were married, he had provided for Ruth in his will. While still having to work part-time, she was able to lead a comfortable life. By the time Paul started his MBA, his father was a recovered alcoholic and working again. He was invited to all family functions and was clearly making an effort to reconnect with his children. Although it was a family with their share of missteps, they appeared to have rebounded from personal strife and to enjoy each other's company. I particularly admired Ruth's strength, clear devotion to her children, and her forgiving spirit, which had allowed her to welcome her ex-husband back into family gatherings. She was also kind to me, in a matter-of-fact way.

While everything, or almost everything, seemed right between Paul and me, in retrospect some events seemed odd. Not, "Oh my God, he's a psychopathic killer, run for the hills!" kind of odd, but enough that they left an impression. It is only now, two decades later, that I finally understand them. They were the red flags people tell you about, so easy to see in life's rearview mirror but so difficult to read as you are speeding down the heady "freeway of love"—in a convertible with the top down, going twenty miles per hour over the speed limit and, unbeknownst to you, with a charming sociopath at the wheel. For me to notice them at the time, the flags would have had to be much bigger, and maybe even fluorescent. Having a friend jumping up and down screaming and pointing to them might have helped, too. (No such luck.) But, newly in love and, like most people, blissfully uneducated about the behavior of sociopaths, I did not see then what is so clear to me now.

Odd red-flag moments, such as pressuring me to stay up with him on New Year's Eve even though I was sick, not helping me with my coursework even when he had nothing else meaningful to do, and offering minimal help with the subsequent insurance and repair logistics after he got into an accident with my car, all had one thing in common—they were situations or moments in which Paul's and my goals conflicted, sometimes over the smallest things. They all started with pieces of a puzzle that I was sure would fit together but which, no matter which way I turned them, refused to cooperate. Even though my conscious mind brushed them off as inconsequential, some part of me was alerted to these "moments of weirdness," as I came to call them, and they lodged in my memory, awaiting resolution.

Make Your Own Damn Sandwich!

I did not extrapolate or act upon these seemingly small moments of dissonance, but I had a friend who did exactly that in one of her relationships. Her decision to trust her instincts and to generalize from one small selfish act to what married life with her fiancé would be like may have saved her from a disastrous marriage, perhaps to a sociopath, and the resulting emotional and financial carnage. Carol called off her marriage to "Mr. Right" because of a sandwich.

Carol was getting her PhD in psychology at Yale when I met her at the squash courts. We became squash partners and fast friends. Carol was smart, motivated, kind, outgoing, upbeat, and gorgeous. She was so gorgeous, in fact, that one day when we finished playing squash, we walked off the court and saw a man staring at us—actually, at Carol. Carol asked him why he was looking at her, and he replied that he had to find out if she was really as beautiful as his friend said she was.

"Well?" Carol asked in her strong, sexy, confident southern accent.

"You are," the stranger replied, and then turned and left.

Carol was clearly a "catch," and she had come very close to marrying handsome, rich, well-connected "Mr. Right"—the son of a congressman from an established, wealthy Texas family.

One day, before she came to Yale, Carol was not feeling well and was lying on the couch, amidst sniffles, cough drops, and tissues. Her fiancé chose that moment to ask her to make him a sandwich.

"If someone's going to expect me to make him a sandwich when I'm the one who's sick, and he just wants to be waited on, well, that's that," Carol told me. In that moment, she knew she was going to end the engagement, and she did.

I remember being shocked by the story. Ending an engagement over who was going to make a sandwich? Maybe *he* wasn't feeling well. Maybe he didn't realize how sick she was. Maybe he just forgot she was sick. Maybe. Maybe. Maybe. But maybe not. Maybe Carol was right. Maybe there was no excuse for her fiancé asking her to make him a sandwich when she was the one who was ill. None! It was a red flag, signaling inherent selfishness, entitlement, and perhaps a lack of empathy. It was a sociopath math moment—a rare gift, a deal breaker. Despite the lost money and dashed

CHAPTER 5

egos resulting from bringing plans for a big Texas wedding to a screeching halt, Carol ended their engagement, and she had no regrets.

At the time Carol told me the story, I was so thoroughly committed to making excuses for this kind of selfish behavior that I was sympathetic to her fiancé's point of view. I thought that perhaps she was a bit narcissistic and selfish or didn't have the big picture in mind. There are two sides to every story, right? Wrong. Carol was right; I was naïve. Carol was wise. She went on to marry someone else, because she knew that even who makes a sandwich is important. I went on to have a horrible, twenty-year marriage to a sociopath that almost destroyed me.

With Paul, I brushed off the "Could you make me a sandwich?" moments, excused them away, and then forged ahead. In fact, I even patted myself on the back for being understanding, flexible, and giving Paul the benefit of the doubt—things my family had always encouraged me to do for people when I was growing up.

Paul and I got the flu over the Christmas break. He got it first, so he was starting to feel better by the time New Year's Eve rolled around. I was still exhausted, so we decided to stay in and have a quiet evening, punctuating the New Year with a champagne toast. Even when I am feeling well, I am not a night owl, so by 10:30, I was fighting sleep and losing badly. I knew I could not stay awake until midnight. I was sure Paul would understand.

"I can't believe it," Paul said, making no attempt to camouflage his cutting tone. Then, shifting to his velvety voice, which distracted me from the content of his words, he continued, "Who can't stay up 'til midnight on New Year's? I love New Year's Eve. It's soooo romantic. Why don't you just make some coffee? I *really* want to ring in the New Year together."

"Paul," I said, "I'm so tired."

"Onna," Paul replied in a caring, gentle tone, eyes in full "puppy dog" mode, "a few weeks ago, Brian invited us to a New Year's party. I know I told you. Anyway, I told him the other day we couldn't come, because you might still be sick. If you really were too sick to stay up, it would've been nice for you to let me know. At least I could've gone to Brian's."

I have a very good memory for concepts (like being invited to a party), although not for details (like the address of the party), and I had no memory of Paul telling me that we were invited to Brian's party, much less that he might want to go. Brian and Paul were hardly close friends. It seemed odd, but I assumed Paul's story was correct. Why wouldn't it be? Perhaps I had not committed the invitation to memory or could not recall it in my foggy state.

In all likelihood, Paul's story about Brian's party was not true. More likely, the story contained a kernel of truth—that Paul had heard Brian was having a party—but that we had not been invited or that Paul had not wanted to go. What was true was that Paul had just "gaslighted" me.

CHAPTER 5

Named after the Oscar-winning 1944 film *Gaslight*, about a sociopath's nearly successful attempt to drive his young wife mad in order to gain control of her estate, gaslighting is a technique used to cause the target to question her memories, her perceptions, and her grip on reality. As a result, the gaslighted person loses self-confidence, feels vulnerable, and even feels guilty about doing things she never did. This guilt puts the victim in the gaslighter's "debt." If gaslighted consistently over time, the victim's confidence wanes, and she relinquishes increasing control over her life as she relies more and more on her trusted partner—the sociopath who is purposely manipulating and eroding her sense of self. It is brilliant, because it works. If you have never watched the movie *Gaslight*, now would be a perfect time to do so.

Caught off-guard and exhausted, at first I did not know what to think about Paul's apparent selfishness. But my need to be nice, to eliminate conflict, and to understand the other person's point of view (all wonderful qualities when dealing with normal people but profound vulnerabilities when dealing with a sociopath) told me exactly what to do—make excuses for Paul. Maybe he was looking forward to sharing our first New Year's Eve together so much that he was just disappointed. Maybe he did not realize how tired I actually was. Maybe he loved me so much that he could not imagine celebrating New Year's Eve without me. Maybe. Maybe. Maybe. Feeling guilty (as he must have intended), I made coffee, struggled to stay awake, and shared a New Year's champagne toast with Paul before collapsing into bed.

In actuality, this was something else altogether: a red flag, although a subtle one. Paul's behavior reflected a complete lack of empathy for me. Even though I was physically and emotionally spent, Paul demanded that I prop myself up with caffeine so as not to disappoint him. He didn't even offer to make the coffee! Someone who really cared about me would have been sympathetic to how I felt and maybe offered to make me a cup of chamomile tea and tuck me in with a gentle kiss on my forehead. Paul did exactly the opposite. Paul's trivial need to have me with him as the clock struck twelve on New Year's Eve trumped my health and fatigue. Sociopath math—remember.

Love Blinds—Really!

If Paul had become annoyed with me for disappointing or inconveniencing him on our first, second, or even third date, I probably would have decided he was a selfish jerk and ended any meaningful involvement with him. So why did this small red flag go unheeded when it occurred on New Year's Eve, a year into our relationship? Because his annoyance and selfishness occurred in the context of what appeared to me to be a loving, mutually respectful relationship. *That* is the problem, and it is not just a problem for me; it is a problem for most of us.

All a sociopath has to do is act *as if* he is a great guy and *as if* he loves you long enough until you believe that he does. Then, once you fall in love with him, his behavior will be interpreted through a rose-colored lens, and red flags, both small and large, are likely to be overlooked or excused away.

Shakespeare's words, "Love is blind" (*The Merchant of Venice*), are part of our collective vocabulary because of their timeless truth. Confirming what Shakespeare noted centuries ago, a 2004 University College London study found that feelings of love dampen activity in the part of the brain associated with assessing the motivations and intentions of others.[21] Being in love creates a dangerous blind spot. This is why so many sociopaths get us to fall deeply in love with them first by representing themselves as our soul mates.

The sad truth is, given the prevalence of sociopaths, especially among men, women should look for these warning signs throughout any developing romantic relationship. That's when the signs are the most important to detect but also the most difficult to see. I discovered about twenty years too late, as I was in the process of divorcing Paul, that one way of magnifying these hard-to-perceive signs is to keep a handwritten journal. Writing by hand is slow, so as I tried to make sense of what was happening in the present and how it related to the past, the tedious process of writing by hand allowed me to make much needed mental connections. This helped me stay grounded in facts rather than the self-serving falsehoods Paul perpetuated. It is much harder to gaslight someone effectively if the person has documented what really happened.

Times of conflict or potential conflict are particularly important to commit to writing. When your needs clash with your partner's, even over something small, what happens? Does he try to balance your needs against his and come to a mutually satisfying solution? Or, like Paul, does he try to get his way via manipulation, minimizing the importance of your needs, questioning the validity of your perspective, making you feel guilty, making you feel you misremembered or misrepresented something, making you feel sorry for him, or elevating the importance of his needs (e.g., "I have been soooo looking forward to sharing a New Year's kiss with you")? Even if a decision feels like it makes sense at the time, be wary if, over the long run, tradeoffs consistently favor him.

Keep in mind that if any self-respecting sociopath is seeking to ensnare you, he will offer compelling reasons to make you disregard any red flags you notice. He may encourage you to view them as "no big deal." He may suggest that you are being too sensitive, selfish, needy, controlling, or that you can't take a joke (e.g., "I can't believe you really thought I was serious about you making coffee and staying up when you were sick. *Obviously*, I was just kidding."). *Any* chinks in his armor, no matter how small, are a big deal if they reflect a lack of empathy or ethics. Early in a romantic relationship, these seemingly inconsequential hiccups may be the only glimpses you get into the hollowness of the sociopath's heart, the blackness of his soul, and his unbridled need to diminish and control.

If you think I am being alarmist, please keep reading.

What's In It for Me?
Another Red Flag Missed

Against the vast, sparkling sea of emotionally and intellectually fulfilling time spent together studying, attending classes, working out, sharing dinners, and looking for jobs, the ripples that appeared in my relationship with Paul hardly registered. No person or relationship is perfect, so of course there would be disagreements, small hurts, and misunderstandings. Only now am I wise enough to know that the root cause of the minor discord in our relationship was the important part —not the mere fact of the discord.

It was easy to think that Paul and I shared important interests and values, because, throughout our second year in business school, our narrow goals (to get good grades and get good jobs) and our lives overlapped almost perfectly. How could I imagine what would happen if our goals ever diverged or conflicted? The only way I could have done that would have been if I had extrapolated New Year's Eve to sharing a life with Paul. However, I did not know why that short interaction with Paul on New Year's Eve left me so unsettled. I just knew that it did.

It never occurred to me that a key reason Paul was sharing so much of his life and time with me was that talking to me about our assignments helped him get better grades with less effort than studying on his own. I just assumed that Paul loved the intellectual banter with me, that he valued my opinions, and that he enjoyed the learning process, as I did—that we were so alike, soul mates. Starting out with these assumptions, and having them reinforced by the rewarding time we spent together, meant it took me far too long to abandon that framework and understand the truth.

I am not alone in being unable to discard firmly entrenched but inaccurate assumptions. People tend to have a "confirmation bias." We interpret new information in the context of an existing framework—looking for evidence that confirms our current viewpoint and discounting evidence that contradicts it. Thinking the world was flat, humankind rejected strong evidence to the contrary for centuries. Old worldviews that have served us well are not cast aside easily, even when opposing evidence abounds.

Perhaps not by accident, Paul and my second-year MBA course selections overlapped almost perfectly, allowing us to study together and even co-author papers and work together on projects. Paul, however, took one class in the fall that I did not take until the spring.

CHAPTER 7

One night in April when I was preparing for class, I asked Paul for help. Paul refused, which struck me as odd. Hadn't we always studied together and helped each other? When I pressed him, he became annoyed and said he had such high ethical and moral standards that he did not think it would be fair to discuss the topic with me or to tutor me, because he had already taken the class and knew the professor's point of view. This would give me an unfair advantage, and, as a highly principled person, he could not do that. It was almost a burden that he was so exceptionally honest, ethical, and honorable, but his integrity, and that of anyone in his life, was of the utmost importance to him.

I backed off and did not ask for any more assistance, but Paul's stance struck me as bizarre, because there was no basis for it. In fact, students who had taken and excelled in a class one semester were often asked by professors to tutor students in the class the following semester. Several professors had asked me to do this, and I was able to earn a fair amount of spending money that way.

What was going on? Although I was blind to it then, I know now that this was one of the few times in our narrow, almost perfectly overlapping MBA lives that Paul's goals and my goals conflicted (as they had for a few hours on New Year's Eve). Paul had already taken the class; so devoting an hour of his time to discussing the coursework with me was of no value to him. There was simply nothing in it for Paul, especially when there was a Mets game on television. Paul's high moral ground was a smokescreen for not wanting to put any effort into something that would not benefit him, even if it would be quite beneficial to me. Sociopath math, remember? No empathy. If it was not a means to a better grade for Paul, and if he could fabricate an excuse that would not blow his cover (his lofty morals and ethical character—brilliant!), Paul had zero interest. None! He'd rather watch baseball, and that's what he did.

Conflicting needs should trigger discussion not annoyance. A person in a mutually loving relationship should not hesitate to help his or her partner, especially when the partner's need is high and the price of helping is low. (Sorry, guys, but missing a Mets game does not qualify as a high price. You can always record it.) Paul wrapped himself in claims of honor, honesty, and integrity to hide exactly the opposite qualities. My love for Paul blinded me to these red-flag, no-empathy moments early in our relationship when the price of getting out was far, far lower than it was two decades later.

I Will Follow Him

Deeply in love, or so I thought, Paul and I agreed to coordinate our job search so we could stay together after business school. In early January, Paul received his first job offer—to work for a niche consulting firm in Minneapolis. I wanted to stay on the East coast, closer to family in Vermont. I hoped to work in public relations after getting my MBA, but almost no public relations companies interviewed at Yale during my graduating year, and I needed to generate my own leads. I did, and I got four offers in my desired field, all in Massachusetts and Connecticut. However, Paul wanted to stop his job search, accept his first offer, and cancel his many upcoming interviews with firms in Connecticut and Massachusetts.

I was confused. Hadn't we developed a joint job-search strategy to generate job offers in a few agreed-upon cities, including Minneapolis, and then make a "what's best for us" decision once all relevant offers had been extended? As a sociopath, Paul needed to appear as if he wanted to cooperate with me, all the while doing only what was best for him. If he had made it clear early in the job-search process, which started at the beginning of our second year in business school, that staying with me was not his priority, it is likely I would have ended our relationship. He would have lost access to all the advantages I provided as his girlfriend—an apartment, access to a car, a study-mate who would help him get good grades with less effort, better food than the cafeteria, and physical intimacy. Why blow that?

"It's a perfect match," Paul explained. "No matter how much I interview, I'll never find any firm or job I like better. I won't make much money, but money doesn't matter. I know I'm going to love it there."

Once Paul played the "it's the perfect job for me" card, I did not want to stand in the way of the man I loved and his ideal first position out of business school with a boutique consulting company. Wanting to be a loving, supportive, understanding girlfriend, I played right into his hand and encouraged Paul to take the job. I would keep looking. I broadened my search to any type of job that I could do well, not just the type of job I really wanted. After a few months, I received a lucrative offer from an investment management company in Minneapolis. Shame on me, but I took the job so that Paul and I could stay together, not because it was a position or long-term career I really wanted. I left those dreams behind back East.

CHAPTER 8

Clearly, I am not the first woman to trade off career in favor of a relationship. Maybe I would not have done it if I were younger with decades of time ahead of me to find Mr. Right and start a family, but I was thirty-six years old when I finished business school. I wanted children, and my biological clock was ticking—loudly. Besides, I was in love with Paul, and I thought he was in love with me. Once in Minneapolis, I hoped I would be able to craft the public relations career I wanted.

In truth, Paul probably didn't care if I got a job in Minneapolis or not. If I, like Jenny, was naïve enough to sacrifice my ambitions to tag along where he was going anyway, that was fine with him. After all, in Minneapolis, we were able to get a bigger and nicer apartment than either of us could have afforded on our own. This was especially true for Paul, because he had a bigger tuition debt and a smaller salary than me. My relocation package was more generous than Paul's, too, and my company was happy to give Paul's belongings a free ride to our new apartment in Minneapolis. The lack of balance in our job search process did not set off alarm bells for me. After all, long-term relationships are full of give and take, tradeoffs, and compromise. I assured myself that the scales would balance over the long term.

What a sociopath says he will do for the benefit of someone else and what he actually does can diverge wildly, especially over time. You can explain away any single incident, but beware of a disturbing long-running pattern. Each decision I made, each trade-off I offered, made sense to me at the time and was couched in logic and long-term purpose. Yet, years later as our marriage dissolved, I asked Paul what meaningful tradeoff in our almost twenty-year relationship he had ever made for me. He could not recall even one.

Neither could I.

Prince Charming Picks Me

I poured myself into my new job, but I was a lightweight compared to Paul. He lived and breathed for his firm, often staying at the office until well past midnight and even spending entire weekends at work. Consulting companies are known to demand insane hours from their new associates. Still, the amount of effort Paul invested in his job was beyond what firms expected even from their superstars. I tried to be as supportive as possible to help Paul fulfill his dream, which was to make partner earlier than anyone ever had in the firm's fifteen-year history. I did not understand his rush; perhaps it was part of his plan to work hard, make money for ten years, and then retire to a university town to teach. Oddly, however, Paul had never mentioned this goal after our discussions that first weekend when we were on the business team together at Yale. (To my knowledge, after getting his MBA, Paul never volunteered to work with underprivileged children or to support any other worthy cause either.)

Night after night, Paul came home after 1:00 a.m., only to go back to the office after five hours of sleep. I tried to be sympathetic and keep us well stocked in Starbucks. I loved him. I admired his drive, ambition, and accomplishments. He was already making a name for himself at his firm. I was so proud of him, but I missed his companionship. I missed our long discussions about our class assignments, which had taken place just months earlier when we were still in school.

Although we saw each other rarely, we made the best of the snippets of time we had together—a bike ride here, a movie there. To compensate for our lack of "us" time, we planned a weekend getaway in Chicago in early January.

Chicago was beautiful even in the cold, windy winter, but I ended up exploring it by myself, because Paul "had" to work on a project over the weekend, banging away for hours on his laptop at the small hotel room desk. Luckily, he was able to break for dinner, allowing us to keep our Saturday night reservation at a restaurant at the top of one of the tallest buildings in the city. Seeing as I tend toward the "no makeup and casual" side of attire and had only packed a few things, I picked out something from my suitcase that seemed appropriate but which was hardly fancy. I was also feeling a bit low after spending a day alone that Paul and I had planned to spend together.

"You're wearing *that*?" Paul asked when he saw my outfit.

CHAPTER 9

I let the comment go. He was tired and had been working nonstop. Letting him know that his comment hurt my feelings might put a damper on our evening together. Paul had also started commenting that I was "too sensitive" and "too controlling." Was I? To prove Paul wrong, I changed my clothes and put on some makeup. It was no big deal. We shared little time together these days, and I wanted us to have a much overdue special evening together. Silly me for not getting more decked out in the first place.

That night, between dinner and dessert, against the backdrop of the colorful, vibrant Chicago lights viewed from what felt like the top of the world, Paul proposed.

"Yes!" I said, giddy with excitement as I answered the question I had been hoping Paul would ask.

Paul slipped a vintage diamond ring on my finger, and we embraced in a deep, long hug. I felt so lucky to have a soul mate who had similar interests and values to mine, a kind man with great integrity who wanted a family, loved the outdoors, was athletic, and was so intelligent that we could share a stimulating life together.

My life, derailed personally and financially by my previous marriage, was back on track. I had an MBA, a good job, and I had found the man of my dreams. We both wanted children, and between our two careers, we were clearly on our way toward a comfortable life and financial security. Or were we?

The Secret Wedding

By the time Paul and I got engaged, we had been living together and working in Minneapolis for six months. Still, virtually everything I knew about Paul was from our time at Yale. He was that busy at his new job. Chronically absent or exhausted from his grueling schedule, he rarely talked to me about his clients or assignments. He had no time to hear about my projects at work either. Couldn't I see how tired he was?

Watching the Mets, the Giants, or the Rangers became the priority when he was home, because, more than anything, he just needed to decompress. To share his company, I started watching a lot of professional sports. The rich intellectual relationship we had shared came to a screeching halt. I was sure the loss was temporary. We were both overachievers at work and wanted to make great first impressions on our respective employers, and that took priority. We were just busy and tired. How could it be anything else?

Because it was a second marriage for both of us, we decided to keep our wedding simple and inexpensive. We did not want our parents to feel they needed to buy us anything, and we wanted to save our money for a house. Paul took things a step further by insisting that we keep our wedding plans private—that it be just the two of us. In fact, he made me promise to not even tell my family where we were getting married, only the date: May 1. He did not want anyone to show up and ruin our much-needed time together. It seemed an odd request, but since it was so important to Paul, and because we were not inviting friends and family anyway, it didn't seem like a big deal to agree.

By mid-April, Paul was swamped at work, and he expected the demands of his job to overflow into May. He asked me to postpone our wedding so he could see an important project through to fruition.

Lisa, a friend from work, looked at me with surprise when I told her we had changed our wedding plans. "Onna," she said, "who changes their wedding date?"

"But it's just the two of us," I replied, "so it doesn't really matter."

She didn't give up. "Is everything okay? Changing your wedding date a few weeks before you're supposed to get married seems *really* weird."

"Of course. Things are great," I said. "It's just that Paul's so busy and so important to the project he's working on."

CHAPTER 10

"But it's your *wedding!*" Lisa continued. "Most people would never do that."

"Lisa," I said, "I've already been through one failed marriage. All that matters is the kind of marriage we have, not the wedding date. Who cares if, years from now, we're happily married and celebrate our anniversary on May first, twenty-first, or even June twenty-first?"

I called the inn nestled in California's wine country and the justice of the peace we had booked to change our wedding date and then shifted my vacation time at work. Now we planned to get married on May 21. I should have realized that Paul's desire to keep the wedding simple and private gave him total control over a very important date in our lives. If no one had booked a plane ticket to be with us, the wedding could be changed or even cancelled at the last minute—whatever he wanted, for whatever reason he wanted.

I'll never know if Paul had legitimate reasons to change the wedding date or if it was an orchestrated performance for the partners at work. As Lisa correctly pointed out, *who changes their wedding date?* By doing so, he became an instant office legend. "Look! Paul not only logs long, hard hours, he is so committed to the firm he even changed his wedding for work. Now *that's* dedication!"

On May 21, with no friends or family in attendance, Paul and I got married. Telegrams and flowers and cards from *his* family flooded in. None came from my family and friends, because I had respected Paul's desire to keep the location private. When I asked Paul why he gave his family and friends information about our wedding but asked that I not divulge our plans, he looked shocked and claimed he did not know what I was talking about—that he had never made such a request. Paul chalked it up to a "misunderstanding" or "miscommunication." What else could it be?

My mind searched for a clear memory about Paul's request, but so much had been happening between both of our jobs and planning for our wedding that no memory was crystal clear. Had I misunderstood? Had I just assumed I should not tell anyone the location due to Paul's desire to have a private ceremony? We had both been tired and working hard, hadn't we? He would never have asked me not to tell my family where we were staying and getting married, all the while telling *his* family and friends. That didn't make sense! It had to be me who had misunderstood.

A little voice in me should have been screaming, "Why would I make up the idea that I shouldn't tell anyone where we were getting married? That's crazy!" But now that Paul was saying he had never made such a request, the idea of such a request seemed beyond bizarre. What else could it be but a terrible misunderstanding?

How would it have possibly crossed my mind that I was being gaslighted by Paul, that this was a purposeful manipulation, one of thousands that lay

CHAPTER 10

ahead, to unsettle me, to make me doubt myself, to erode my self-confidence, and to test me just to see if he could get me to do it? This is how sociopaths operate. This is how Paul operated, each deception couched as a misunderstanding seeded with the suggestion that I was too sensitive, too controlling, too unreasonable, or had simply misunderstood or misremembered.

The Honeymooners

We spent our honeymoon hiking, horseback riding, wine tasting, and sleeping in. I had wanted to go on a particular hike, but we never did. Finally, I told Paul that I was concerned that we were leaving without going on the one hike to which I had so looked forward. Paul looked at me, incredulous. With his loving eyes engaging mine and his voice gentle and silky, he explained that I must not have expressed my needs clearly. Of course he wanted me to be happy and to do things I wanted to do.

I was confused. How could Paul have misunderstood that this hike was the number one thing I wanted to do on our honeymoon, aside from getting married and spending long, lazy mornings in bed with my new husband? Hadn't I brought it up multiple times? I replayed the week in my head. I had mentioned it to Paul, and each reason Paul gave for not going on the hike had made sense at the time and had been expressed considerately. One day he had a headache. The next afternoon he was tired. Another day he said he had heard about a prettier hike, saying we could go on "my" hike tomorrow. But when tomorrow came, he wanted to go for a bike ride. Shouldn't we add some variety instead of hiking two days in a row? Hadn't we done enough hiking already? The next day, he wanted to go into town and do some shopping. It seemed strange that somehow we had not done the one thing I had wanted to do most, yet we had done everything on Paul's priority list. I let it go. I thought, "It's no big deal," and I had just married my Prince Charming. We did lots of things I enjoyed. Why sweat the small stuff?

The truth is, I *had* communicated my desire to go on the hike clearly, and Paul had steered away from my preferred activity for the simple reason it was the activity I had chosen. Sociopaths lie and manipulate simply to lie and manipulate. Perhaps it makes them feel superior and powerful to get capable, intelligent people to make sacrifices and take both the smallest and the largest actions against their own best interest—from not going on my preferred hike or not telling my family where I was getting married to compromising the type of job I really wanted after business school. Sociopaths enjoy being puppeteers. They manipulate for the rush of feeling in control and weakening others so they can manipulate and dominate them even more in the future. It is as if they are on a marathon of erosion. Like

CHAPTER 11

raindrops on a mountain, each small sacrifice I made or wave of self-doubt I felt shaped me so that over time, no sacrifice for Paul was too big and my self-confidence was eroded completely.

Why did I fall for Paul's manipulations, which—in hindsight—make me look like a spineless sap? I am only human, and under similar circumstances, the majority of women would have fallen for them, too. Ask any introductory psychology student, and he or she can tell you about the concept of "cognitive dissonance." We dislike inconsistency (i.e., dissonance) and we strive for consistency, especially within ourselves—our attitudes, behavior, perceptions, thoughts, etc. If, for example, we become aware that our attitudes and/or our behavior are inconsistent, we are motivated to make a change to create consistency.

When my honeymoon came and went without us going on "my" hike, I experienced cognitive dissonance. If Paul truly loved me, the honeymoon should have reflected my interests and preferences as well as his, but it did not. To make the unpleasant feelings associated with this mental disharmony dissipate—to resolve the dissonance—I had several options. I could have lowered the importance of one of the factors creating my mental discord. Perhaps the hike *really* had not been important to me. Alternatively, I could have added an element or reframed the situation to eliminate the dissonance. Perhaps, as Paul said, I had not communicated my preference properly, so he was not at fault. I could have also reminded myself that overall Paul was a wonderful guy and worth a little sacrifice here and there. Another possible way to resolve the dissonance was to conclude that I had just married a lying, manipulative weasel.

Unfortunately, for me to decide that Paul was, in fact, a dishonest, scheming, controlling rat was highly unlikely at that moment. With the wealth of information I had telling me that Paul was a wonderful, empathetic, honest guy, and the fact that I had just made the immense emotional investment of marrying him, a misunderstanding about a hike a few days earlier was unlikely to trigger that conclusion—although, in retrospect, I wish it had. With that avenue to resolving the dissonance blocked, I was left with the alternatives. And there was nothing stopping me from engaging in the mental gymnastics of tapping all three of these strategies—the hike was not that important to me, I was an ineffective communicator, and Paul was worth the sacrifice. Case closed! Cognitive conflict resolved! My new husband was a wonderful man. Onward!

In isolation, any single dissonance-creating episode would have been inconsequential. Yet, the fact that this and future incidents appeared so trivial made them inordinately dangerous, because they slipped under my radar. As a result, they did not sound an alarm that might have caused me to resolve the dissonance by recognizing that Paul was dangerous and controlling, and that I needed to get him out of my life as soon as possible. Mountains do not turn to rubble in a day. Each drop of rain and gust of wind slowly erodes until, hundreds of millions of years later, there is little left. In the same way, insidious, slow erosion is part of a controlling, abusive person's toolkit, and it was a major part of Paul's. From one day to the next, I would not experience a perceptible shift in what I considered "normal" for me and for my relationship with Paul. Yet, from one year to the next, the cumulative effect proved ruinous.

Although human beings are wired to resolve cognitive dissonance, very few people understand their minds work like this, and few people, therefore, think this can happen to them. They are stronger, smarter, better educated, more perceptive, and more psychologically astute than those naïve victims, right? News programs and reports are brilliant at blaming the victim by pointing out the victim's naiveté, and, through the nature of the questions asked, assuring us that the victims chose to blind themselves to reality and should have known better. These commentators and investigative reporters do us a tremendous disservice. They need to become better educated about how the human mind really operates. Unless we seek to understand and counteract the automatic workings of our brains, we are vulnerable to the manipulation of these master puppeteers. Sociopaths count on that.

What Just Happened?

Paul and I arrived back in Minneapolis late on a Saturday and spent a leisurely Sunday together. Both of us needed to return to work on Monday morning. I had not worked the entire vacation or even checked in with the office. My co-workers and team leader knew I was on my honeymoon and that I would not be in touch. Still, before I left, I had been working with an out-of-town client headquartered in Cincinnati. Some weeks we were with the client in Cincinnati, others we worked out of the Minneapolis office. I had to know where I was supposed to be on Monday morning and if I needed to book a flight to Cincinnati.

I delayed checking in with my colleagues until early Sunday evening. If I could not get in touch with someone on my team, I might wind up in the wrong location the next morning—a potentially suicidal career blunder. Why had I waited so long?

So as not to disturb Paul, who was watching TV in the living room, I made the call from our makeshift home office (no email in those days). Luckily, Brad, one of my co-workers, picked up right away. He said the team would not be travelling that week. Concern about my close call with career suicide faded. I could relax and enjoy the final evening of my honeymoon.

When I got up to head back to the living room, Paul was standing in the doorway.

"Who was that?" he snapped, face red, shoulders tensed.

"Just Brad, from work," I replied, taken aback by Paul's anger.

His face grew tighter. "Why are you calling Brad? Who's Brad to you?"

"Our honeymoon's over, and I just needed to know where to be for work tomorrow. You've met Brad. He's just a colleague. I already waited too long to call. I was getting worried."

"Our honeymoon isn't over!" Paul said, his jaw tight and his piercing eyes trapping me like a predator immobilizing its prey. "Our honeymoon isn't over until *I* say it's over!"

I flinched. My pulse quickened. Carol, my friend from Yale, would have known what to do—look for an opportunity to leave quietly the next day, stay with a friend, and have the marriage annulled. But I did not understand what had just happened. All I knew was that I wanted Paul's anger

CHAPTER 12

to go away.

"I'm sooo sorry," I said. "I didn't mean to upset you. I don't need to make any more calls tonight. Let's just make the rest of the night special."

"You've already ruined it," Paul said and then left the room.

My head felt light, and my heart pounded. I returned to the living room, where Paul was watching TV. His eyes never looked away from the screen. His tight face and closed body language made it clear I was not to join him on the couch. Clearly unwelcome, I returned to the office.

My thoughts racing, my pulse pounding, an automatic attempt to resolve the cognitive dissonance between my perceptions of Paul's behavior and my beliefs about Paul ensued. To hold onto the assumption that my new husband was a great guy, I had to conclude there was a good reason he was upset. *Maybe he's stressed about returning to work tomorrow. Maybe he's sad our honeymoon is over. Maybe I was inconsiderate to call then. Maybe. Maybe. Maybe.* Still, I could not shake the upsetting interaction. That night, there was an icy distance between us in our bed. I slept fitfully.

The next morning, as is common to sociopaths, Paul acted as if our tense exchange the night before had never happened. Not wanting to bring up an upsetting topic before we both returned to work, I tabled the subject until the end of the day.

"You're so silly," Paul said, his tone soft, gentle, even playful when I broached the subject after dinner that evening. "Especially when you're tired, you can make a mountain out of a molehill. It was nothing. I haven't given it a second thought. I wasn't angry. I don't know what made you think so."

"But you said, 'Our honeymoon isn't over until *I* say it's over,' and it really upset me," I said.

"I'd *never* say something like that," Paul replied.

"Paul, it really upset me."

He looked at me. "Do you really think I would say that?"

"You just sounded really angry with me for making that call."

"What do you think I said?" Paul asked.

"Something like, 'Our honeymoon isn't over 'til *I* say it's over,'" I replied.

"Onna," Paul continued with the softest, smoothest, most caring voice, "I don't remember saying that, and if I had said anything like that, *I could only have been kidding.*"

"It didn't seem like that," I replied.

"Why are you giving me such a hard time?" Paul asked. "*You* were clearly over sensitive last night. But now you're getting *me* upset. It seems you're calling me a liar."

That stopped me in my tracks. I started to doubt myself. Had I been

CHAPTER 12

tired? Had I been too sensitive? What did Paul actually say? Maybe he was right. I replayed the evening in my head. My recollection did not match Paul's at all, but he was so confident and calm in his retelling of events, his recall unwavering. The clarity of the interaction the previous night receded. What had actually happened? I anchored on what was clear to me—the Paul I knew, the man I married, could never have said anything hurtful like that on purpose. It must have been me.

"I'm so sorry, Paul," I said, anxious that I had gotten Paul upset with me. "I don't know why I was so bothered last night. I guess I was just tired and disappointed that our honeymoon was over."

"It's okay," Paul said, his silky voice returning. "I love you. Don't worry. It's no big deal."

He leaned over and gave me a gentle, lingering kiss on my forehead.

I sighed. "Thanks for being so understanding. I love you, too."

With the conflict between Paul and me officially over, I was flooded with emotions—befuddled about what had just happened, confused about my recollection of the previous evening, and embarrassed that I had been upset to begin with. But, I also felt "off"—a low-lying sense of anxiety that I could not attribute to anything specific. Paul and I had had a misunderstanding. We had talked about it. We had resolved it. I loved Paul, and Paul loved me. Everything seemed fine, but the not-so-subtle feedback from my emotions signaled that everything was not right, that something was terribly wrong.

Knowing, Without Knowing We Know

A chronic, subtle sense of unease, anxiety, and feeling that something is "off" are classic symptoms of being in a relationship with a sociopath. These feelings became my constant companions.

The Iowa Gambling Task is a classic study designed by neuroscientists at the University of Iowa and discussed at length in a book[22] by Antonio Damasio, one of the researchers. It demonstrates how we can sense that something is wrong and feel anxious without understanding what is making us feel that way.

In their study, subjects were given four decks of cards, play money, and instructions to draw cards from any of the four decks until they were told to stop. Each card in the deck triggered a payout or a loss of varying amounts. The decks were rigged so that two of the decks had positive expected payouts while the other two were downright punitive and would result in large losses for the participant. Players' anxiety and tension were measured via the electrical conductance of their skin, the same technique used in many lie-detector tests.

At first, a player's choice of decks appeared random. But soon, players experienced tension and anxiety while reaching for the decks with negative expected payouts. Players also started avoiding these decks long before they had a logical explanation for their choices. One of the things this experiment shows is that our anxiety and tension can signal that something is legitimately wrong long before we realize it consciously or can offer some sort of explanation.

What do the results of this card experiment have to do with living with a sociopath? A relationship with a sociopath is just like thinking you are drawing cards from a fair deck when, in fact, you are drawing cards from a deck that is stacked against you. You will feel anxious and on edge. Although participants in psychology experiments are debriefed so they understand what has actually transpired, in real life there is no guarantee that you will ever understand the root cause of your negative feelings. Without understanding the root cause, you may never remove yourself from the person or situation triggering the feelings, hence feeling anxious and on edge become chronic.

Let me elaborate on this finding by conducting a simple thought experiment. Imagine the tension in the study's participants if they had been required to keep choosing from the punitive deck, not all the time but as frequently as they did from the nonpunitive decks. Their anxiety and tension would have persisted and likely escalated. Imagine now that, due to heightened tension and anxiety, a player asks to avoid these decks. When the experimenter asks why, the player explains that certain decks seem associated with big losses.

Imagine if the experimenter appears to listen with great empathy and compassion (as a sociopath would) but then explains that the decks have been balanced carefully. If the player perceives differences, it is just a matter of being unlucky early on in the study or that she is one of *those* people who is overly sensitive to negative feedback. In fact, the experimenter was just like her; he had a similar impression when he went through the experiment himself, but almost no other player has made that comment. Further, it is important to the study for her to continue, and the lead experimenter will not pay her for doing the study unless she completes it—although the assistant experimenter would be happy to help her out if he could.

In light of the information that there is no valid reason to be upset, and with her ego on the line to prove she is not "overly sensitive," the player persists. Several outcomes, none of them good, are now likely. Her anxiety and tension will persist and build as she is required to take actions she senses, accurately, are contrary to her interests. As her anxiety mounts, maybe she will stop the experiment again and reiterate that she is sure two of the decks are minefields and ask permission to avoid them. To reassure her that the decks are, in fact, balanced, the assistant will offer (although he suggests he might get in trouble for it) to take the decks aside and check them. Maybe they got scrambled. She waits. He returns, assuring her that the decks are even. Again, maybe it is just randomness that made some decks appear more or less favorable than others.

Alternatively, maybe, as the assistant suggested earlier, she is just overly sensitive to negative feedback. In fact, another experimenter is looking for people who consider themselves exceptionally sensitive and tend to "over react." Maybe she would like to sign up for this study as well. Not wanting to appear unusually weak or overly sensitive, she persists with the experiment in spite of mounting anxiety every time her hand reaches for the two punitive decks.

In this scenario, her body is in constant "fight or flight" mode, because she is in a negative situation. But since someone she trusts, someone who seems to show considerable empathy for her, is telling her she is misreading the situation, she does not leave. By the experimenter discounting the player's perceptions and reasoning, not only does she experience ongoing anxiety, she has less confidence in her ability to perceive and assess the friendliness or hostility of her environment. Her self-confidence and self-esteem take a hit. Her hard-wired fight or flight mechanism, crafted over millions of years of evolution to signal danger, is dampened.

If this is truly just an experiment that takes a half-hour of her day, no long-term damage is likely. But living with a sociopath is like being stuck in a rigged experiment that never ends. Being in fight or flight mode is great if you are trying to outrun a nasty dog. Living in fight or flight mode constantly is profoundly unhealthy—both physically and emotionally. In addition, having someone you trust continually contradict your perceptions and undermine your decisions is intellectually and emotionally corrosive.

Other potential outcomes to this thought experiment exist. Choosing not to experience constant anxiety and having all of her efforts to understand what is going on fail, our player might continue to go through the motions but give up emotionally as she realizes she can do nothing to control a situation she perceives as negative. This possibility sounds a lot like "learned helplessness," a term introduced by psychologists Steven F. Maier and Martin Seligman.[23] Learned helplessness is linked strongly with depression. To avoid expending energy in an unwinnable situation, it might be best to just resign oneself to one's unpleasant fate—to give up, to not care, to disconnect. The problem is that once a person learns that it is futile to try, this behavior is not easily unlearned. As a result, the person does not attempt to exert effort to advance his or her interests in future situations, even when the situation is different and new efforts are likely to yield positive results.

Being in an environment for an extended time in which the connection between effort and results is severed can change a person, leaving him or her chronically depressed. Is it any wonder that more than ninety percent of women involved in long-term relationships with sociopaths become depressed or anxious?[24]

Danger! Bridge Out Ahead

"Our honeymoon isn't over until *I* say it's over" was not just a red flag, it was an oversized, florescent red flag accompanied by blaring sirens and fireworks. Why did I miss what is so obvious in hindsight? I did not understand that people like Paul really exist in the world, not just in movies or as someone else's husband on shows like *48 Hours*. It wasn't that I thought I was special or immune to negative experiences, I simply had no idea how common sociopaths are, what amazing actors and manipulators they are, that *anyone* can become a target, and that everyone needs to know the signs that may signal they are involved with a sociopath. It was not something I ever considered, especially not on the final day of my honeymoon, but how many of us would have dissolved a one-week old marriage on the basis of a single comment? I should have. Paul's comment was a rare gift, because it illuminated a fatal flaw. It was a glimpse into the real Paul. It was not the comment of a good guy having a bad day or being stressed out from work or overly fatigued or anything else for that matter. His remark demonstrated that Paul viewed me as a possession to be controlled. This is not normal, and it is certainly not healthy. This is how sociopaths view those they are grooming for future exploitation.

I was not so naive as to think that good marriages should be devoid of conflict and compromise. To the contrary, I realized that living in such a way that allows two people's needs and long-term goals to be accommodated is a difficult dance, requiring the resolution of conflicts and misunderstandings, solving problems, and probably shedding a few tears along the way. However, not all marital problems are equal. Some are solvable and common even in the healthiest of marriages. Alternatively, some are symptoms of malignant, cancerous people and relationships. It is important to understand if a lack of empathy, a lack of a conscience, and a need to control are the root cause of any conflict. These are deal breakers. They are perilous and cannot be fixed. If you find yourself in such a situation, you must escape.

Think of a small boat heading out into the ocean, suddenly taking on a small amount of water after leaving the dock. Before heading farther out to sea, away from the safety of land, wouldn't it be prudent to understand if the leak can be patched easily or if it is a symptom of a dangerous problem

CHAPTER 14

that is guaranteed to get worse? Patching things up, not understanding the root cause of the problem, and sailing off into the sunset may feel good at the moment, but it will be disastrous and even deadly in some cases. The same is true of a relationship with a sociopath. There is no fixing it. It will not end well, and the farther you get from shore, the more likely it is that when you finally see the problem for what it is, you will be in grave danger—emotionally, financially, and even physically.

The reason I should have ended the relationship after the "Our honeymoon isn't over until *I* say it's over!" comment and the subsequent discussion with Paul was that these interactions contained clear signs of sociopath math at work. In Paul's mind, I existed to serve his needs—a relaxing final night to his honeymoon. My need to preserve my career by finding out where to be the next morning counted for *nothing*. It is hard for nonsociopaths to comprehend that such behavior could be caused by an inability to feel empathy for another person. This is something that most of us do not even know to consider. We have empathy, so it never crosses our minds that many people do not—and never will. Instead, nonsociopaths persist in concluding: "I must have misunderstood," "I must be missing the big picture," "There are always two sides to any conflict," "I must have done something wrong," and "He must have been tired." However, once you understand a sociopath's ever-present mental equation, it is time to stop asking these questions or explaining away or excusing his selfish, controlling behavior. When someone assigns no importance to other human beings, the most self-serving behavior, even over the littlest thing, becomes possible and, ultimately, the norm.

One person wanting to control another and placing zero value on another person's needs, when those needs clearly should be the priority, is dangerous! This is how many women end up dead, by getting involved with or marrying someone who needs to control them. No one but you should control your destiny. If another human feels entitled to govern your thoughts, opinions, relationships, actions, or movements, run fast, run far, and don't look back! Keep in mind, however, that getting out of a relationship with a sociopath can be treacherous and may require guidance from experts.

He Always Tells the Truth— Even When He Lies

Much as agents in the *Men in Black* movies used "neutralizers" to erase any recall of alien encounters, Paul dazzled and distracted me with brilliant linguistic gymnastics to obscure any glimpses of his true, dark, soulless self. He was masterful at talking his way out of anything and creating an alternate reality to get me to buy into his version of events and to distrust my own recollections. Sociopaths, in general, are experts at this, because they are highly motivated to succeed and have more practice at this than a nonsociopath can even imagine. The people they target typically trust the sociopath and, hence, are not prepared to counter the manipulation unleashed upon them.

Getting someone to question him or herself is easier than you think. Perception and memory are tricky, malleable things, even without the presence of malicious intent. Two well-meaning people often recall even recent events quite differently. Haven't we all experienced this? Moreover, thanks to advances in forensic science and DNA testing, eyewitness testimony is no longer considered reliable—because, on average, it isn't. The Innocence Project considers faulty eyewitness recall the most important factor that leads to wrongful convictions.[25]

Our brief exchange the next day to discuss what had happened illuminated how Paul, like so many sociopaths, used language to dominate, influence, and obscure the truth. When it happened to me, I did not understand Paul's techniques (shared by other sociopaths and fellow manipulators). Yet, a word-by-word dissection of my conversation with Paul reveals the manipulative tools he employed so often.

When I recalled that Paul had said, "Our honeymoon isn't over until *I* say it's over!" and he replied, "I'd *never* say something like that," those six words comprised three techniques that are effective at creating misperceptions:

1) framing the conversation to blind me to what was in clear view,
2) creating cognitive dissonance that I would likely resolve in his favor, and
3) deceiving without technically lying.

By starting out with "I'd never ... " Paul encouraged me to frame his behavior in the context of who I believed Paul to be—a good, loving, honest, and honorable man. The fact that he made a point of presenting himself as so moral while we were dating, and I believed and loved that about him, provided a smokescreen of perceived honestly to conceal his dishonesty. This alone gave him an incredible advantage over me. For me to have shed my entrenched view of Paul's nature was all but impossible at that moment. I had just married him and had a vested interest in believing in his inherent goodness. Before you judge me as naïve or stupid, keep in mind that we *all* perceive the world through a lens forged from our interpretation of past events and present expectations. For this and other reasons, it is almost impossible for us to see what we are *not* looking for, even when it is right in front of us.

A comical 1999 experiment conducted by psychologists Daniel Simons and Christopher Chabris that became the inspiration for their book on misperceptions we have about our mental abilities, *The Invisible Gorilla: And Other Ways Our Intuitions Deceive Us*,[26] demonstrates our blindness to what we are not expecting. Their study involved two teams with three players each, two basketballs, and one gorilla (actually, a person in a gorilla suit). Subjects were asked to view a short video of the two teams passing a basketball back and forth. The task was to count the number of times the team wearing white passed the ball. In the middle of the short game, a person in a gorilla suit walked into the center of the scene, stopped, faced the camera, pounded its chest several times, and then lumbered away.

When the brief video concluded, viewers were asked how many times the white team had passed the ball. Then the experimenters asked if they noticed anything unusual about the game. Believe it or not, about half of those who counted the passes as instructed did not even notice the gorilla. Even when asked if they saw a gorilla, most of those who viewed the tape laughed, because the idea of a gorilla being part of the video was preposterous. This study and its findings have been repeated consistently. It has become a classic and has been used to make several points about how our minds work, including that we tend not to see what we are not expecting to see, even when looking straight at it. After all, the task was framed as counting passes among players with white shirts, not finding a big, out-of-place, faux, hairy primate. Similarly, as Paul's new bride, without even knowing that I was doing it, I was framing each interaction by looking for confirming evidence that I had selected a wonderful spouse. I certainly was not looking for signs that Paul was a lying, manipulative sociopath.

Still, Paul's caustic comment that he, and he alone, determined when the honeymoon was over did not fit my "Paul is a wonderful person" framework. So, like any other human being, I was motivated to make a mental adjustment so that my perception of Paul's behavior and my understanding of Paul's character were in harmony once again. In other words, I had to resolve the dissonance between his statement that "I'd *never* ... " and the fact that I thought he had just done something he said he would

CHAPTER 15

never do. To this end, it was easier for me to shift my perception of what I thought Paul said the previous night to fit the assumption that my new husband was a wonderful man than to hold onto my initial, albeit correct, memory of the tense exchange. To hold onto that correct memory would have required me, within days of our wedding, to have drastically deflated my assessment of Paul's character and to have concluded I had just made a horrible mistake by marrying him. Tall order!

In addition to framing his comment and employing cognitive dissonance to make it hard for me to conclude that Paul could ever lie to me, he actually lied to me without technically uttering any words that were untrue. Think about what Paul said and what he did not say. Paul never said, "I did not say that." If he had, that would have been a lie. Perhaps because it made the game of deception more engaging, Paul preferred an orchestrated misperception to an outright untruth, although he was comfortable with downright lies when necessary. What did Paul say? Simply that he would " ... *never* say something like that." That is not the same thing. In fact, if at the very moment he spoke that sentence Paul did not intend to say something like that, his statement would have been technically true.

Paul's next line, "Do you really think I would say that?" employed the technique of answering a question with a question. And it was not just any question but a question that redirected my focus away from Paul's behavior to defending my character (i.e., Am I the kind of person who accuses my husband of being purposely hurtful?). This was another effective evasion technique. Without being aware of this tactic, I was immobilized. Paul succeeded in getting me to feel defensive, as if *I* needed to explain and justify my words. Without resorting to an outright lie, Paul had cleverly diverted me from the truth, made me question my memory, and made me feel guilty for doubting him.

Imperfect memory is another technique Paul used to obfuscate. When I pressed the point, he countered with, "I don't remember saying that ..." Again, that was true technically. Neither Paul nor I have a photographic memory. Absent a recording, neither of us could have remembered exactly what was said the previous day.

When I persisted and commented that I remembered him saying something like that, Paul employed the "I was just joking" defense. In other words, if I was correct that Paul had said anything even close to what I thought he said, it could only have been a joke, because Paul was such a nice person that he would never have done something hurtful on purpose.

When I clung to my correct perception that Paul had not been kidding, Paul's defense turned to subtle character assassination that made me question myself by suggesting that I was oversensitive and couldn't take a joke. "*You* were clearly over sensitive last night," he said. Bullies often use this technique to shirk responsibility for their cruel acts. If the bully's behavior hurt his target's feelings, it was only because the target lacked a sense of humor or was neurotically defensive or sensitive, not because the bully did anything a reasonable person would have ever taken seriously. Then, to prove that he or she is not overly sensitive or lacking a sense of humor, the target of the hurtful behavior often reneges on the assertion that the bully's behavior was caustic. Score one for bullies everywhere!

When none of these approaches sealed the deal, Paul used the sociopath's ultimate trump card—pity. He seduced me into feeling badly for him. "But now, *you're* getting *me* upset." By design, this pulled at my heart strings and got me to disengage.

To buy a little extra insurance, Paul repackaged his attempt to turn the tables and to get me to sound the retreat by saying, "It seems you're calling *me* a liar." Gavin de Becker calls this type of subtle character assassination "typecasting."[27] By labeling me again in an unflattering way—as someone who is not only overly sensitive but who would also call her new husband a liar—Paul set me up a second time to prove an unflattering label untrue. The ultimate irony here was that, although he had lied, I had not called him a liar. By accusing me of doing so, he distracted me yet again from his lie and put me on my heels as I sought to reassure my new husband that, as a kind person who loved him, I would never call him a liar.

Once we reached this point, there were only two likely endings: my capitulating and apologizing for being upset and for upsetting Paul, accompanied by an unsettling "What just happened?" feeling, or Paul getting angry with me for unreasonably persecuting *him*. Either unsatisfying conclusion would create a negative association with my attempt to discuss an upsetting situation with Paul, thereby reducing the likelihood that I would try to have such a discussion again. It was exhausting—and it was meant to be. Final score: Paul 10 – Onna 0. The sociopath wins!

Although Paul did not use the technique in this particular conversation, another ploy he used often was to distract and discredit with irrelevant details. As if in a court of law, once he established that he *believed* I had misremembered something trivial (like recalling that we had started dinner at 6:30 p.m. when he was sure, whether or not he was actually correct, it was closer to 6:10) then, by implication, the rest of my memory was also flawed, rendering all of my concerns and observations moot, because clearly they were not grounded in reality.

Many sociopaths are wordsmith wizards, skilled storytellers, and expert debaters. Beware, because the yarns they spin and the arguments they win tie you up in knots and leave you deflated, however, they have little to do with the truth and nothing to do with constructive conflict resolution. If you are unaware of the manipulative techniques involved (as I was), such conversations are "crazy making," as if you are being spun on a perpetual merry-go-round. If this is how you feel after trying to resolve conflicts with your partner, start keeping a journal, because befuddling, unsatisfying, and chronically one-sided "resolutions" to conflicts may be a strong indicator you are dealing with a sociopath. Your written record will help establish that fact long after your memory of past events begins to fade or is distorted beyond recognition through your sociopathic partner's manipulations.

"You Have But Slumber'd Here While These Visions Did Appear"[II]

I chalked up Paul's honeymoon comment to the shock and stress of us both returning to our grueling careers after our wedding and week off in California. Like a dream, the clarity of the incident and subsequent confusing and unsatisfying conversation with Paul faded. Life went on. Perhaps because Paul and I saw so little of each other, our marriage seemed to work. The primary demand our relationship put on Paul was a fifteen-minute phone conversation each day, because we were rarely home at the same time. Even on days when I was not traveling, I typically fell asleep alone. Paul arrived home consistently well after midnight.

Although I cannot say I loved my job, I was good at it and received a promotion a year after joining the firm. Paul continued to invest inhuman hours into his consulting career and advanced from associate to manager an unprecedented year earlier than anyone in the history of the company. We spent most of the limited overlapping free time we had together looking for a house. Like studying together at Yale, we had a common goal once again. I felt a resurgence of our relationship. I enjoyed sharing time with Paul as we learned about the various neighborhoods and suburbs in Minneapolis, went to open houses, and looked for the perfect starter home. We were thinking about the house in the context of wanting to start a family.

To accommodate Paul's work demands, we bought a house ten minutes from his office, increasing my commute considerably. Ironically, Paul did not seem to be able to spend any more time at home, even though our new address cut his round-trip commute by over an hour. Around the house, the workload that had been split fairly evenly at first in our apartment quickly devolved to ninety-five percent me and five percent Paul. When I asked him to pitch in more, he pointed out how much harder he was working than I was and that he was too tired and needed some downtime. (Sociopaths have an inflated sense of their importance. Once they have you where they want you, helping around the house with everyday tasks is not going to be high on the list of an inherently entitled person.) To be supportive of my superstar husband, I let him off the hook.

Although I rarely saw Paul even after we bought our house, if I wanted to be reminded of just how awesome he was, all I had to do was to stop by

---
II Puck in Shakespeare's A Midsummer Night's Dream

his office on a Saturday to say "Hi," or to bring him lunch. His dedicated team, mostly young, attractive female junior associates, were always there working alongside Paul. They adored him. To them, Paul was saint-like. He was so helpful, smart, kind, and patient. Such a great mentor. When I met them, they could not say enough wonderful things about Paul. Sally, one of the analysts on Paul's team, told me that she didn't mind working past 1:00 a.m. night after night on Paul's projects, because he would never ask someone to do anything he was unwilling to do himself. He was simply the most amazing man she had ever met. She felt fortunate to be working with Paul and gave him her unquestioning loyalty and time. I felt lucky to be married to such a wonderful person, such an unrivaled superstar.

Reports like this from his young, female work associates made me dismiss the sinking feelings I had about my odd and upsetting interactions with Paul. He was a wonderful man. Everyone thought so. Still "moments of weirdness" (or, in retrospect, examples of sociopath math) continued.

One night after completing a six-month assignment, I was having a celebratory dinner with my team from work. While at the restaurant, my pocketbook was snatched from my chair, but I did not discover it missing until I got up to go considerably later.

My license (which showed my home address), car keys, house keys, cash, and credit cards were gone. The restaurant manager let me use his office phone to alert my credit card companies and cancel the cards. (This was before the days when everyone had a cell phone.) The thieves had acted quickly and had already racked up thousands of dollars of charges. As I hung up the phone with the last credit card fraud-protection agent, I felt a little panicked. This theft had been carefully orchestrated. These people knew what they were doing. Now that my stolen credit cards were no longer useful, would they target the house?

I was twenty minutes away from home with no way to open or start my car. I called Paul at his office, told him what happened, and asked him to pick me up. It never occurred to me that he would say anything other than, "Yes."

But he didn't. Without hesitation he said, "No." He did not even seem concerned about me or sorry about his inability to come to my aid. It was 9:00 p.m. He explained that he was still working on a deadline and would be at the office for several more hours. He could not leave. I could figure it out, right? There must be someone else who could help, right?

My colleagues had already departed, because I assured them I would call Paul and everything would be fine. I had no money to pay for a cab. The kind manager of the restaurant—a man I had never met before that evening—did what my own husband would not do: He invested a significant amount of time to help me. He arranged to have someone cover his responsibilities at the restaurant and then drove me to Paul's office.

CHAPTER 16

The manager waited in the parking lot while I found Paul. Paul hardly stopped working long enough to toss me his house key so the manager could drive me home to get a spare car key and then drive me back to the restaurant to get my car. No hug from Paul, no "I'm so sorry this happened" or "How are you doing?" Nothing! It was clearly an inconvenience for *him* to take a minute of his time to retrieve his house key and give it to me.

It seemed surreal. I felt unsettled. Sure, Paul was working late to meet a deadline, but I had just been robbed and was going to be returning to our house, only about ten minutes from his office, in a situation in which two shady, unscrupulous characters had our address and house keys. Shouldn't there have been more to Paul's reaction, to his concern for me? Shouldn't he have been willing to make some sort of tradeoff for my safety and benefit? Shouldn't there have been some expression of empathy? There was no reaction on Paul's part other than subtle bristling at the inconvenience it caused him to deal with me calling and stopping by his office while he was working. His lack of reaction penetrated me, and it lingered.

A few days later, shaken more by Paul's reaction than by the theft itself, I talked to Paul about it. I explained that our brief interaction the night my pocketbook was stolen left me feeling trivialized and unimportant. Paul looked surprised. With the gentlest, silky voice, he suggested that if I was in any way upset due to his reaction that night, it must be that *I* was too sensitive, too demanding, too needy. After all, the thieves had not come to our house and, due to my credit card companies' policies; I was not responsible for covering their spending spree. So, other than losing some cash and an easily replaceable pocketbook and wallet, it was really no big deal. Alternatively, *his* work demands were very important, pressing, and nonnegotiable. He did not see why on earth I would feel any other way. His feelings and decisions had been totally right. My feelings, on the other hand, were clearly wrong.

To bolster his argument, Paul used a couple of handy tools from his sociopath's toolkit—diversion and putting me on the defensive. He suggested that if I could not see how important it was for him to stay focused at work that night, perhaps it was because I was jealous of him and subconsciously wanted to undermine him. We both knew how competitive *I* was—Yale, Harvard, formerly top nationally ranked squash player, promoted early at work, and so on.

To support his view, Paul pointed out that while he adored his career choice and new firm, I didn't seem thrilled about the job I had taken. While I was probably in the top ten percent of new hires at my firm, Paul was in the top one percent—the type of employee who was becoming legendary in his excellence and devotion to the company. Everyone was sure he would make partner in less than six years, while the typical fast track was seven. No one had ever made it in less than six years. But Paul was special. Paul was superhuman. I should be happy to be married to someone as wonderful, accomplished, and successful as him. I should understand that diverting him from his superstar path for even an hour could only reflect, subconsciously of course, competitiveness or selfishness on my part. Maybe it bothered me that he was even more successful than me. Now, what was it that *I* was concerned about?

Not only was I immobilized on this occasion by the not so subtle suggestion that I could possibly be jealous of and therefore not supportive of Paul, but, in general, I was naive and far too trusting (the perfect wife for a sociopath). The theft episode aside, it never occurred to me to ask why Paul needed to put in such grueling hours at his consulting firm. Other people from our class at Yale were also working at Paul's company. Every one of them was working long and hard, but he alone was constantly at the office past midnight. To prove himself, was he taking on more work than the other new hires? Did he have such high standards that it required considerably more of a time investment for him than for any other new MBA?

Twenty years later, when I ran into a woman with whom Paul had worked during his first year in Minneapolis, she expressed regrets about my recent, horrible divorce from him. As she walked away, she turned and said, "You know, Paul worked hard, and he's very smart, but he never worked as hard as you thought he was working."

I wanted to vomit.

The Twilight Zone

With my biological clock ticking loudly, once we had been at our new jobs for eighteen months, Paul and I decided it was time to have children. After just two months of trying, the pregnancy test registered positive. I danced around our house. At last, I was going to be a mother!

Oddly, Paul showed little interest in our developing child. He had no desire to accompany me to any of my doctor appointments, not even the ultrasound or amniocentesis. Although my obstetrician's office was no more than fifteen minutes from Paul's office, I attended each checkup alone. I tried to convince myself that I did not mind. After all, as a rising star at work, Paul was simply too busy for such things. I was grateful that at least he attended Lamaze classes with me on weekends.

In preparation for the birth, I started maternity leave two weeks prior to the due date, allowing me to transition my assignments smoothly to my colleagues. Paul did not scale back at all. Just days prior to the official due date, labor pains started late in the night. Apparently, baby Jessica was not positioned correctly. As a result, my baseline pain was agonizing, and the accompanying labor pains unbearable. At 1:00 a.m., as I lay in a warm bath to try to take the edge off the assault on my body, Paul sat in the hallway just outside the bathroom with his computer balanced on his lap working on a presentation for a client. There wasn't much he could do to help me right now, he reasoned, other than keep me company and remind me to breathe. He could do *that* while clicking away on his laptop.

Trying not to be disappointed by Pauls' lack of attention, I took pride in my stoicism and attempted to breathe as I had been taught to avoid screaming from the pain. I was such a good, supportive wife for an ambitious consultant. This was just another example of how independent I could be, how understanding I was of Paul's grueling work demands and his goals. He loved me for how much I supported him, his ambitions, and his dreams, right?

Wait! Wait! Wait! For God's sake, wait! I was in labor with our first child. It was one o'clock in the morning, and I was in agony. Was it asking too much to have Paul focus exclusively on me? Apparently, it was. But he had already conditioned me to demand little and accept less. Now that I was about to give birth, why would I expect more?

CHAPTER 17

Jessica's birth was complicated medically, but she greeted the world healthy and beautiful. While at the hospital, Paul was the perfect doting husband and new father. Our time together there was a wonderful reminder of the man I had married and why I loved him so much. He was so thoughtful and kind, captured perfectly in pictures as the proud, loving new father and devoted husband. This was the man with whom I fell in love at Yale. This was the man I married. This was how he would be all the time if he did not have such a demanding boss and if he was not so dedicated to his firm. I was smart and ambitious. I loved and respected him for being smart and ambitious, too. Once he had accomplished what he wanted in his career, he could put this career on autopilot, and things would calm down. There would be more time for us and for our new family. I was sure of it.

I could not have been more wrong. Jessica's birth became another notch in Paul's belt at work. He made sure everyone knew that he had worked on a presentation throughout my labor; all framed as a demonstration of his incredible dedication to his firm, not his being an inattentive husband. Within days of my return home, he decided he had to attend an optional out-of-town, weeklong seminar. My mother had planned to visit after Jessica's birth but had to cancel due to my father developing unexpected health problems. Ruth, Paul's mom, moved up her visit. I was grateful for her help and much needed advice about being a new mother. This was the first time we had spent a lot of time together, just the two of us—or the three of us, including Jessica. I felt close to Ruth, as if I had a second mother.

As in the hospital, in front of his mother, Paul was a doting husband and father who couldn't wait to make me a cup of tea or cuddle with Jessica. Yet, once we dropped Ruth at the airport to return home, Paul's attention waned. He was consistently too tired and too busy to help with Jessica, to talk to me about any of his work assignments, to listen to my concerns or triumphs as a new mom, or to be a meaningful, loving husband and companion. But he wasn't too busy to criticize me for choosing to breastfeed Jessica, to find the dinner I made boring, to think my choice of clothes was "off," or to express annoyance that I picked out an outfit for Jessica that he did not like. I wanted a partner in life, a husband, a co-parent for our beautiful baby girl. Isn't that what I had signed up for?

It might have been what I signed up for, but no sociopath can ever be a loving husband, much less a loving, engaged parent. Remember, they are not capable of love or empathy. If a sociopath cannot care about or love his own children (unimaginable to nonsociopaths but simply an extension of sociopath math), why have children at all? Aren't children just an unwanted distraction and financial drain?

Among the reasons sociopaths have children is that children provide sociopaths with something they crave—power and control. Not only does being a parent give someone complete control over the developing life of his or her children, even better, it gives the sociopath almost complete control over the other parent. If you want to hurt or control a loving parent, there is no better way than by hurting or manipulating the child the parent loves.

"Stand by Your Man" may have worked for Loretta Lynn and Tammy Wynette, but if your man's a sociopath, it's a really, really bad idea. If I had been collecting data and fed it into a statistical regression model to help me understand Paul's behavior, what would have been clear was a significant correlation—that Paul's conduct was exemplary in public yet increasingly dismissive and even contemptuous of Jessica and me in private. He wasn't a doting husband and father. He was an actor performing when he had an audience. I had entered a twilight zone of subtle erosion. I didn't realize that, so, instead I struggled to understand what had happened to the man with whom I had fallen in love at Yale.

Could Paul be depressed? Sleep-deprived? Could something else be wrong? Clearly not. To see "wonderful Paul," all I had to do was to watch him interact with someone other than me, such as his team of junior associates at work. When they visited our home to see Jessica, I saw the man with whom I had fallen in love—attentive, helpful, kind, and soft-spoken. That begged the question, "What's wrong with *me*? What am I doing wrong?" followed by, "How do I need to change to encourage the loving, attentive man I married to focus on me and our child? How do I fight for a marriage that all too quickly has lost its luster?"

Perhaps these are understandable, even admirable, questions when dealing with a normal person—to look for the role I played in the loss of a connection or spark with my husband. But these are self-destructive queries when your partner is a sociopath. A sociopath's relationship to a targeted individual is akin to the relationship of a black hole to the surrounding cosmos: It sucks in all matter, energy, and light, returning nothing. It is never satisfied, emerging from every cosmic meal demanding, "MORE!" Asking "What can I do to make things better?" or "What more do I need to do to make our marriage work?" just brought me closer to the black hole's gravitational pull, from which escaping with my soul would prove almost impossible. Gravity always wins!

Of Economics 101 And Frogs In Hot Water

You need not have studied economics to know that scarcity drives up value. A sip of water for someone parched in the desert is immensely more valuable than the same sip of water at the end of a meal at a white tablecloth restaurant where an attentive waiter refills your glass constantly. Is love any different? A single gesture of kindness or expression of love in a flowing stream of affection goes all but unnoticed. The value of that same gesture in a love-deprived environment, however, is immeasurable.

Because human beings value love, many of those who seek to control others use love or the promise of love to control and weaken others emotionally. Taking a chapter out of the "Sociopath's Playbook," Paul began by getting me to love and to trust him. Next, he exploited my trust as he changed my world from love-rich and positive to love-starved and negative. This gave him power over me, because it left him as the primary source of something I valued but rarely got—affection.

Why would any self-respecting, confident woman tolerate such behavior? At a basic level, I am no different from a frog, and sadly, neither are you. I have been told on many occasions, typically in business settings, that if a frog is put in hot water, the frog will jump immediately to safety (if it can). The frog's mental arithmetic is pretty simple:

Hot Water → Ouch! → Jump! → Live!

However, if that same frog is placed in comfortable water and the heat is turned up ever so slowly, the frog will stay in the pot until it is boiled to death, because the life-threatening change is too gradual for the frog to detect. In the absence of the perception of danger, the frog's self-preservation instincts do not kick in and tell it to jump to safety. In the frog's brain, the situation probably looks something like this:

Nice Water → Warm → Warmer → A Bit Warmer → Hot → Really Hot → Boiling → Dead Frog!

The moral of the frog story is that it is difficult to sense changes in the environment when the change is subtle but continual. However, it does not take long for small changes to accumulate, adding up to meaningful

CHAPTER 18

shifts and, ultimately, profound and possibly disastrous alterations in the environment. If a company fails to sense these changes, it cannot take the required actions. Even if the owner is aware of symptoms of poor health, such as declining profits, he or she may not understand the root cause behind them and, therefore, may not be able to make the required course corrections. Eventually, the business dies.

I am no expert on frogs, but if the frog is anything like me, it is possible that due to the gradual nature of the change, by the time the frog senses danger, it has been too weakened by the hot water to jump out. Alternatively, the frog may want to jump, but it is being cooked on a gas stove, and the frog is not sure that it can clear the flames as it tries to reach safety. Similarly, the most dangerous time for a woman trying to escape an abusive relationship is when she actually tries to leave. Hence, the question, "Why didn't you just leave?" is insultingly ignorant. In either case, maybe the frog wants to get to safety but cannot. It needs help if it is going to survive. Someone must either turn off the stove or reach in and pull the frog out of the pot. If not, the frog knows it is weak and in danger but must resign itself to a terrible fate. This echoes the sense of helplessness many emotionally and/or physically battered women feel, and it is among the many reasons why it is so hard for them to leave abusive relationships. I understand it now, because, due to my relationship with Paul, I am one of those women.

To make matters worse, you can probably get the frog to jump willingly and happily into a pot of comfortable water if it is disguised to look exactly like the perfect frog habitat, complete with everything the frog needs for its long-term survival and well-being (food, a mate, shelter, nice temperature, and so on). Should the frog have known better than to pick a habitat that looked so perfect? Is the frog weak and pathetic to have stayed as the environment changed, even if there was no conscious perception of the changes until the frog was too weak to leave? Did the frog really *choose* to stay in such a toxic environment if it was unaware of the toxicity?

I pose these questions, because if, as you read my story, you dismiss me as pathetic or weak, then you make the assumption that what happened to me could never happen to you or someone you love (assuming you do not think you or your loved ones are weak and pathetic). But this would be a mistake. Just watch ten episodes of a crime show like *Murder by the Book* or *48 Hours*. What percentage of the close family and friends of individuals who turned out not just to be sociopaths but sociopathic murderers thought the killer was anything other than a wonderful parent, child, sibling, or community leader?

Yes, it makes great drama to focus on "who done it" and "how they solved the crime," but wouldn't it do greater public service to unearth the warning signs? How could others have known, for example, that the head

CHAPTER 18

of the recreation committee, father of two, and little league coach turned out to be a sociopath who had grown tired of his wife and killed her simply to avoid the financial consequences and personal inconvenience of a divorce? Normal people do not do such things, but sociopaths do! What were the red flags? How could the people involved have known? What signs suggest we might be in a similar situation?

"My husband is considerate and caring. He simply couldn't have murdered his third wife," the fourth wife says on national television, standing by her man even when the evidence against her husband is overwhelming. "*The man I know* is simply not capable of such a thing."

Yes, it makes for good television drama, but the problem with vouching for someone's character is that it assumes what you know about a person in certain situations generalizes to all situations. This is not even a good assumption when it comes to nonsociopaths, but it is a terrible assumption when it comes to sociopaths. It is the same as assuming that just because Meryl Streep persuasively portrayed an emotionally tormented World War II concentration camp survivor in *Sophie's Choice* that she could never convincingly play British Prime Minister Margaret Thatcher in *The Iron Lady*. She won an Oscar for both roles. Like Meryl Streep, Sociopaths are accomplished actors, but the real world is their stage. Sociopaths are that good at masking who they are and playing whatever role is required to get what they want, including a long-term marriage to provide a warm, cozy home base and the illusion of normalcy.

TV stories about sociopaths make such compelling drama, because virtually no one suspects ahead of time what these individuals really are. The doting fourth wife, for example, truly loves her husband and sincerely believes he could never have murdered anyone. But if experts are right, that between one and four percent of humans are sociopaths, then our only defense against falling into a sociopath's trap is to understand the prevalence of sociopaths in our everyday lives, to be wary of the subtle signs, and to understand what aspects of our humanity they are using against us.

Of Social Isolation, Pigeons And Food Pellets, Slot Machines, And Intermittent Reinforcement

Isolating a woman is a classic strategy that physically and emotionally abusive men use to make her easier to control. It is a red flag that should never be ignored. My move to Minneapolis to be with Paul, distancing me from family and friends back East, was an ideal place to start. Paul built on that. He refused to visit my family on Thanksgiving, explaining that he did not like my overly intellectual brother who always returned to our parents' home for the holidays. Paul insisted that he was working so hard (note the pity play) that if he was going to take time off from the demands of his grueling career, it only made sense for him to be with people *he* liked so he could relax. (What about my needs to be with my family?) In the almost twenty years I was married to Paul, I never spent a Thanksgiving at my parents' house.

Due to Paul working so much on weekends, we had virtually no social life as a couple, even prior to Jessica's birth. Interestingly, before we started a family, if I went out with friends alone, Paul was often home early that night waiting for me. Here is a typical exchange.

"Hi, Paul, it's great you're home. I thought you wouldn't be home 'til after midnight."

"We got done early," Paul said, his face devoid of any "nice to see you" smile. "I was *really* hoping you'd be here … the one night I'm back before midnight …"

Note that I had made perfectly reasonable decisions and had nothing for which I needed to apologize, yet Paul encouraged me to feel that I had been insensitive because *he* had been home alone for a short period of time.

"I'm really sorry," I said, genuinely regretting losing a rare chance to spend time with my husband. I joined him on the couch and gave him a kiss. He returned it halfheartedly. The fun of a rare evening out with colleagues evaporated.

"You just abandoned me, again," Paul said. Then he shut off the TV and walked out, leaving me alone in the dark. That deflated "What just happened?" feeling enveloped me. I would talk to him tomorrow. Isn't that what married people did—talk about their problems and misunderstandings? I had already started making excuses for him in my mind. Maybe he was just exhausted and disappointed because he had hoped to see me when he walked through the door. Maybe he'd had a bad day at work. Maybe. Maybe. Maybe. It did not occur to me that this was a deliberate setup on his part to control me by making me feel guilty about having a life of my own and not being at his beck and call.

When I talked to Paul the next day, he said, with an appropriately caring but incredulous tone, that of course he had just been kidding about feeling abandoned and that he couldn't believe I took his comment seriously. "I don't even know what you're talking about. Of course it's great you went out with friends."

Yet, when you consider that most communication is nonverbal[28], what had Paul actually expressed? Something like, "Don't you dare have a life outside of me or I will withhold my love and affection from you." Would he ever admit to that? Of course not! After all, what he *said* was " ... It's great you went out with friends." Yet, Paul's unmistakable nonverbal message in this case, and in countless others, exerted subtle influence below my level of conscious awareness. Just like the subjects in the rigged card experiment, I started to feel tense whenever friends suggested I do something with them or when I considered calling them to make plans.

As a result, I started isolating myself by going out less, especially when it might interfere with my time with Paul. If I did go out, I would leave unusually early, just in case Paul beat me home. It did not take long before invitations to join colleagues after work began to wane. Too often my answer was "No," or a guarded, "Okay, but I have to leave early." Anything that weakened me and isolated me made me more malleable, more dependent on Paul.

Looking back, another ploy Paul used to isolate me and to keep the world from responding to me positively was to imply that my friendships with male colleagues were inappropriate. Ironic, don't you think, seeing as he had a virtual harem at work, disproportionally picking young, attractive women as the junior associates for his assignments? I worked in financial investments, so many of my colleagues were male. I was an outgoing, attractive woman in her thirties in great shape with a killer figure, but Paul encouraged me to dress conservatively in dark, drab colors (he loved brown) and in professional but not flattering clothes. He implied often that, by wearing makeup, I was trying to attract other men. I started to feel bad when I even considered putting on mascara, and at some point, without making a deliberate decision, I stopped.

While helping me craft my love-starved, negative environment, Paul did not completely withdraw his love. Were it clear that Paul did not love me anymore, never would, and perhaps never had, I am sure I would have sought a divorce. Instead, he expressed his love sparingly, and, as a result, inconsistently—a small act of kindness here when least expected, a nice dinner together there. Psychologists call this type of reward system "intermittent reinforcement." Intermittent reinforcement is inconsistent and unpredictable, and it has a dark side. It is strongly linked to highly addictive behavior. It is our response to intermittent reinforcement that keeps us playing a game that is stacked against us, because the occasional win keeps our hope alive.

Decades ago, the famous psychologist B.F. Skinner observed in his experiments with rats and pigeons that intermittent reinforcement of something of value (e.g., food) creates highly addictive behavior. I knew about this from the psychology 101 class I had taken during my freshman year at college. What I did not know, however, was that it was being used successfully on me, and that it is a cornerstone of emotional abuse.

A slot machine is one of the best and most intuitive examples of how intermittent reinforcement works. These machines have varying financial payouts at unpredictable times. When a player wins at a slot machine, he or she feels good and gets money—two things the player values. The only way to achieve this success is to play the game again and again and again, enduring failure after failure along the way. Like all gambling games, the odds are in favor of the house and against the player. Still, it is hard for the player to stop, because a big, exciting reward might be just one lever pull away. Because there is no exact correlation between the gambler's actions and the payout of the next pull of the handle, the slot machine could even be broken and unable to issue any positive payout, but the player would have no way of knowing this. Once the addictive behavior has been established, the player will likely persist at the game for a long time.

Now, think of Paul as the slot machine and think of the payout not as money but as love—something fundamental to human existence and happiness, and something I value as a normal, healthy human being. I particularly valued Paul's loving attention, because his maneuverings and my decisions had put me in a love-starved environment, isolated from family and friends. Just like the person pulling the slot machine lever and hoping for the next big payout, without even deciding consciously to do this, I continually tried to please Paul and connect personally with him, hoping to stumble onto something that would trigger him to act in a loving way toward me again. I knew he was capable of showing me love and affection, because he had directed those feelings toward me in the past and I saw him acting in a caring way toward other people. Believing I would receive a positive response eventually, I persisted. The payoff I got, albeit infrequently and unpredictably, only served to keep me in the game, hoping for the next payoff—maybe it would be the next time, or the time after that, or the time after that ...

What Double Standard?

Blinding me even further to how emotionally vacant my relationship with Paul was becoming was the joy and exhaustion of motherhood. It was beyond anything I had ever experienced, anticipated, or imagined. My love for Jessica was so profound and deep, as if I had discovered a hidden, untapped well of joy inside me. Once Jessica was born, I knew I could not return to work full-time.

My unexpected shift in priorities wasn't the only thing that nixed the possibility of returning to my firm. A new career opportunity for Paul added to the mix. Within two weeks of Jessica joining our family, Paul's firm asked him to open an office in New York City. It was a huge compliment and reflected the high esteem in which the partners held Paul. His senior partner and mentor would be the lead partner in the office, and Paul would be his right-hand man. I resigned and became a full-time mom and logistics coordinator for our move back East.

The New York metropolitan area is exorbitantly expensive, so we bought a small house in a suburb that allowed Paul to commute into the city. He continued to work around the clock, often staying in the city overnight to establish the new office or travel to service his out-of-town clients. I did not mind. In fact, we got along better when Paul was away, because the white space in our relationship was less apparent when he was not there. When he was away, we spoke on the phone each evening. I updated him on Jessica and other issues. He rarely talked about work, other than telling me about his long hours, demanding senior partner, and how little sleep he was getting.

It was a happy time for me. Not only did I have Jessica and the excitement and fulfillment of watching my child grow and blossom, I found Renee, a wonderful woman to care for Jessica a few days a week. I used this time to launch a small advertising and public relations consulting service. It was perfect. I could work at 9:00 a.m. while Jessica was with Renee or at 9:00 p.m. after putting Jessica to bed.

With Paul rarely home, my odd working hours had almost no impact on our marriage. I booked between twenty and thirty hours a week, and because Jessica was asleep during at least half that time, it allowed me to be an almost full-time mom to her. Becoming close friends with several moms

Husband Liar Sociopath   53

in the neighborhood who had children Jessica's age came easily. My family was now only about a five-hour drive away, and Paul's mom was only two hours away. While in Minneapolis, I had been running on fumes. Now I had a full tank of gas and was out cruising in a red convertible on a perpetually brilliant sunny day. Life was good. I felt lucky, successful, fulfilled, and even joyous at times.

Paul rarely informed me of his travel plans for work—just what day he'd be leaving, what day he'd be returning, and about what time. Business trip after business trip, he neglected to give me any specific information. He had a cell phone now. Why did I want to know what plane he was on or what city he was visiting or the hotel at which he would be staying? If I needed to get in touch with him for any reason, I could just call his cell and leave a message. He'd get back in touch with me when he could.

I trusted Paul. I certainly did not want to appear overbearing or controlling, as he accused me so often of being when I asked for specifics. I wanted to be a great wife who understood and supported the career demands of her superstar husband. Why should I care about what flight he was on or where he was staying as long as he came home safely? A colleague of his joked that he had never known any husband who was given such a "long leash." This comment was a welcome reminder that I was not a controlling person. Yet, if my behavior suggested to others that, in fact, I was the opposite of controlling, why did Paul consistently accuse me of being controlling? I had no answers. It was just another nagging data point that refused to fit within my current framework. I would have to wait over a decade for a "light bulb moment" of resolution.

One night, I was expecting Paul home from a three-day business trip. At about 10 p.m., I was seconds from being finished with my work when I heard the door open.

"You're home!" I called from my home office so Paul could hear me. "I'm just finishing up. I'll be right there."

Paul did not respond or pop into my office. Instead, I heard the television go on. I finished the last sentence I was writing, saved the file, and powered off my computer. No more than a minute or two later, I greeted Paul in the family room.

He scowled. "I've been away for three days, and you can't even get up to say hi?"

As always, I stupidly went into defensive mode, explaining myself and assuming he had some valid reason to be upset with me instead of labeling his complaint as a setup to establish that I was somehow selfish and inconsiderate, when that was far from the truth.

"Paul, I didn't know when to expect you home. Anyway, it's great you're here. How was your trip?"

CHAPTER 20

"I can't believe you didn't even get up to say hi," Paul repeated.

"Paul," I replied with as caring a tone as I could muster, even though I was growing annoyed, "I was just finishing up. I don't understand why it's such a big deal. We're talking about sixty seconds. You could've come in to see me. I just needed to finish the thought I was writing down. I didn't want to lose it and—"

"It's pretty disappointing after how hard I'm working for you so you can spend time with Jessica."

I could not change Paul's perception that I was being uncaring, inconsiderate, and unappreciative. The absurdity of Paul's accusations in light of what had actually happened—that I did not immediately stop my work to jump up and see him when he could have easily walked into my office to say hello—penetrated me. What was really going on? My mind percolated. Did Paul view our relationship as so lopsided—he entitled to come and go as he pleased but me needing to be available to him the second *he* was ready to talk to me or wanted something from me, including to simply not be alone? I did not sleep well that night.

This was sociopath math in action. Yet, even when Paul's behavior grew more extreme, it would take me years to label it as such. If it was not evident to me that in Paul's mind he was allowed to change our wedding date, work on vacations and while I was in labor, be in the office all weekend, and stay in the city night after night, cancelling personal plan after personal plan for the sake of his career, but that I could not be busy or distracted the second he wanted something from me, a mis-delivered UPS package a month later made it unmistakably clear.

To accommodate a client deadline, I was expecting an overnight package on Friday with materials I needed to work on that day to prepare for a client conference call first thing Sunday morning. I had agreed to the weekend conference call to help my client, a business school friend, prepare for a last-minute but critically important Monday morning meeting. Ironically, over the weekend, Paul had promised not to work on Saturday so we could hang out, have some quality time together with Jessica, and then go out for a grown-up dinner—just the two of us. Paul rarely kept such promises. Still, I had scheduled Renee to stay with Jessica on Saturday evening so Paul and I could go out to dinner.

Unfortunately, the client's assistant wrote down my address incorrectly. By the time UPS and I figured out where the package was, the best they could do was deliver it on Saturday morning. I told Paul what had happened and that I would need to work for about four hours during "our" Saturday together. I had no choice. It was either work on Saturday to meet the Sunday morning deadline or let down an important client and business school friend. As Paul had worked through vacations, weekends, evenings,

CHAPTER 20

and holidays—even through my labor pains—I naively expected mutual respect for my work demands.

Paul's reaction caught me off-guard. "I can't believe you'd do this! You're going to ruin the time I took off for us to spend together?"

Nothing I said seemed to appease Paul. Our bed on Friday night felt icy cold. I got up early Saturday morning with Jessica. Paul slept in.

As soon as the materials arrived, I got to work so the project would not loom over the day. The plan had been to work on it on Friday when Jessica was with Renee. I asked Renee if she could come during the day on Saturday, but she could not. Nor could a few other baby sitters I called. With no one to watch Jessica while I worked, I hoped Paul could help. But when he finally got up, Paul crashed in front of the TV. Couldn't I appreciate how tired he was after working so hard all week?

The assignment took longer than I had hoped, especially because I had to keep Jessica occupied as well. I felt horrible, putting in toddler movie after toddler movie to keep her distracted so I could get some work done. Finally, by midafternoon, I was finished. For dinner, I got dressed up—washed and styled my hair, put on makeup, a nice dress, and jewelry. Paul looked handsome. I was looking forward to some rare and much needed one-on-one time together.

"I can't believe you worked today," Paul said as soon as we pulled away in the car.

"Paul, I explained what happened," I said. "I didn't plan it to be this way. It was just a mix-up. The project should've been done by Friday, but the client made a mistake."

"Still, the one time I put aside time to be together, and *you* work!"

"Paul, this happens to me all the time with your work demands. Cancelled plan after cancelled plan, and I just roll with it. I understand that things happen and clients and partners can be really demanding."

"But you said it would take you about four hours, and it took a lot longer."

"I did my best," I said. "What was I supposed to do? And besides, I was distracted a lot because I had to watch Jessica."

"So you're saying it's *my* fault," Paul snapped.

"That's not what I said. Can't we just try to enjoy our dinner together?" Paul sulked.

"I'm sorry," I said, hoping Paul would reciprocate and apologize for his lack of support and understanding and that we could put the incident behind us and enjoy dinner.

But "I'm sorry" never crossed his lips. Sociopaths do not apologize, at least not in a sincere way. If someone made a mistake, it was not Paul. If he felt bad, someone else was to blame—me.

CHAPTER 20

Puppeteer Paul was at it again, pulling strings and manipulating me into feeling apologetic and sorry for him when *his* behavior was selfish and unsupportive. Although I understand many of his techniques now, back then I was clueless. As a result, I was no more than a marionette, being controlled by the tug of twine or, more accurately, by a disapproving tone or look, by the withdrawal of attention or affection, or by just by the right choice of words.

Once we were at the restaurant, in view of other people, Paul acted like the perfect doting husband. I put on a brave face and went through the motions of enjoying a rare evening out. Inside though, like a flower deprived of sunlight and water, I was dying.

A Second Look

What was Paul really doing? What were the specific tools and techniques the master puppeteer employed that are also used by fellow sociopaths and manipulators? Paul started by using the technique of *devaluing* or *minimizing my needs*. As a sociopath, this came naturally to him, because a sociopath truly places zero value on anyone's needs but his own. By Paul—someone I loved and respected—placing minimal or no value on my work, and without even knowing this was happening, I began to question the value I placed on my work and how important it was for me personally as well as for our family.

If I valued my client and my career, with a meeting scheduled Sunday morning and a package that was delayed, what option did I have but to work on Saturday? If my need was reasonable, which it was, then Paul's behavior was unreasonable. To prevent me from reaching this conclusion, Paul went on the *distraction offensive*. He suggested that I misrepresented how long the project would take. Not only did this *distraction* technique create a temporary blind spot to the real issues, it also undermined my credibility (clearly, I could not accurately estimate how long my work would take) and my integrity (perhaps I misled Paul on purpose). This kept me on the defensive, and defending myself diverted me from Paul's selfishness, arrogance, and sense of entitlement.

When I pointed out that it took me longer than expected because I had to juggle caring for Jessica and work, Paul accused me of accusing him of being the reason it took longer than expected to complete the assignment. This technique of *accusing me of attacking him* also put me on my heels and averted my focus from his selfish choices and behavior. He used this same technique after returning from our honeymoon when he said, "It seems you're calling *me* a liar."

Paul's entitled attitude and the fact that he acted so superior were also subtle methods of manipulation. He spoke and acted on the assumption I was never to inconvenience or disappoint him, but he was permitted to inconvenience and disappoint me at will. He also placed himself above watching his daughter while I worked. By acting so superior, Paul actually increased the likelihood that I would view him as superior and capitulate to his views.

CHAPTER 21

Then Paul *invoked my pity* by pointing out how hard he worked. He upped the ante by implying that he was underappreciated. Since I am an empathetic person, I am hardly going to kick someone when he or she is down. In fact, if I feel badly for someone, like most people, I will try to make that person feel better. So, what did I do? I apologized! But through all the selfish behavior and the ruining of our one-on-one time together, Paul did not apologize for anything he did or said. He took no responsibility. It was all *my* fault.

Never having to say, "I'm sorry," is not a sign of love, as that ridiculous line in *Love Story* suggests. Quite the contrary, it is a clue you may be dealing with a sociopath. Sociopaths do not apologize, or if they do, the apology is insincere (and your intuition is likely to tell you this). It comes down to sociopath math. In Paul's mind, my needs did not count. As a sociopath, he felt no empathy for me. Why should he apologize when I did not matter to him, other than to serve his needs, a duty at which I had just failed miserably?

Regardless of whatever Kool-Aid I had been drinking in the past, the clarity of the double standard was unshakable that weekend. There was no way to excuse it away or reframe it. Yet, while the double standard in our relationship was clear, what was not clear was what to do about it. If I had known about sociopaths and realized that Paul's behavior was sending out huge warning signs that he was a sociopath and had only married me so I could be the logistics coordinator for his life and that he would never put my needs or the needs of our daughter before his, then I should have left Paul right then. I could have easily rebuilt my life as a single mother. I had a wonderful education (my MBA was only a few years old), a career on which I could build, a family not too far away, and supportive friends down the street. Also, I was in my late thirties, athletic, and still quite attractive, so there remained a strong possibility that my future might still involve a loving and meaningful relationship.

I did not know that sociopaths "walk among us" and that I was getting clear signals that Paul was one of them. Instead, I struggled to understand how big a deal this double standard of Paul's was and what I should do about it. After all, for the first time in years, I was happy in other aspects of my life—I loved being Jessica's mom; I had a successful new business venture that gave me the flexibility I needed to function as a full-time, stay-at-home mom; I had good friends and a nice house; and I thought Paul and I were building considerable financial security together. Although Paul was rarely home, we talked each night when he called, and we did share intimate time together when he was home. It was unclear if this double standard was worrisome enough that I should put the rest of my life at risk.

What was clear was that if I did not want to incur Paul's disapproval,

CHAPTER 21

my work and personal life had to be invisible to him, one hundred percent of it conducted when Paul was away, engaged in a project of his own, or asleep. But with Paul away so much, how much of a sacrifice was that on my part? Surely, I could do that to keep the peace and to keep our family intact, especially because after a year of trying unsuccessfully, and with my fortieth birthday on the horizon, I was pregnant with our second child.

The Show Must Go On

"Where secrecy or mystery begins, vice or roguery is not far off."
— Samuel Johnson

 Keeping my life all but invisible and inconsequential to Paul was not the only pillar upon which the "success" of my marriage (i.e., lack of tension) depended. Another pillar was accepting living in an information void. Secrecy is symptomatic of sociopaths. They use it to cover things up—gambling, other women, and various self-indulgent pastimes of which the average spouse might not approve. Perhaps they also tend toward secrecy because it makes them feel powerful to withhold information—to know something to which no one else is privy. No matter the reason, I learned to live with only scraps of information about where my husband was on any given day or night.

 Whether because I was almost forty when I had Daniel, our second child, or for some other reason, my second pregnancy was complicated. Daniel was to be delivered by planned C-section. Unless Daniel decided to come into the world exceptionally early, Paul and I knew our son's birthday in advance. Yet, with the C-section just days away, I did not know where Paul was, only that he was out of town traveling on business somewhere in the US. Emotionally, I felt minimized and abandoned. Rationally, I told myself it was no big deal. If Paul was out of town and there was a crisis, how useful could he be to Jessica and me until he returned anyway? I was just being foolish and needy to want more information. It would be okay, especially because my mother had come to help.

 I loved having my mother at the house, because it was such a rare event. We spent a few days shopping for Daniel and Jessica and stocking the house with food. We wanted to make sure Jessica would feel like an important big sister, not a displaced sibling. My mom had not been at my wedding to Paul, and she had not been there for Jessica's birth, due to my father being ill. Also, because Paul disliked my brother, I never saw her at Thanksgiving anymore. As a result, I was overjoyed to be spending rare mother-daughter time with her at such a special moment in my life.

 The day before the C-section, everything seemed to be going as planned. Paul arrived home well after I had put Jessica to bed, and I was tired and

CHAPTER 22

fighting sleep. I tried to stay awake, but with my eyes heavy, I said goodnight to my mom and Paul and went upstairs to bed.

A few minutes later, Paul joined me in the bedroom. As he closed the door behind him, it seemed to shut with a particularly loud thud.

"Are you going to explain this?" he snapped.

"What are you talking about?" I asked, truly shocked by Paul's anger and clueless as to the cause.

"You're excluding me from everything! You aren't paying any attention to *me*. You're making me feel like a stranger in my own house!"

"*What?*"

"You heard me," Paul said, simmering with anger.

"I'm about to have a C-section tomorrow. I'm exhausted. I don't understand!" My pulse quickened, and my mouth went dry.

Paul left the room, closing the door hard but just short of slamming it so as not to alert my mother. I heard his footsteps go down the stairs, and then the TV turned on.

I burst into tears. Like a child reprimanded by her father for something she did not do, I wanted to run to my mother for support, to feel the warmth of her arms around me and hear her soft voice telling me it would be okay. But I was an adult, almost forty years old. I didn't want my mother to worry about me, and I was ashamed to be in a situation where on the eve of giving birth to my second child, the man I married would treat me so poorly. And why?

What had just happened? What had I done? Had I really pushed Paul away? He had been working around the clock, like usual. He had not taken any time off to get things ready for the baby. That was his choice. I wished he had. But asking Paul to focus on me and "us" never went particularly well, so, as usual, I had gone about doing all the preparation for our second child myself, with a little last-minute assistance from my mother. He was the one who had chosen to be so remote. Why was he angry with me?

Sleep that night was elusive; the interaction with Paul kept replaying in my mind. When Paul came to bed hours later, I pretended to be asleep. I did not want to talk to him. I remained as still as I could, curled up in a near fetal position, positioned as far from Paul's side of the bed as possible without falling off the edge. I did not want him to touch me, even by accident. At such a precious and precarious time in my life, on the eve our second child's birth, he was being a selfish ass.

The next morning, exhausted, deflated, and profoundly hurt by Paul's verbal attack the night before, I got Jessica ready, and my mom and I drove her to her half-day preschool. On the morning of my second child's birth, I should have been feeling a mixture of joy and tension. Instead, I felt frightened, unnerved, and was battling back despair. When Paul finally awoke,

CHAPTER 22

I hugged him and told him I loved him but that I was unsettled by our interaction the night before. I was certain he would shake off the insanity of the previous evening and focus on making sure I was feeling positive for the big day ahead, hug me, and say he was sorry. He didn't. Sociopaths are never sorry. They have no remorse, and they are never wrong. If they are angry, it is always someone else's fault.

It did not matter that I was going to have a C-section that morning. Paul's needs had not been met the night before. As a result, Paul felt abandoned, overlooked, minimized, hurt, and not in control.

Many of us have been taught that for someone like Paul to have feelings like this, he might have been treated poorly as a child. Perhaps his mother or father did not give him the love and attention he needed, and this resulted in oversensitivity or a feeling of emptiness. If this were the case, than perhaps, insight, understanding, and love would help make Paul feel whole again.

Having studied psychology as an undergraduate, I certainly thought this was plausible—that love and understanding were likely antidotes to Paul's "moments of weirdness" (i.e., self-absorbed nastiness). From what I knew about Paul's childhood, Ruth had children so close in age that at one point she had three children under the age of four. Perhaps, as the oldest, Paul felt increasingly displaced and craved the attention he wanted but could not get from his overwhelmed mother and inconsistent, alcoholic father.

Such potential explanations actually distracted me from the truth, made me believe change was possible when it wasn't, and kept me in a toxic relationship far longer than if I had known to consider that Paul might be a sociopath. Wondering if someone involved in a difficult relationship might be a sociopath is a question we should all know to ask, because even though they comprise just one to four percent of the population, by their very nature, sociopaths must be even more common in high-conflict relationships. Sociopaths can come from loving parents or abusive parents, intact homes or broken homes, rich parents or poor parents. Sociopaths are simply hardwired differently, with studies indicating that a significant amount of their nature is genetically determined[29].

If I am right and Paul is a sociopath, no elaborate explanation is required to account for his behavior. It just comes down to sociopath math. In Paul's world, Paul is the only one who matters—ever. If his needs are not being met, that is unacceptable, and someone else is to blame. Seeing as he truly cared for no one other than himself (including Jessica, me, and our unborn child), it was of absolutely no concern to him that his behavior might upset me at such a critical time. Should he have been concerned that I would tell someone about his acerbic behavior? Of course not. He would just deny it, and seriously, who would believe me?

CHAPTER 22

My mother stayed behind to pick up Jessica from preschool and bring her to the hospital to see her new brother and me. As Paul drove me to the hospital, my despair was unshakable. I fought back tears. It was another moment of clarity. No matter what Paul was feeling in this situation, wasn't my physical and emotional health—as well as that of our unborn child—paramount? Paul had not taken any time off from work until the day of the C-section. If he had wanted to be involved in any of the shopping or preparation, all he had to do was ask. How selfish and contrived to say now that I had pushed him aside, that I had been ignoring him, that I had kept him from being involved.

Paul did not talk to me in the car, but his body communicated his contempt—eyes straight ahead, jaw and shoulders tight. When we arrived at the hospital, I struggled to speak during the admittance process, and my voice cracked continually. My eyes pooled with water, releasing an occasional droplet down my cheek. As I wiped each tear away, I apologized to the admitting nurse.

"She's just tense and worried about the C-section," Paul explained with a tender tone to his voice and a charming, relaxed smile. He put his arm around me and drew me close. "You'll take great care of her, right?"

"Aren't you lucky to have such a great husband," a nurse said. "He's a keeper."

I felt sick.

This quick change in persona from monster to nice guy (or nice guy to monster), and the failure to acknowledge it subsequently, is characteristic of sociopaths. The monster was the real Paul, who was now evident more and more, but only when there was no adult audience other than me. Even though the evidence of Paul's true self was mounting, I still had no idea to what I should attribute his behavior. I still had no idea that the "nice Paul" was, in fact, fake. As in the hospital, sociopath Paul was rarely visible to anyone but me. His public persona was saint-like. This meant I was all alone in my observations.

Since no one else seemed to witness this callous behavior, it made me doubt myself. Maybe it *was* just me. Maybe I was losing it. Maybe Paul was right that I was selfish, controlling, and overly sensitive. If that were true, shouldn't I try to change? Shouldn't I feel lucky to have a Prince Charming in my life who cared about me in spite of my considerable failings? If I was really as flawed as Paul thought, would anyone else ever love me? If not, shouldn't I do everything possible to hold on to my marriage with Paul?

If I told my mother or a friend what had transpired the night before, would they have said, "I bet Paul's a sociopath, that your marriage is a fraud, and that you should end it now before it gets worse and ends badly"? Probably not. Even a friend or my mother would find my reports

CHAPTER 22

of Paul's behavior so incredulous that it would be easier to assume I was simply overly emotional on the eve of a C-section, that I had blown some interaction out of proportion, or that it was just a misunderstanding. Such exchanges with Paul left me more and more emotionally raw, "off," and overly sensitive, so this conclusion that "it was me" would probably have seemed more reasonable than the possibility that, without provocation, my husband had acted so callously on the eve of our son's birth.

Devil Woman

Unable to abandon the premise that Paul was fundamentally a good, loving, honest man who truly cared about me, I had to explain his behavior in some other way. Still not ready to conclude that I was an essentially selfish, controlling person, as Paul often suggested, the more extreme Paul's moments of weirdness became, the more I assumed he must be under severe stress or depressed. I needed to love and support him through whatever was going on.

Having children changes the dynamics of a relationship and puts stress on a marriage. Sleep deprivation darkens moods and compromises cognition. Could that be what was wrong? With Paul averaging less than five hours of sleep a night, perhaps that was why he was so irritable at home and why he paid so little attention to Jessica and Daniel. Wasn't he working around the clock to provide for us? If he was chronically and profoundly starved for sleep, if he was missing our one-on-one relationship, if past childhood hurts needed mending, shouldn't I respond by focusing as much as I could on him by being loving and supportive?

Within days of Daniel's birth, Paul returned to his super-human work schedule. As before, Paul's focus and relentless dedication to his firm left little time for our relationship. At least Paul's Herculean work schedule was financially rewarding. For him, the payoff was to treat himself to a new two-seater BMW that he just had to have. (Again, note the self-indulgent, impractical, status-oriented, expensive purchase.) I thought it extravagant and impractical, but he was the one working so hard. If he wanted to splurge on himself and we had the money, he encouraged me to think it would be selfish of me to oppose it. For me, the payoff of Paul's financial success was that I could continue to be as much of a full-time mother as I wanted. I found being the mother of my two children the most joyous experience of my life, so I counted my blessings for Paul's lucrative compensation and the freedom it afforded me. I continued to spend most of my week being Jessica and Daniel's mom and worked part-time for myself, finding a steady flow of freelance advertising and public relations projects.

I did projects for people I liked and worked on assignments I enjoyed. I had a group of close female friends who were also mothers of children under five. Paul's long hours and considerable travel made it easy for my work life and my social life with other moms to stay invisible to him. As long as I arranged my life to fall under Paul's radar and focused entirely on him on those rare occasions when he was home (and awake), our relationship was workable.

The New York office continued to grow and thrive. Paul was offered an unprecedented partnership after only five years with the firm. It was unimaginable! I was so proud of him. He truly was a superstar.

With Paul so busy and my days brimming with my own work and caring for Jessica and Daniel, I rarely got into the city to see him. One day, however, after Paul had been a partner for two years, I stopped by for lunch. He introduced me to the newest members of his growing team of consultants. Paul had been raving about a new consultant named Anne-Marie. She was a top graduate of New York University's Stern School of Business, and Paul had convinced her to join his firm over other lucrative offers. She did, ostensibly under the condition that she would work on Paul's projects exclusively. According to Paul, she was the smartest, most capable, hardest working consultant he had ever met. She was the only person Paul had ever met who was willing to match the insane hours he was willing to work. She was the next Paul. She was a superstar.

Anne-Marie was not at all what I expected. She had a decidedly unattractive horsey face framed by dull brown hair that was in need of a cut. Carrying at least thirty extra pounds on an already big frame, she moved awkwardly. Her choice of frumpy clothing did not enhance her appearance or make her look polished. But as Paul turned toward Anne-Marie at the appropriate part of the, "This is my wife, Onna. Onna, this is Anne-Marie" introduction, Paul was transformed. As if bewitched by a sorceress' spell, his tone softened, becoming lyrical and velvety. His eyes seemed to caress her large frame as his glance lingered upon her for an uncomfortably long moment. Her response to me felt overly polite and sweet, downright saccharine. Something primal in me stirred. No way, I assured myself. Just no way! I glimpsed her left hand and sighed when I saw a wedding band. A flood of guilt followed the relief. Paul was honorable, honest, and incredibly hardworking; how could I doubt his fidelity and integrity? How silly of me to feel threatened. I was being ridiculous.

To avoid any awkward silence, I asked her about a project she was working on with Paul. My take on her after our interaction was that she was smart for someone from a good business school but not in the rarified atmosphere of "brilliant," as Paul asserted. Still Paul continued to sing her praises week after week and month after month. Annie-Marie could do no wrong.

About a year after Anne-Marie joined Paul's firm, he informed me that his consulting firm was considering branching out into a new business area,

CHAPTER 23

and the partners were willing to allow him to start a separate, sister company to address this new opportunity. Paul wanted to invest in the new company and be its CEO. In fact, the whole thing was his idea—actually his *and* Anne-Marie's.

My heart quickened, and the blood coursing through my body instantly made me feel several degrees hotter. Inside, a voice screamed "Noooooooooooooooo!" With Paul making partner, we were on financial easy street. We wouldn't be just okay; we would be well off. We had already repaid all of our debts, and if Paul worked just five more years (and we were financially conservative), we would have enough money to do a major "regroup." We could move to a college town, where Paul and I might be able to teach or work at the college (taking a huge cut in pay), and we would have a wonderful quality of life and a wholesome place to raise Jessica and Daniel. Putting our money at risk and Paul becoming an entrepreneur was not part of the plan.

Any startup is risky, and new ventures require that the founding cast of characters devote insane hours to these fledgling companies to try to make them profitable. Was this ever going to stop? Was I ever going to have a somewhat normal marriage and family life? I wanted to support Paul's goals and dreams, as I always had, and starting this company was Paul's dream, so I swallowed hard and gave Paul my blessing for his new undertaking. I told him how much confidence I had in him and that we would make it happen, if this was what he really wanted.

Paul handpicked the employees for the new company. In spite of her mere one year of post-business school experience, Anne-Marie would be his second in command. For her and her alone, he promised a huge pay raise and more prestigious title. I was relatively friendly with Sally, a woman who had worked at Paul's company, starting at a junior level in Minneapolis. Sally was also going to be part of the new venture. She told me in private that rumors were circulating around the firm that Paul was lobbying to more than double Anne-Marie's salary, while everyone else had been asked to take a pay cut to keep costs low for the new venture. To pull this off, Paul had used up incredible personal "capital" with the investing partners and had agreed to an eighty percent pay cut himself. So much for making partner in five years and all the commensurate financial security! He had just decided to gamble it all on this new venture. The only person guaranteed to be better off financially—a lot better off—was Anne-Marie.

I was worried. Something seemed very wrong. I talked to Paul about the wisdom of this decision, but his icy response and dismissive tone made it clear that his decisions to put Anne-Marie's career in overdrive and to take a gargantuan pay cut himself were not only sound business decisions but also none of my concern. After all, I was ignorant about all the relevant details, including her brilliance. When I pressed the point, he redirected the discussion to ensure I would retreat from the topic.

"You're jealous of Anne-Marie."

"No, I'm not," I said. "It just seems odd that she's the only one to be promoted to a level far beyond what she ever would have been even if she stayed with your consulting company or if she got a job anywhere else. People in your company are talking."

"Are you spying on me? She deserves every penny, and she's vital to the success of the startup. I can't do it without her."

"Paul," I said, "it's a startup. You're hardly making more money than she is, and you've been a partner and out of business school for almost seven years now. She's had her MBA just a year, and you're making her almost equivalent to you. It just doesn't add up. Won't it create resentment among people who've worked with you a lot longer than she has?"

"Clearly you're the only one who's resentful," Paul replied. "You're jealous because Anne-Marie's so successful and you're just a mom."

Tied up in knots once again, I did not know how to respond. I was happy with the decision I had made about balancing work and being a mom. I had not just done it for me and for the kids; I had done it to preserve my marriage. If I had continued to work full-time as a financial consultant, placing as much of a priority on my career as Paul did on his, Paul and I would never have seen each other, much less the kids. How long would our marriage have lasted? How would Daniel and Jessica have been impacted? I knew of no partners in Paul's firm who were married with kids who had a spouse with a full-time, demanding job. For most people, it was not a stable long-term solution.

Not understanding Paul's manipulative trap, his accusation that I was jealous of Anne-Marie made me want to prove to him that I was not. (Notice I was totally distracted from the topic I wanted to discuss with Paul and had been put on the defensive yet again.) The best way to prove that I was not jealous of Anne-Marie? Support Paul.

Paul's Dream

Sociopaths generally have a high need for stimulation, which experts believe stems from the shallowness of their emotional life. They cannot and do not experience the love, affection, attachment, and happiness that create the rich tapestry of a normal individual's interpersonal and emotional life. Sociopaths fill the resulting void with action and distraction. They loathe boredom and downtime, so they are prone to making quick, risky decisions and pressing for immediate action. For sociopaths, it is as if the downside of any decision they make simply does not exist.[30]

I am somewhat the opposite. I make decisions by gathering data and considering my options, often overthinking the negative consequences of a decision and wondering about the road not taken. As a result, I admired Paul's propensity for and comfort with quick decisions, taking risks, and never second-guessing himself.

There are several reasons why sociopaths have unshakable confidence in their quick, risk-laden choices. Unlike mere mortals, they lack fear, including fear of failure. They have no concern for the impact of their choices on other people. Sociopaths also have such a grandiose sense of themselves; they feel superior to others and are certain they will succeed.

This constellation of characteristics—quick decision-making, risk-taking, action-oriented, lack of fear, and complete confidence in oneself in the face of uncertainty—does not scream *sociopath* to most of us. Instead, it suggests something we admire—*leadership*. Unfortunately, instead of seeing these characteristics and running in the opposite direction, we are drawn in as if to a gravitational force. This is particularly true with sociopaths, because they are often charismatic and charming, highly skilled at telling people what they want to hear and excellent at getting even the most intelligent, experienced, and capable people to march to the beat of their drum. Is it any wonder that there are countless examples of individuals and groups who have had their lives derailed by a charismatic sociopath?

At first, a genuine leader and a sociopath may look identical—just as one's true soul mate and a sociopath may also look identical. And for all the reasons noted, since you assume the person who is influencing you is a well-intentioned, talented, dynamic leader—as I did when I first worked with Paul and for almost two decades afterwards—you can often be emotionally and

CHAPTER 24

financially past the point of no easy return before you realize the bitter truth. Then, because sociopaths do not play by the rules and are often vindictive and vengeful toward anyone who has seen them for who they really are, getting away from the sociopath and getting on with your life can be a nightmare.

Another consequence of sociopaths' unique hardwiring to being stimulation-seeking, able to experience pleasure (but not happiness), risk-prone, devoid of empathy, and having no conscience is that they do not constrain their sexual appetite. As a result, they can be sexually promiscuous and adventurous. Not only do they seek sex for the sake of pleasure, they use the illusion of love and physical intimacy to manipulate others.

Those primal feelings when I met Anne-Marie were triggered for a reason, but I suppressed them. Men and women could have mentor-mentee relationships without sleeping with each other, right? Paul was a man of great honor and integrity, right? Back in business school he refused to help me with a class for fear of appearing unethical. An affair would have been far, far worse. There was no way Paul would do *that*.

The perfect sociopath storm was forming. Not only did Paul want to invest our money in this new company, take on the professional risk inherent in any startup, and take a huge pay cut—all with Anne-Marie at his side, squirreling away an obscene amount of money for someone with her nascent credentials—he insisted that the company be based in Connecticut. It would be less expensive than New York, he argued. This would require us to move as soon as possible. In fact, he had already scoped out office space and put a hold on the first floor of a building.

Paul and I had moved three times since receiving our MBAs several years earlier—our apartment in Minnesota, our house in Minnesota, and our house in the New York suburbs. I did not want to move again. With Paul's work demands getting the company off the ground, I knew the entire move would fall on me and put my life, my work, and my clients at risk. Yet, relocating to Connecticut would put us closer to my family. And with two young children, being closer to grandparents was something I valued, even if it meant leaving behind my newfound friends and happy life in the New York suburbs. If this were *the* move, the final move to put us where we really wanted to be, then maybe it was worth it. Reluctantly, I agreed to relocate.

Paul's House

Paul's ideas about our next house and my ideas could have not diverged more. He wanted to build a $1 million dream house from the ground up. To me, it was absurd. Houses take money, time, and energy to build. We had none of those to spare. It was already March. I wanted to be settled into a new house by July to allow Jessica to make a few friends before starting kindergarten. That wasn't enough time.

Paul started staying in Connecticut during the week to work and commuted back to our home on weekends. In typical Paul overachieving style, he worked nonstop on the start-up, often not even having enough free time to call home in the evening. It was not as if I was swimming in free time either. I was scrambling to prepare our house to sell and to look into towns, school systems, and preschools in the area surrounding Paul's new office. I also needed to purge, pack, and organize our belongings, continue to be a mom to Jessica and Daniel, and spend some final quality time with friends I would never be living near again, not to mention finish projects for my clients. If I had any free time, I wanted to keep my business alive and ensure a smooth move for Jessica and Daniel, not build a house.

Our financial present and future were gutted overnight. Not only had we invested a considerable amount of our money in the new venture, Paul's gigantic pay cut made my income jump from inconsequential to meaningful. The time and effort required by such a quick move with two young children, not to mention building a house from scratch, would crash my income to almost zero, just when we needed it most. To keep our overall financial and personal risk at acceptable levels, it was clear to me that we needed not only to avoid building an expensive house but rather to buy a small, conservative house or rent. I even suggested that the kids and I stay in New York and that Paul rent a small apartment in Connecticut until the new venture proved viable.

Paul would not hear of it. He would not consider living apart. (Remember Jenny's role in Paul's life as maid, housekeeper, and sexual partner?) Paul was certain the new venture would be wildly successful. Didn't I have faith in him? He insisted the family stay together. How could I value our family so little that I was willing for us to live apart? Case closed.

Paul found a builder with a lot on a remote road and a floor plan that

CHAPTER 25

the contractor promised could be built in three months. Paul loved it. Including all the extras Paul wanted, it would cost a "mere" $1,000,000. To humor Paul (a stupid idea), I agreed to look at it only as part of a broader house-hunting effort that also included much smaller, less expensive houses.

I hated the lot and the floor plan. I knew it would take significantly longer to build than the contractor claimed, and it certainly would never be done by July. Every house in which I had ever lived had brimmed with character and warmth. This house was big, boxy, isolated, dark, and cold. Not a neighbor in sight. Not a child to play with. Not even a good place to put up a swing set for Jessica and Daniel. Nothing. It was completely uninteresting—big, remote, and expensive.

Paul saw it differently. It made a statement. It had lots of room for entertaining his current and future employees and for his family to visit. It would also have ample space for both of us to have a home office. Paul did not care that it would be dark, because he was rarely around during daylight hours anyway. He did not care if it was isolating for the kids and me either, because he would not be the one driving twenty minutes to the closest park. For Paul, it was ideal. He had to have it. And he was so busy that he wanted to seal the deal immediately and not waste another minute looking for other houses. He had a company to run. Decision made!

I could not agree to buy this house. It was light years beyond my comfort zone for financial risk. It was also wrong for the kids, and it was wrong for me. I knew I would be miserable there. Besides, despite what the builder said, I was certain it would not be finished in time for Jessica to start the school year there. Therefore, it would require an interim move and result in even more disruption in our lives. With great confidence and conviction, I told Paul, "No."

He was shocked. He wanted the house. It was his dream. Weren't we supposed to support each other's dreams? He came up with a plethora of reasons why I should not even think twice about the expense. Think about all the money we had saved that *he* had made! He assured me that he had complete confidence his new business venture would be successful, telling me about all the milestones the business had already reached on time or even ahead of schedule. Soon, he'd be making the same level of money he did as a partner in his former firm. I'd been to business school, too, though, and I knew the odds of any new venture succeeding. It was risky. It would take a lot of time, and it might even fail.

Further, when I pointed out the people I knew who had built even small houses from scratch and that none had been completed within the timeframe our builder was promising, Paul told me how distrusting I was and that I didn't understand that this house would be the builder's sole priority and that the target date was totally feasible. According to Paul, I was being an alarmist. I just did not "get it." If I did not want to be involved in the day-to-day decisions about the house, he would take care of it all.

I did not back down. Even if I thought spending the money was prudent (which I did not), and even if I thought the builder could finish on time for us to move directly into the house (which I was sure was impossible), and even if Paul would be the one to coordinate all the work with the builder while I orchestrated the move and all the logistics with the kids, it still did not matter to me, because I DID NOT EVEN LIKE THE HOUSE.

"Paul," I said, "I get that this is *your* dream house, but if we're going to spend a fortune building a dream house, then it should be *my* dream house, too. It isn't. I don't even like the house. I don't want to live there. Maybe we should rent."

"I don't have time for this, Onna," Paul snapped. "I'm exhausted. I have a business to run. I'm working 'round the clock. Not just for us either. I have people depending on me for their livelihood, to pay their mortgages, to feed their kids. I can't spend any more time looking for a house when people need me and I've found a perfect house for us!" (How odd that he insisted he did not have time for more house hunting but that he had time to make all the decisions involved in new construction. Hmm ... Sociopath math!)

"Paul, no," I insisted, clear in my logic and convictions and holding my ground calmly.

I did not realize it at the time, but Paul had been using multiple manipulative techniques to get me to see it his way. These included trying to make me pity him for how hard he was working, and making me feel guilty because he needed to get the house decision behind him so he could focus on the start-up's success and make sure his employees could get paid. He had tried to make me question my assessment of our assets and the amount of financial risk with which I should be comfortable. He told me that I was simply wrong about how long it would take to build a house, even though I had researched it and had overwhelming data to support my view. In other discussions, he even tried to convince me that my understanding of the rotation of the earth and the seasons was incorrect by arguing that a north-facing house set tightly among tall trees would be full of natural light.

He argued that we could get around the horrible school system in town by sending the kids to private school. The fact this would involve time-consuming admissions applications for me to do at an already stressful time and would entail me driving Jessica to and from a private kindergarten in another town instead of her getting on a school bus for the local public kindergarten did not concern him. That private school would be another

CHAPTER 25

huge financial commitment at a time when our income had been slashed did not register to him as problematic either. To me it was all beyond crazy. It was so insane that I could not believe Paul did not see it. He had to be so stressed and tired from working on this startup that he wasn't thinking straight. What else could it be? All I had to do, I was sure, was point out all of the issues to Paul when we were together on the weekend and when he was rested, including that I did not even like the house, and the issue would be put to bed. How could it end any other way?

Paul's Way Or The Highway

Paul agreed to discuss the house with me when he was back from spending the week in Connecticut. The conversation was brief.

"Onna, this is simple," he said. "I've more important things to do than to keep looking for a house when I've already found the perfect one. I don't know why you're being so difficult and melodramatic."

"Paul, I've explained why I don't want that house, and it's my house, too," I said.

"The house is perfect. You're being ridiculous!" Paul said in an icy tone. "I'll make this really simple. I'm buying the house. The paperwork's waiting for my signature. If you and the kids want to move there with me, great. If not ... " a penetrating stare punctuated a long pause, "I'm buying it and moving in with or without you. You can't stop me. I don't need your approval. *You* have a decision to make."

Paul glared at me as he pushed his chair back from the table. Then he got up, walked out of the house, and drove away.

I started to shake. Like a dam overrun by raging storm waters, tears poured from my eyes and down my cheeks. Was Paul serious? Was he really saying that if I did not agree to the monstrosity of a house he was leaving Jessica, Daniel, and me? My mind flooded. I had always been so supportive of Paul's dreams and goals. How could this be happening? Daniel was two, and Jessica was five. I knew we did not have the perfect marriage, but weren't we making it work?

Our house in New York was already under contract to be sold. I had put my business on hold and had no income of my own. My medical insurance and the insurance for the kids were all through Paul. (This was prior to health care being universally available.) So much of our net worth was now invested in Paul's new company and future. What was I going to do? Where would I go? Where would I live? Was I going to be divorced twice? Was I going to become a single mom? All over a house?

Panic gave way not to clarity but to self-doubt. Why was Paul doing this? Was he under so much stress that he needed to check the house off his list so he could focus on other things? Was he right? Was I being unreasonable? Unsupportive? Selfish?

Then a completely different thought bolted through mind. Was this

CHAPTER 26

about Anne-Marie? Was he leaving me for her? I was the one who had made the sacrifices, but would she be the one who would benefit romantically, emotionally, and financially?

Others have noticed that sociopaths try to make their partners jealous. It is as if they are signaling that their partner had better meet all the sociopath's needs or they will move on to someone else who is clearly enamored with the sociopath and waiting in the wings.[31] Paul had been using this technique on me for some time, but I did not know it. All I knew was the panicked stream of thoughts coursing through my head. Should I fight for my marriage? For my family? What was best for Jessica and Daniel? Would Paul try to take our children from me? Would Anne-Marie end up being a stepparent to by children? It was all a blur.

I was terrified of the idea of my marriage and family falling apart—of the possibility of losing full-time contact with my kids, and over what, a house? Was any material possession worth that?

Although no material possession is worth losing an important relationship, this was not about a material possession. It was not about a house. It was about power, control, and who Paul truly was and is. When charm, deception, gaslighting, lying, and other nefarious manipulation techniques did not get Paul what he wanted, he threatened, bullied, and attacked (emotionally, psychologically, and financially). I had given Paul everything he'd wanted so consistently by succumbing almost seamlessly to his manipulations that I had rarely encountered the aggressive, bullying Paul, so when I did, I was ill prepared. I did not know what was going on or what to do. All I knew was that I was scared.

Two agonizing hours passed. Finally, Paul's car pulled into the garage, and he walked into the house. Part of me was sure this was all a bad dream and that Paul's position and disposition had softened while away. Another part of me knew he was serious. I had glimpsed this heartless Paul before—on the last day of our honeymoon and on the eve of Daniel's birth—but I had shaken it off and assured myself that I had been tired, confused, oversensitive, or high on ready-to-give-birth hormones.

"Well?" he said. His jaw was tight, his eyes cold and emotionless.

There had been no change of heart. Fearful of how the man standing in front of me might explode my life, I swallowed hard before answering. "If the house is that important to you, we'll make it work."

"Right," he said. Then he went to the family room, sat down, and turned on the TV.

Too bad it was not until fifteen years later that I read and truly understood Gavin de Becker's words in *The Gift of Fear and Other Survival Signals that Protect Us From Violence*.[32] In his book, he asserts that if you allow someone to disregard you when you clearly say "no," you are essentially signaling to them that they are in charge. Although Mr. de Becker wrote this regarding criminal behavior, it seems applicable to my situation with Paul as well. I had said *no* to the house, but Paul refused to hear it. He wanted and expected total control over not only our home but also over my life. The red warning flags were flapping loudly, but I was too afraid to stand my ground—too afraid that my relationship with my children might be at risk. No one who loves you would ever put you in such a position. No one who loves you would ever force you to make an important decision quickly and out of fear. Paul did not love me and never had. I was just too afraid to see it.

Nightmare On Elm Street

While Paul worked in Connecticut and the kids and I were still in New York, I barely saw him, although we talked on the phone in the evening when we could and saw each other on alternating weekends. On those weekends, he proudly showed me all the expensive light fixtures, granite countertops, hardwood floors, and other items for the new house. From the decisions he had made, it was clear that he regarded the house as *his* not *ours*. If I did not like something or if I felt he was spending too much money, he either ignored me, told me the decision had already been made, or accused me of having bad taste. I never won. I gave up. If he wanted black pedestal sinks for the bathroom, he was going to get black pedestal sinks for the bathroom. I wanted a counter so I would have a place to put my toothbrush and toothpaste and storage space below. He thought counters didn't look upscale and classy enough. His objective was appearance, appearance, appearance. Mine contained a large dose of convenience, convenience, convenience. But, just like everything else in Paul's dream house, getting impractical black pedestal sinks was nonnegotiable.

I overheard him talking to our builder, confirming the pedestal sinks he had selected. Paul joked that he was getting them because he wanted to be sure that *his* bathroom would never be cluttered with "his wife's stuff." What stuff? A toothbrush, toothpaste, and a hairbrush? I didn't even wear makeup anymore. According to Paul, that would have made me look whorish. Heaven forbid that anyone, including me, regard me as attractive.

Paul's treatment of me became increasingly contemptuous and dismissive. If I shared with him that the purging of no-longer-needed possessions, organizing, and packing was hard and emotionally draining at times, he said I was just a complainer. He and Anne-Marie were the only ones who were really working hard. His whole demeanor changed as he spoke of her—his eyes became almost dreamy, the muscles in his face relaxed, and his tone softened. Anne-Marie worked around the clock side-by-side with Paul. Anne-Marie was brilliant. Anne-Marie had a valuable perspective on any business issue. Anne-Marie was willing to jump in and do anything for Paul. Anne-Marie never complained.

I didn't get it. Anne-Marie was neither attractive nor charming. She was smart and hardworking, but I had graduated near the top of my MBA

CHAPTER 27

class at Yale, even ahead of Paul; how much smarter than me could she be? Paul never talked to me about business, and he certainly never solicited my opinion about critical decisions.

No matter how much the gap between Paul's treatment of me and his regard for Anne-Marie grew, I could not bring myself to think that he was having an affair with her—not even when Paul told me that the company rented an apartment near their office so Anne-Marie would have a place to stay on those evenings when she and Paul worked 'til the wee hours of the morning. Not honorable, honest Paul, not the man who bristled at any inkling from anyone else of dishonestly or lack of integrity.

Our New York house closed in mid-July. With tears in my eyes, I said good-bye to my home, my neighborhood, and my friends. It was difficult. Even though our builder had promised that our new house in Connecticut would be ready for a July closing, it was clear to me that we would be lucky to be in the new house by Thanksgiving. As Paul insisted that we would close "next month," then "next month," and then "next month," he refused to rent an apartment or house. Instead, Jessica, Daniel, and I moved in with Paul in his extended stay hotel. It would have been fine for a week or so. We were there for almost five months.

Paul often returned from work well after midnight. When he did come back earlier, he had nothing positive to say. He would ignore me, snap at me about some trivial issue, or criticize me for the slightest thing. I tried often to reach out to connect with him about something, anything. But if I tried to talk to him about his day, he rebuffed me and disparaged me for sticking my nose into his business. What did I know about *his* business? I wasn't a part of it. He reminded me of that often.

I was not trying to pry but to stimulate conversation. I enjoyed talking about business issues, too, not to mention the fact that our financial future was riding on the success of Paul's venture. If I tried to talk to Paul about the kids, he couldn't believe that I didn't see how tired he was. Why couldn't I just respect how exhausted he was and leave him alone? He missed Halloween night with Daniel and Jessica. He missed Jessica's sixth birthday celebration. Just too busy. Had to work. I understood, right? On the few occasions he did join us for dinner, he brought his laptop to the table, clicking away on the keyboard and checking emails while the kids and I ate. He would feign not being hungry. I think it was just a nonverbal way of communicating to me how little the kids and I mattered. Message received!

Living in a tight space, away from family and friends, ignored, dismissed, or criticized on a daily basis by Paul wore on me. When I was talking to my mother on the phone one day, I dissolved into tears. Throughout my life, I had not been someone who cried easily, except perhaps when my

CHAPTER 27

dog died or when my grandparents passed. A friend of mine had become clinically depressed following business school. While I supported her as a friend and I understood depression intellectually, I had never experienced anything like it personally, not even in my post-partum months. I always viewed problems in life as challenges that I was confident I could tackle. But now? One teary day followed another. What was happening to me? I had long daily phone conversations with my mother, trying constantly to make sense of Paul's latest slight, criticism, or "setup," in which it seemed he was looking for excuses to accuse me of being selfish, inconsiderate, controlling, or incompetent. Nothing I said could convince him that my motives were not suspect or that my judgment was sound. I found myself pouring a glass of wine at the end of each day, anticipating it longingly just to take the edge off. Prior to that, I was a virtual teetotaler, only drinking wine or champagne on special occasions—perhaps, at the most, seven glasses of wine or champagne a year. Now I drank that much in one week, week after week.

Frequent crying, increases in alcohol consumption, and feeling sad and anxious are signs of depression. I wasn't depressed though, I reasoned. I only felt sad, scared, unworthy, and constantly apologetic around Paul. Once away from Paul, perhaps to visit my parents in Vermont, my normal confidence and feelings of self-worth and hopefulness rebounded. They evaporated the moment I reentered Paul's world.

I told myself that it was just an exceptionally stressful time in our lives and that I needed to be strong, not sweat the small stuff, focus on what was important—my kids and my marriage—and soldier on. Paul had started a new business, we had moved, we were living in cramped quarters, we were building a house, and our income had been decimated. It *was* a stressful time, but it would pass. I was not depressed; it was just that my life was depressing. I needed to make some changes, and if I did, the tears would stop. Hopefully, moving into the new house would be a step in a positive direction.

We moved into the house in late November. I had almost no help from Paul emptying boxes and setting up the house. I had no close friends yet who could lend a hand. My ability to service my previous clients waned. Most of my work was concentrated on three major clients. I lost one of them due to my unavailability.

Soon after the holiday rush, I went to the bank to get some cash. My mind scrambled when I looked at the account balance on the withdrawal slip. It couldn't be right. I went to see a teller. It had to be a mistake. But it wasn't. Paul had withdrawn $50,000 from our checking and savings accounts two days earlier, and there had been no automatic deposit for Paul's salary that month.

CHAPTER 27

When Paul got home that night, I asked him what was going on at work. He said he had no idea what I was talking about. When I told him about my trip to the bank, his countenance changed.

"I've been trying to protect you from this," Paul said, eyes down, looking crestfallen.

A sinking, hollow feeling encased me. What now? He explained that the startup was having cash-flow issues. He told me it was caused by the tardiness of the investing partners to supply him with the promised next round of financing. He assured me the startup was achieving its sales goals, but its costs had been much higher than expected. To take care of his employees, Paul had not paid himself and had taken money from our personal account to meet payroll. He had meant to tell me, but he was just so distracted at work and worried about his employees that it slipped his mind. Also, before the investing partners would provide the next wave of financing, they wanted him to reduce costs even further. Everyone was going to take a twenty percent pay cut, and he had agreed to forfeit his own salary for an indeterminate time.

Blood pounded against my forehead. My jaw tightened. Was I even breathing? As I tried to form a sentence that would express how I felt—a cocktail of anger, betrayal, and fear about our finances—Paul blurted out, "I'm doing the best I can."

He seemed to be fighting tears. "I can't believe they're holding me hostage by withholding the financing," he continued in a strained voice. "I *had* to pay all the people who are working so hard. You know how important it is to me to follow through on my promises. I promised those people jobs and salaries. They've all gambled their careers on me. I can't let them down. I'll repay the money when the financing comes in. I just wanted to do the right thing. That's all. It's *so* important for me to do the right thing."

"Is that why you've been so nasty lately?" I asked. Not aware of his tactics until almost a decade later, Paul's pity play was working. As he tapped my empathy, my anger receded, giving way to concern about Paul and his employees.

"Have I?" Paul let out a long, audible sigh. "I thought I was doing the right thing by shielding you and *not* talking to you about it," he said with soft, almost pleading eyes. "Especially after you've worked so hard to move us. I'm so sorry if it seems like I've taken it out on you—I'm just so tired, so worried."

Notice the wording. Paul never actually took accountability for anything. He just said he was "sorry if it *seems* like I've taken it out on you."

My heart melted. All the pain of the past year was trumped by my empathy for Paul. He was in trouble, and I was his wife. I wanted to support him. I wanted to help. I reached out and hugged him.

CHAPTER 27

"I wish you'd let me know when you're under that much pressure," I said. "We'll get through it. But you have to tell me what's going on, because it comes out in other ways, and it's really hard on me, especially not knowing why you're on edge all the time."

"You're right, I should talk to you more," Paul replied. "I really thought the cash flow problems wouldn't reach this point. But I guess I've been so stressed, so worried about paying and providing for *everyone else* at work, and so exhausted. You're my rock. It's one of the things I love and admire about you. I'm so grateful for everything you've done. I don't really deserve you."

Paul's kind words and praise felt like he had opened a window in a long-shuttered attic. Warmth and a feeling of connectedness engulfed me, pushing out the stale, stagnant darkness. Paul and I held each other tightly. Even though we were in crisis, it felt good to be in it together. Paul pulled away slightly.

"I have to talk to you about something else," he said, his face stern, his tone somber. "I hope you'll be relieved and not hate me."

"What is it? What's wrong?" I asked. My brain scrambled, my breath caught, and energy left my body—what else could it be? Then I inhaled deeply, steeling myself for whatever words Paul might utter next.

"We need to sell the house," he said. "The mortgage is too big now that I've agreed not to be paid. I may not get paid again for a very long time."

Sure, I hated the house. It was big, dark, and expensive. But moving again so soon? Selling a house again? Moving the kids again? Looking for a new home again? All the time, all the disruption, all the stress, all the logistics. I had just finished unpacking boxes! I had just gotten my life off hold, and now it was going to go on hold again to facilitate another move, triggered by Paul's my-way-or-the-highway decision! I felt weak, numb, hollow, followed by an unpleasant mixture of disbelief, anger, betrayal, and frustration with myself for not talking Paul out of the house. Hadn't I tried—really hard? Why hadn't Paul listened to me about the house? But I knew bringing this up would do no good.

The kids would be impacted profoundly—a new house, a new school, new friends. It was too much too soon. Not only that, Paul had gone "top of the line" on everything in the house. He wanted everything to be perfect right away. No phase-in process. No long-term plan. All perfect. (All perfectly sociopathic—I want it now! Now! Now! Now!) I had given up discussing his spending, because I never prevailed when we had conversations about his dream house and, such topics only fueled the growing tension between us and left me defeated and fighting tears. The housing market had dropped since we had committed to building the house a little less than a year before. With all the extras, which certainly would not be

CHAPTER 27

valued by someone else, we might lose $200,000 or more on the house. I couldn't believe it. Would we have any equity left?

But what other choice did we have? Now that Paul wasn't bringing in any money, we had to sell the house. I also needed to focus on ramping up my income as much as possible. Losing a client could not have come at a worse time. We could not buy a single thing we did not absolutely need, and we had to start cutting coupons for the things we did need. I had done it before business school. I could do it again.

"Paul," I said, "I'll support you under two conditions: that you sell the BMW and that we go to marriage counseling. Things have been horrible. I can't continue like this."

"You're right," Paul said. "I'll put the BMW up for sale tomorrow, and if you pick a marriage counselor, I'll go."

I sighed. As I exhaled, a damn burst inside me, unleashing suppressed pain, doubts, and fears, and sending tears cascading down my face. This wasn't bad, this was good—Paul had agreed to go to marriage counseling. Maybe we had hit rock bottom. If we could survive this, we could survive anything. Maybe everything was going to be okay.

All The World's A Stage
—For A Sociopath

I researched marital therapists, searching for a male counselor (hoping to make Paul more comfortable) with an office near Paul's work so appointments would be minimally disruptive to his stressful, all-consuming job. And so the charade began.

Marital talk therapy with a sociopath is like an art appreciation lecture for the blind. Those who have unknowingly taken this path with a sociopathic partner are doomed to their own personal version of *Gaslight*, an eerie sense of unreality, a gnawing sense that something is "off" that you can't quite articulate, all topped with a healthy dose of self-doubt. Talk therapy is a stage for a sociopath, and Paul's performance was brilliant. Paul knew me inside and out. To him, it would be a fun game and easy to win. He had no intention of playing by the rules. He did not want to make our relationship better; he wanted to win and to make me more pliable. I was already emotionally and physically drained, so his victory was all but assured. The only question was how long he would find the game entertaining.

My goal in therapy was to heal a strained marriage in which I felt there was no "we," just Paul, with me functioning as an apparently incompetent, underappreciated stagehand to a performance in which he was both director and star. To do this, I knew I would have to be willing to see my role in the dysfunctional marriage and be willing to change. I was so miserable and felt I had so much to lose by the marriage ending that I was highly motivated to understand the current situation, my role in it, and what needed to change.

What I did not understand was that no matter my failings, no matter how sincere I was about preserving my marriage, being involved with a sociopath meant self-reflection and self-improvement had to wait (unless they were needed to gain the personal strength to leave the relationship). Understanding that you are married to a sociopath and getting out of that marriage safely should be steps one and two. But I did not know about sociopaths then, and I certainly did not know I was married to one.

Few people, even trained therapists, think to question whether a difficult relationship and a person's eroding sense of self may be a result of being intimately involved with a sociopath. But this is the first question we should ask. Think about it. Sociopaths must be disproportionately involved in difficult relationships and divorces. In fact, a characteristic of many, but not all, sociopaths is an inability to sustain long-term relationships. Hence, if sociopaths comprise up to four percent of the population, they probably represent a much higher proportion of failed marriages and doomed relationships. Let's guess conservatively that it is ten percent. If you are in a troubled marriage in which you feel you are turning to dust and there is a one out of ten chance that the root cause is that you are married to sociopath, shouldn't you rule this out before venturing further into marital therapy and self-reflection? Unfortunately, most people do not even consider such an option.

In emotional pain and with diminished self-confidence, I entered therapy motivated to improve our marriage. What about Paul? He entered therapy unburdened by emotion, empathy, or conscience. He was motivated to do what all sociopaths are motivated to do—prevail and win. His agenda, therefore, was to use the therapeutic setting to increase his control over me so that I would stay on as the needed stagehand for his show. He could have employed any number of strategies. He chose one that was maximally dismissive of me and probably highly entertaining to him—gaslighting.

"It Depends Upon What The Meaning Of The Word 'Is' Is"[III]

Paul manipulated the well-intentioned therapist into becoming complicit in Paul's self-serving altered version of reality—to view Paul as the perfect, calm, devoted, caring father and husband, while I was clearly on edge emotionally due to my declining mental health and jealousy over Paul and Anne-Marie's business partnership. Paul positioned me as emotionally fragile and overly sensitive, that I cried often and for no reason, and that he was a saint for standing by me through these dark personal times. Paul said he only came to marriage therapy because I wanted him to come. Paul thought what was really needed was individual therapy for me, because something was clearly wrong with me—perhaps I was depressed or worse. To him, I seemed unhappy, because I had given up my career. As evidence of this, Paul brought up my alleged jealously of his hard working, devoted, very successful colleague, Anne-Marie.

Fighting back tears, because that would only confirm Paul's portrayal of me, I was taken aback by Paul's recounting of past events. I tried not to appear too incredulous, because that would make me look reactive, overly sensitive, and untrusting. As calmly as possible, I pointed out why I was concerned about Anne-Marie and why I wondered if she and Paul were "involved." The way he talked to her and about her, all the late nights with Paul and Anne-Marie alone in the office, the apartment near the office funded by the cash-strapped company ostensibly for Anne-Marie's sole use, the unusual promotion of Anne-Marie so that only she was at no financial risk by working for this start-up. I even mentioned that Paul came home sometimes almost voracious for sex, and I knew it had nothing to do with his feelings for me. A woman just knows!

The therapist looked at me. "Have you ever asked Paul if he's having an affair?"

"No, I guess not," I responded.

"Maybe you should."

"Now?"

"Why not?" the therapist replied.

My heart quickened, my throat tightened, and my brow glazed over with a thin film of sweat. The part of me that knew what was about to hap-

---

III From Bill Clinton's grand jury testimony about his relationship with Monica Lewinsky, a young White House intern.

pen, without knowing that I knew, predicted that this was a setup.

"Paul," I said, "are you having an affair with Anne-Marie?"

What followed were a series of evasive techniques sociopaths and other liars use. Not even the therapist was schooled in them, so he became an unwitting co-conspirator in allowing Paul to use therapy as a stage for manipulation, empowering Paul with his implicit endorsement.

"I am so hurt that you would even think that," Paul replied, appearing genuinely concerned. Notice, he did not answer the question. Instead, he used the diversion tactics of trying to elicit pity and putting me on the defensive and implicitly attacking my character for hurting *him*.

"Paul, I hope you understand why I need to know. You seem almost obsessed with her, and I feel nothing but ignored and criticized."

"You know how honest I am and how much I value my integrity. I'm not that kind of person," Paul said. To add support for this, he told the therapist about his many accomplishments and past volunteer work. (Ironically, Paul had done no volunteer work since business school and probably only did it before school to pad his application.) Once again, while Paul appeared to address my concern, he had actually released a smokescreen of evasion, misleading by providing evidence of his character, as if a person who "does good" in one setting cannot be a lying, scheming, cheater in another. Trust me, they can.

"Paul," I said, "it all seems to add up. I need to know."

"I can't believe you think that I'm cheating on you," Paul said, appearing convincingly hurt by the accusation. "Anne-Marie and I are working 'round the clock to make this company a success, to give our employees paychecks, to give the kids and us the life we want. It's that simple. It's your obsession with her and your jealousy of her that have me worried." Again, Paul had not addressed the question. Instead, he tried to elicit pity, to put me on the defensive, and use his perceived "character" to address the question that still remained unanswered.

"Paul, are you sleeping with Anne-Marie or not?"

With the most humble, honest, "great guy," hurt look in his arsenal, Paul turned to the therapist and then to me. "No, I'm not sleeping with Anne-Marie."

By trying to ask a highly specific question to counteract all the times Paul responded to my questions without actually answering them, I fell into another of Paul's traps. Clearly, I wanted to know whether Paul was currently or ever involved in a sexual relationship with Anne-Marie. By Paul not really answering my questions, I asked a more specific question, but I did not ask the "perfect" question. This enabled Paul to answer in a way that misled and misrepresented without actually lying—one of his favorite techniques and one at which he excelled. In retrospect, I know this

CHAPTER 29

was almost a game to him, to see if he could lie by telling selective truths. Is he sleeping with Anne-Marie? Of course not, because that would imply it was happening right *now*, and right *now*, Paul was in a therapy session with me. Also, it was possible that they actually never fell asleep together but just had sex, so Paul could argue that his interpretation of the phrase "sleeping with" could "honestly" have been different than the intended meaning in my sentence (i.e., having sex). If he could argue, even in his own mind, that he understood my question to be asking if he and Anne-Marie were *asleep* somewhere together *at that very moment*, then his answer was not a lie. "Honest" Paul had prevailed again.

If I realized I had stumbled into a trap, and if I, therefore, asked the question another way, such as, "Paul, have you ever had sex with Anne-Marie?" then Paul would have likely not answered the question but accused me of hounding and harassing him like a prosecutor with a hostile witness. Most people would agree with Paul, that he had already answered the question multiple times. But had he? He had evaded, deflected, ignored, and become indignant about my question, but he had never really answered it. Throughout this entire surreal scene, I appeared to be a shrew for battering poor, kind, sweet, caring, honest Paul.

Words and language are not universal constants. They mean different things to different people, and meaning depends on context. As a result, sociopaths orchestrate words to obfuscate through selective "truth telling." A classic example of misleading with language is found in President Clinton's response when questioned about his testimony regarding Monica Lewinsky. He said—"It depends upon what the meaning of the word 'is' is." I am in no way saying President Clinton is a sociopath. In fact, I highly doubt he is, but his language skills were and are masterful. Paul's are, too. Many sociopaths have this gift. Sociopaths are chronic liars and are highly skilled at verbal deception. They have years of practice honing the skill of telling undetectable lies and diverting, deflating, and discrediting those who glimpse the truth.

By offering a totally different representation of our relationship, Paul twisted our therapist into viewing him as the doting, caring husband whose kindness and compassion were evident in the fact that he still loved and was concerned about helping his depressed, anxious wife. No matter what example I used to explain my sense of being minimized and dismissed, calm, collected, manipulative Paul always had a different twist. Paul was able to tell his version with complete conviction, devoid of tension or agitation. Remember, sociopaths do not experience fear, particularly fear associated with lying. Meanwhile, my version was laced with hurt and sadness and occasional tears I no longer had the strength to contain. This only made Paul look like a rock and made me seem like shifting sand. When all

CHAPTER 29

else failed, I used the example of Paul insisting that we purchase the house as indicative of how off kilter our relationship and ability to communicate had become. Paul twisted even that to his advantage.

"I'm so worried about Onna. She seems so sensitive to everything and to feel she needs to be in complete control," Paul said. "Yes, I'd wanted to buy that house, and yes, I knew Onna had reservations, but I never knew her reservations were so serious. I just thought they were part of a healthy discussion, and we had to weigh the pros and cons."

"But Paul," I said, "I told you I hated the house and that I didn't want to buy the house, and I gave you all my reasons for feeling that way. You said you were going to get it without me, leaving me and the kids if necessary."

With the most caring, compassionate look, Paul leaned forward and touched me gently. His eyes connected with our therapist's and then switched soulfully back to me. "Onna, I was just joking if I ever said *anything* like that. How could you think I was serious? I'd *never* do that. Why would I ever ask you to buy a house you didn't love as much as I did? If I ever thought you didn't know I was just joking, I would've clarified it. I can't believe we bought a house that you didn't like. Don't you remember I was worried so much about this and your happiness that I told you that we didn't have to buy this house if *you* didn't want to? You remember that, don't you, honey?"

If a therapist is unwilling or unable to look for the signs of a sociopath in a failing marriage, marital therapy is a useless, expensive, and potentially damaging exercise, just one more tool a sociopath can use to weaken, dominate, and control. Save your money; don't bother.

Paul was too good. It was true that he had told me we did not have to buy the house if I did not want to buy it, but he had told me that in September, when getting out of the contract with the builder would have been a legal and financial nightmare, when we had already invested a considerable amount of money in extras that Paul just had to have, and when it would have meant house hunting again just as the kids were starting pre-school and kindergarten. Under that scenario, continuing with a house that would be done in less than two months seemed like the best decision to minimize the chaos in our lives and to avoid a heinous legal battle along with the resulting financial strain. Like so many sociopaths, Paul's misrepresentation was built on a kernel of truth. He had actually uttered the words "We don't have to buy this house if you don't want to." His story was simple, my explanation complicated. He seemed steady and caring. I seemed unnerved and in denial. Paul's version prevailed, because our therapist never questioned Paul's steady, clear, confident version of events.

Unfortunately, not only do most of us have a lot to learn about sociopaths, so do most therapists. Therapists may even have a built-in bias that allows them to be hoodwinked by sociopaths. Perhaps therapists think their education gives them a unique insight into who people really are and whether or not a person is telling the truth or lying. But if they have not studied sociopaths and deceptive techniques, even trained therapists are no match for a sociopath's masterful manipulation. Actors are good at their craft, and sociopaths are accomplished actors.

Secondly, to be a therapist, you must believe in an individual's capacity to change. Yet, because sociopaths do not care how their behavior affects others and cannot experience the happiness that comes from genuine human relationships, what is their motivation to change? There is none. In fact, some have suggested that therapy only makes sociopaths more effective manipulators, because it builds their expertise in talking and acting *as if* they care, thereby adding to and increasing the effectiveness of their devious toolkit.[33]

Sociopaths brilliantly and convincingly create false impressions with other important people, like lawyers and judges, on whom we rely to know better but who have not been educated about sociopaths. In her insightful forward to Tina Swithin's book *Divorcing a Narcissist: Advice from the Battlefield*[34], Dr. Rebecca Merritt Davis describes how those with Narcissistic Personality Disorder (the closest official diagnosis to what laypeople refer to as a *sociopath* or *psychopath*) are often calm and convincing in court while the nonnarcissistic parent comes across as anxious, agitated, and depressed due to prolonged emotional abuse. In this context, reports that the narcissistic parent has neglected or abused his children are typically viewed as false and even recast as inappropriate (and unlawful) attempts by the nonnarcissistic parent to alienate the children from the narcissistic parent. As the impressions given by the narcissistic parent (calm, loving, and in emotional control) and of the nonnarcissistic, but emotionally abused parent (upset, agitated, worried, depressed) are the reverse of what untrained, unknowledgeable people expect, the courts often make highly flawed and potentially dangerous custody and visitation decisions. It is hard to believe how wrong "experts" (e.g., therapists, psychologists, family lawyers, and judges) can be until you've lived it.

Down The Rabbit Hole

Paul had agreed to therapy under the condition that I would not tell anyone we were going. With the expectation of keeping my word, I promised. Normally, I honor my commitments, and secrets are safe with me. But I broke my promise to Paul after two months. I did it, because I felt like I was going crazy. I needed a reality check from an outside source to calibrate what had really been happening in our marriage. Paul's version of events was too bizarre and devoid of any hint of his escalating selfishness and insensitivity. I know memory is biased and imperfect. Was my recollection totally off or were the "memories" Paul was sharing with our therapist not memories at all but purposeful distortions to paint him as a prince and me as a mad woman?

I needed a second opinion, and to get it I betrayed my promise of confidentiality to Paul. I am not proud of my decision, but what if a spouse is truly devious and untrustworthy? Was Paul's insistence on not telling anyone that we were in marital therapy a sincere concern about privacy or was it more akin to a bully or abuser telling his victim not to "tell" in order to keep the victim isolated, perpetuate a charade, and have a green light for future abuse?

I called my mother. She remembered clearly my strong dislike of the house and my calling her in tears about Paul's veiled threat of divorce if I did not buy the house and let him do everything he wanted to bring his dream house to fruition. She and my dad had been aghast but were determined to not interfere in my marriage and my decisions.

A "happy birthday" phone call from my parents brought a much-needed end to the marital counseling charade. Apparently, my dad had overheard my mom talking to me on the phone about Paul and me being in marital therapy. Whether or not he was asked to keep that information confidential, I do not know. When he was on the phone wishing Paul a happy birthday, my dad made an awkward attempt at conversation, asking Paul how his business was doing, how selling the house was progressing, and if Paul was finding marital therapy helpful.

Paul hung up the phone and, with one sweep of his hand, launched a plate of homemade oatmeal cookies off the counter. The plate and cookies shattered on the unforgiving tile floor.

CHAPTER 30

"Liar!" Paul screamed and then stomped out of the room.

After that, Paul refused to return to marital therapy. The strain between us grew. I felt so guilty for betraying Paul's trust at such a sensitive time that, like a good soldier, I continued trying to sell the house and being as accommodating and supportive of Paul as possible, hoping to win back his trust.

When the tension between us lessened somewhat, I told Paul how scared I had been when he sent the plate of cookies crashing to the floor. Paul insisted his behavior was totally normal. He said that my broken promise, and my betrayal of him, was the cause of the broken plate and cookies, so why on earth should he feel he did anything inappropriate or wrong? Not surprisingly, aggression, verbal abuse, a temper, and/or inadequate control of anger are among the signs that someone might be a sociopath.[35] I had grown up in a household in which I rarely heard a raised voice and nothing was ever thrown in anger. After this episode, Paul tried to convince me that my childhood was incredibly odd, because yelling was a normal part of life for which my wimpy family had not adequately prepared me and that I was being a baby for not just getting over it. Nothing seemed right. Normal seemed abnormal. Weak seemed strong.

My mind grasped for some reference points on what a healthy relationship looked like. Seeing as about half of all marriages end in divorce, was this bad enough to seek a divorce when kids were involved? Was this something through which I had to work? I was becoming increasingly confused about what *normal* should be. How did I know what was going on behind the closed doors of other married couples' homes, anyway? When was getting a divorce selfish? At what point did you decide to stop trying to work on your marriage? On the flip side, with kids in the picture, when was leaving the *right* thing to do?

Answers eluded me. All I had were questions, self-doubt, and pain.

Not Your Everyday Walk In The Park

Soon after the cookie incident, I was in a park near Paul's office when I noticed two people who worked for Paul eating a bag lunch while sitting on the park swings. Neither of them recognized me. The only time I had met them was at a holiday party, and I had been dressed up with makeup, contacts, and my hair down. With blue jeans and a sweatshirt, no makeup, glasses, and my hair pulled back in a ponytail, even casual friends often told me I did not seem like the same person. No wonder it did not register with these two virtual strangers that I was Paul's wife. No wonder they continued their conversation at normal volume, easily overheard.

"What does he see in her? She's a witch."

"Yeah, like the Wicked Witch of the West."

They laughed.

"She even looks like a witch—beady eyes, pointy nose. Just hand her a broom."

More laughter.

"She's awful. Paul says she's brilliant. Is he blind? Deaf? She's the meanest person I've ever met. Anne-Marie even made Sally cry yesterday when she called her 'stupid and lazy' in front of everyone. Paul lets her treat everyone like shit. He must be screwing her. What else explains it? The thought makes me sick."

"I know. Have you heard how he talks to her? Like she's a goddess. 'Yes, Anne-Marie. Whatever you want, Anne-Marie. He gets all glassy eyed, like a puppy. Gross!"

"I used to have so much respect for him. It's pathetic. She's disgusting. He's disgusting."

"And the pay cut thing. We all took pay cuts to keep the company going, and Paul gave her a promotion, a fancier title, a bigger office, and—someone said—a huge pay increase. And that apartment for only Anne-Marie to use when she's working late, but no one else can ever use it! I can't believe it. Anne-Marie just got a fancy new car. The investing partners must be going nuts."

"Poor Sally. She's worked with Paul since she started as an analyst in Minnesota. She told me that she went to Paul when Anne-Marie started treating everyone like shit. Sally was sure Paul didn't know and would do

CHAPTER 31

something. Like, what else could explain it? But I saw her in tears this morning. Paul fired her for not being loyal to Anne-Marie. Sally's in shock. She said she has no idea who Paul is anymore."

"I'm updating my resume."

"Me too. I can't take this anymore. Who knows if this startup's even going to make it another month? Before, I thought the world of Paul, was sure anything he touched turned to gold. Now? What an ass! He's making horrible decisions, probably so he can keep screwing that bitch."

The two got off the swings and headed back in the direction of Paul's office. My heart pounded. Blood coursed through my veins with such violence I thought my head would burst.

I called Sally. She and I had been friendly since our days in Minneapolis together. She had always admired Paul and been one of his most loyal supporters. When she answered the phone and realized it was me, she burst into tears.

"Paul fired me," she sobbed. "He said I wasn't loyal to him, because I don't respect Anne-Marie enough. Onna, she's horrible! Paul lets her run everything, and all she does is stomp around, scream at people, and humiliate them. She has no idea what she's doing. Paul tells everyone to do everything Anne-Marie says, but she doesn't know what to do half the time. And if something goes wrong, she rips into people. Everyone's miserable. Stupid me, I thought Paul didn't know. So I talked to him. Everyone hates Anne-Marie. People are losing respect for Paul. He backs her up on *everything*, even when she's totally out of control! Even when other people know much more than she does, he ignores them. When she makes a mistake, she blames someone else, and Paul defends her. It's like he gets off on it in some twisted way."

"I'm so sorry," I replied. "I don't know what to say. I know the company's having cash flow issues and that Paul's under tremendous pressure."

"I used to admire him. He was my mentor. I almost worshiped him. I worked around the clock for him, to help *him* succeed, to help *him* get promoted and make partner. He's a monster. When he called me into his office, he looked hateful." Sally paused before continuing. "Onna, I've never seen someone look like that. It was almost ... almost evil. It scared me. I can't believe I've been so devoted to him. I don't know who he is. How can anyone be like that?"

"Do you think they're having an affair?" I asked.

"Everyone does. She's often in his office with the door closed. They leave for lunch together all the time. They're gone for a long time. There's something sexual there, but who knows if they are actually 'doing it.' Does it matter? It's sick. She's ugly inside and out. No one gets it."

"How can I help?" I asked.

Husband Liar Sociopath

CHAPTER 31

"There's nothing you can do," Sally said. "He's not who I thought he was. He said I'm never to contact him or anyone from the office ever again. I've worked for him since I got out of college. I helped him make partner after only five years. So many of us did. Now I don't even have a recommendation if I apply to business school or law school or ... What about you?"

"I don't know, this is all so fast, and with the kids ... I just don't know." Sweat beaded on my forehead. My body felt alarmingly hot. My heart pounded. What was I going to do?

So Close And Yet So Far

Having validation that my perception of Paul was as real as any perception could be and not distorted by my bias and any personal baggage was inordinately helpful. Paul had always played the "I have no idea what you are talking about" or the "You must be jealous" cards with me when I broached the subject of his and Anne-Marie's behavior. I was always too willing to see the grey in any situation, to give Paul the benefit of the doubt.

This is one of the reasons cults and abusive spouses isolate their victims. The world is not black and white; it includes countless shades of grey. To create meaning and clarity out of the grey, we use past frameworks (e.g., Paul is a good, honest person) to process incoming data (the fact that he's working late constantly reflects his dedication to his career, loyalty to his firm, and commitment to support his family). The problem is that once this framework has been established, and once we create an explanation (accurate or not) for how an event fits into the framework, we have created a *pathway*.

At first, this pathway is weak and inconsequential. Yet, like all learning, if we visit this pathway repeatedly, what started off as a goat path in our brain, connecting "working late" to "Paul's loyalty and dedication," becomes a dirt track, a country road, and then a two-lane highway. Ultimately, the connection in my brain between Paul working late and the excuse I provided for him in my mind based on the false assumption that he was an honest, wonderful man had become a superhighway, allowing me to travel on it automatically, at lightning speed.

As discussed at length in the seminal book, *The Talent Code*[36], the same learning process that allows an elite athlete like Peyton Manning to throw a football accurately under pressure (i.e., lots of practice that creates super-fast neural connections) was likely at work in my brain, making an instantaneous connection between Paul's behavior, such as working late, and the excuse I made for him in my mind when I was 100 percent convinced he was a great guy.

Here's the scary part: The way our brains work, we cannot blow up that super highway *even when we realize the assumption on which it was built is faulty* (i.e., that Paul is not a good, honest, loving man). The highway remains. The best we can do is to erect a "STOP" sign in front of the highway's on-ramp and start the difficult process of making other connections and methodically reinforcing them instead. Doing this is hard, because even when we get information that is screaming at us to put up that STOP sign, sociopaths are experts at dampening those screams and reducing them to faint whispers. Did I really hear what I thought I heard? Did I really see what I thought I saw? It is not always easy to tell. The world abounds with uncertainly. Consciously and unconsciously, we all attempt to validate our perceptions by seeing how they compare to others' perceptions, and these adjusted perceptions become part of our unique reality.

Sociopaths, and others who strive to control people, fashion their victims' world so that the sociopath is the main source of their victims' continuous, automatic calibration. This is another reason why abusers attempt to eliminate or minimize their victims' contact with other people. If you doubt that people can influence others so easily, a classic psychology experiment performed by Solomon Asch[37] in 1958 may shock you.

In Asch's study, subjects were asked to look at eighteen sets of cards. The first card in each set showed only one line and a second card in the set showed three lines of various lengths, one of which was exactly the same length as the line on the first card. The other two lines were of noticeably different lengths. These cards were shown to groups of eight to ten students, but only one of these students was an actual subject. The others were in on the experiment. For each pair of cards, the students in the group were asked to indicate which line on the second card was the same length as the line on the first card. The first two times, the confederates gave correct answers. This gave them initial credibility. Then, for later trails, the confederates all gave the same incorrect answers. The actual subject in the experiment always went next to last so that he or she would hear the other students' faulty answers.

The disturbing result of the study is that we tend to see what others see. About seventy-five percent of the subjects conformed to obviously incorrect answers at least once. About thirty percent conformed on seven or more of the eighteen trials. This happened in groups as small as three to four people. Interestingly, if just one other person gave the correct answer, the subjects conformed to the false majority view only one-fourth as often as they did if no dissenter was present. In light of this, is it any wonder that sociopaths and others who seek control isolate their victims physically or emotionally? If we tend to see what others see, the sociopath wants to be the only other opinion available, since having just one other person who sees things the way we do gives us confidence in our observations and convictions. If you want to control someone, isolating him or her really helps, because even one ally can undermine the sociopath's control.

Keep in mind that the confederates in the experiment were just students of a similar age whom the subject neither knew nor held in particularly high regard. Imagine the impact if the other members of the group comprised people the subject held in high esteem or viewed as an authority or an expert.

Unfortunately, we know from the disturbing but revealing Stanley Milgram experiments conducted at Yale in the early 1960s [38] that human beings are influenced strongly by those viewed to be in authority. In this experiment, subjects were asked to deliver an electric shock when a person in another room did a task incorrectly. (The person in the other room was a confederate of the experimenter and no shock was actually administered.) At the direction of a man in a white lab coat, someone who was viewed by the subjects to be in charge and knowledgeable about the experiment, subjects were instructed to increase the voltage as punishment for wrong answers, ultimately reaching dangerous levels (if the shocks had been real). Even with screams of protest coming from the person being "shocked" in the next room, over sixty percent of subjects continued to deliver high level shocks for incorrect answers. The experiment is considered a disturbing classic in demonstrating how easily most of us are influenced by someone we consider an expert or authority.

The sociopath's inflated, grandiose view of himself, the extreme confidence and clarity in his convictions (because he lacks doubt and fear), and the sociopath's ever-present self-confidence and self-assurance tend to elevate the sociopath's status in other people's minds. Undermining the credibility of other potential sources of influence also enhances the relative influence of any sociopath. To this end, Paul encouraged me to question the motives of any threatening source of information (e.g., "Don't listen to your brother; he's always been jealous that we make more money than he does." "Your father just doesn't know how things work in the real world'." "Your mother is too sensitive; she gets over emotional."). These are just some of the reasons why living with a sociopath like Paul made me question my perceptions, lose confidence in myself, and fail to come to obvious conclusions—even when relevant information was staring me in the face for prolonged periods of time. As these experiments demonstrate so dramatically and shockingly (no pun intended), it is likely that the same fate would have also befallen many other smart, capable people under similar circumstances.

Prior to overhearing that conversation in the park and talking to Sally, I lacked external validation of my feelings. The mockery of our marital therapy only added to my self-doubt and paralysis. The discussion with Sally and the one I overhead in the park gave my deflated confidence a much-needed boost.

I was not too sensitive. I was not controlling or jealous. This was simply

CHAPTER 32

unacceptable. How had it taken me so long to see what had been in front of me all along?

Paul was leaving on a short business trip (with Anne-Marie, of course) that afternoon. It would give me time to regroup. If I was honest with myself, I didn't even care if Paul came back. In fact, I wished he wouldn't. I was scared of him.

The Question Is Not What You Look At But What You See[IV]

For months, I had to fight the impulse to recoil whenever Paul touched me. Yet, if we did not have frequent sex, Paul's impatience with me grew even worse. Instead of sharing intimate moments with my husband, I felt like I was feeding a beast. If I did not feed the monster, it would devour me. I had to keep him satiated to keep myself alive. Not surprisingly, our sex life was still not frequent enough or satisfying enough for Paul, so he added this to my growing list of shortcomings, which included: bad gift-giver, poor cook, complainer, incapable of meaningful conversation, lazy, controlling, demanding, and jealous. Due to my broken promise to Paul, he also made it clear that he considered me dishonest and a liar. Who was this person Paul kept describing? Certainly not me! Equally importantly, who was Paul?

While Paul was away, I stumbled across another major withdrawal from our accounts that he had failed to run by me ahead of time. This time he had taken money from our brokerage account. No matter how scared I was, no matter how deflated I felt, no matter what the consequences, this could not continue.

The night Paul returned, I waited until after the kids were tucked into bed, and then I told him I could not go on like this any longer. I did not care what the therapist said. I was sure Paul was having an affair, that he placed no importance on the kids and me, and that he was making key financial decisions without consulting me. I was miserable. Our marriage had to change or end.

Paul denied any inappropriate involvement with Anne-Marie. He launched into a smokescreen of diversion and distractions by telling me that he was certain I was accusing him of having an affair to cover up my own string of infidelities. I know now that it is not unusual for sociopaths to project their own unethical, tawdry behavior onto their victims, but I did not realize it at the time.

"Who with, the mailman?" I snapped. "I hardly see another person. I'm either running the kids around, attempting to keep my own business on life-support, trying to keep the house spotless so we can sell it, doing everything else around the house, because you're too busy to rake a leaf or

---

IV Henry David Thoreau

CHAPTER 33

shovel a snowflake!"

Paul listed the multiple affairs he suspected me of having—my boss in Minnesota, my dentist in New York, and now he wasn't sure who it was, but he was sure it was someone. (Notice the attempt to avoid dealing with the issue at hand by attacking my character, putting me on the defensive.) He rationalized the money as just another oversight and would not admit to forcing the monstrosity of a house on me—still insisting that it had been *our* decision and that I was an adult and could have said "No."

When Paul refused to acknowledge that any of my concerns—including those about Anne-Marie—had even an iota of validity, I mentioned what I had overheard in the park. Paul diverted the conversation immediately by grilling me about who the employees in the park were. I refused to give him descriptions or even the genders of the two employees. At midnight, after a tearful two-hour conversation in which I felt like I was hitting my head against the wall, I got up and walked across the room toward the foyer, leaving Paul sitting alone on the couch.

"Where are you going?" Paul demanded. "We're not done!"

Paul was not convinced that he had pounded me sufficiently into submission, into buying his twisted version of events. This included that Sally had betrayed him and was undermining his authority and needed to be fired, and, if I were a loyal wife, I would never talk to Sally again.

"I'm leaving, Paul. I've already talked to my parents. I'm taking the kids and driving to Vermont. Now. Whether you're screwing her or not, you clearly care more about Anne-Marie than you do about the kids or me. When the house sells, we'll split the money and get a divorce. I'm done."

It was a perfect time to leave. I felt clear and strong. My family was relatively close. I still had a career that could be resuscitated. More importantly, Paul had so depleted our assets with his investment in this company and the debacle of the house that we had few assets remaining about which to argue.

As I crossed the oversized, ostentatious, totally wasteful foyer to head upstairs to get Jessica and Daniel, I felt Paul's hand on my arm—gentle, not aggressive. "Don't leave me. Don't leave me."

I turned to face him. Paul looked crestfallen and dejected, as if every muscle in his face had lost its tone. Still, I felt ice cold, resolute. I didn't care.

Sobs exploded from his body, and he doubled over and collapsed to the floor, clinging to me and pulling me down with him. "You're right! You're right! I've been too tired and stressed to admit it, but I've been a horrible husband. I'll change. I promise. From now on, you and the kids will be my top priority. Just don't leave. Don't leave me. You are the only one I've ever been able to count on. I know I haven't shown it for a long time, but I love you. I know you still love me. We were great together once. We can be again. Don't go. Don't leave me." Paul's body heaved violently. Tears

CHAPTER 33

fell on my shoulder as he cradled against me, holding me like a child holds a precious doll in a storm.

I realize now that this was all an act—just pulling out "I'll change" and "pity me" from his sociopathic bag of tricks. But then …

"Paul, I can't do this anymore," I replied stoically, my body stiff and unwelcoming.

"Onna, please, please don't leave," Paul begged. "Everyone's deserted me. You're the only one I can count on. I don't know how I'll go on without you. I don't know what you heard, but I had to let Sally go, because she was undermining my credibility. She was worried everyone was working too hard. She was being too mothering and too protective. You know she's like that. I talked to her; I asked her to stop. She couldn't. It's just too much in her nature to care too much, but we had work to do, and she was eroding my leadership. I did everything I could to avoid it, to work with her. It was devastating. I've worked with her for years. Letting her go was horrible."

I felt my resolve weaken as the part of me that has way too much empathy for others started to connect to Paul's apparent pain. My body relaxed slightly as he continued.

"And the investors are being so unreasonable and demanding results that I don't know if I can deliver. I'm working 'round the clock. The reason I'm so loyal to Anne-Marie is that she's loyal to me. She's the only one who understands the dire situation the company's in and is working and sacrificing as much as I am to save this startup. I know it looks bad. I'll never put Anne-Marie in front of you and the kids again. Just don't leave me. Don't leave me alone. From now on, we'll make every decision together. I promise. I'll update you every week. I'll never take our money for the business again without asking you. And if I do, you can take everything we have and I'll let you and the kids go without a fight. Just don't leave me. "

Paul's limp body folded in on itself, and he collapsed into my lap like a terrified little boy. My resolve melted. I had never seen anyone so vulnerable, so in need.

Something inside me stirred. Finally, he tapped the part of me that I valued most, but the part of me that, if unprotected, could be turned against me—my empathy. Once he tapped my empathy, he could unleash one of the ultimate weapons sociopaths have used throughout history to get kind, loving people to take actions and make decisions that are against their own self-interest—pity. He was my husband, the father of my children, and he needed help, a lot of help. He was expressing profound remorse and promising to change. Doesn't everyone deserve a second chance? If I turned my back on him now, what would that say about me?

"I'll stay, Paul," I said. "But things have to change, and they have to change starting tomorrow."

The Illusion Of Hope

As a sociopath, Paul's black, vacant soul is not capable of change, but as a good actor, he transformed his behavior quickly and profoundly. He just had to dust off a character he had already perfected—that of a doting companion. If he wanted me to continue as his stagehand, and if he wanted to avoid a divorce that was not on his terms and his timetable, he needed to put on a good show. He could do that, and he did.

After we slashed the asking price of the house, it finally sold. Paul was too busy to help pack, organize, and clean the house to make it ready for its new owner. Fortunately, his mother, Ruth, came for a week to help. Sharing the work with someone was so much better than facing the time-consuming, thankless task alone. I appreciated her help with the purging, packing, and cleaning as well as for giving me much needed reassurance and emotional support during an exhausting time.

Almost two years to the day after leaving New York, and just over one and a half years after moving into Paul's dream house, our moving van pulled out of the driveway to take us to our new, much more manageable home in a town forty-five minutes away that was known for its good, up-and-coming public school system. Ostensibly to deal with his struggling startup, Paul still worked nonstop, leaving me in charge of the closing for both properties and settling the kids into our new life. The rest of my life—including my career—stayed on hold. I had no other choice.

Paul's obsession with Anne-Marie seemed to cool, and his behavior around her and his references to her became those of one professional to another, not someone obsessed. A few months before the house sold, Paul told me that the startup was now meeting all of its revenue milestones and profit goals but that the investing partners wanted out. Apparently, they did not want to continue supplying the cash required for the business to grow. All of his explanations seemed odd, because the investing partners had deep pockets and had known Paul since his uber successful days as a consultant. If the startup was meeting all agreed upon milestones, why terminate their involvement prematurely? Part of me was sure I was not getting the full story. Could the investing partners be noticing alarming, financially irresponsible decisions Paul was making involving Anne-Marie? Could this be why they wanted out? I would never know the truth. Who would ever tell me?

CHAPTER 34

Paul found a buyer for the startup. Prior to the sale, Paul elevated Anne-Marie to be equal to his position, and one of the conditions of the sale was that Anne-Marie would get a position equally lucrative to Paul's at the acquiring company. Thanks to Paul, only three years out of business school, Anne-Marie now had a senior director title and a salary equal to Paul's in a large public company. To seal the deal, Paul forfeited any immediate payout for his share in the start-up in return for a payout for both him and Anne-Marie if they helped the acquiring company meet certain goals. Again, I thought Anne-Marie got an amazingly sweet deal, but Paul's relationship with her *appeared* professional now, and I did not want to pour salt in an open wound. Also, Anne-Marie was pregnant with her first child. I hoped that, whatever had gone on between Anne-Marie and Paul, it was in the past, and that Anne-Marie's budding family would distance her further emotionally from Paul.

Yet, the ink on the deal was hardly dry when Paul and Anne-Marie grew dissatisfied and wanted out. In retrospect, it was hardly surprising given the need they both have to be in control. They claimed the new company had rearranged their responsibilities and compensation in violation of their employment agreement and the conditions of the sale. They resigned, and major legal action ensued. Ultimately, Paul and Anne-Marie prevailed. Yet, the lawsuit cost us two stressful years and plunged our cash flow to almost zero when Paul resigned to work exclusively on the legal case. Not only did the household bills add up quickly, the legal and forensic accounting bills also grew to alarming levels, tapping virtually all of our assets.

Still, a common enemy creates strong alliances. It was financially frightening, but aside from the nagging suspicion that Paul had been involved romantically with Anne-Marie, I had always considered him a man of high integrity, exceptional intelligence, and business acumen. With the lawsuit challenging Paul's integrity and our remaining assets, I stood by Paul and his effort to defend himself.

One day he returned from testifying to report that his lawyer had praised him for being the calmest person under pressure he had ever witnessed in his entire legal career. (Little did I know that was *not* a sign of having the truth on his side, because sociopaths like Paul do not experience fear and hence can lie calmly and often with impunity.) Apparently, a string of email communications were so damning to his former boss that she had been reduced to tears while testifying about them. These emails and Paul's testimony were a big factor in convincing the arbitrators that his former boss, not Paul and Anne-Marie, was lying, and that Paul and Anne-Marie were exemplary employees who this large firm was trying to cheat out of the payout they were due. I was so proud of Paul for taking the ethical and moral high ground, standing up for what he knew was right, and prevailing

CHAPTER 34

to the end. David had slayed Goliath.

And yet, I'll never know what really happened. In retrospect, it is more likely that Paul's depiction of his boss and his carefully orchestrated, but difficult to refute, lies were what brought his former boss to tears, not guilt about her supposed attempt to undermine him. Years later when I became Paul's adversary during our divorce, I realized that not only is he a dangerous opponent due to his considerable intelligence and intense motivation to win, he is also truly gifted in his ability to twist the truth, misrepresent facts, and lie so convincingly that it would never occur to you that he was lying.

Paul crafted email after email during our divorce, leaving "evidence" of events that had never occurred. He referenced facts selectively and distorted them to make it appear like he was taking the high ground and that *he* was the wounded, aggrieved party. All the while, he was violating any semblance of ethical behavior in addition to, at times, violating the law. Had I not learned to document my understanding of even my most trivial interactions with Paul, his emails would have laid the groundwork for proving behaviors and communications on my part that he had hoped to use against me, but which had not, in fact, ever occurred.

The Weeds Always Win

When Paul and Anne-Marie found themselves with some available time, they hung out a shingle for their own consulting company—A-M-P Consulting Solutions. About this time we discovered that, although Daniel was an exceptionally bright child, he had some severe learning challenges and developmental delays that would mean years of work with specialists, daily therapy at home, and bi-weekly professional help. I orchestrated all of his diagnoses, care, and therapy. Paul never got involved and never seemed all that concerned. I assumed Paul was just too busy starting his own company, that he completely trusted me to take care of Daniel's needs, and that he was calm in the face of adversity. Not knowing that Paul was and is a sociopath, how would I have ever attributed his behavior to total indifference regarding the welfare of his own son?

It would have been nearly impossible to do justice to Daniel's issues if I had been working full time. I felt grateful that Paul and Anne-Marie's time together seemed professional now and that their new company was making money, allowing me to focus on Daniel's substantial short- and long-term needs. Yet, just beneath my feelings of gratitude, a sea of melancholy and irritability was growing that could not be denied.

Comment by apparently innocuous comment, to which I was obviously just "too sensitive," Paul's critical, dismissive behavior returned. As a result of habituating to slowly elevating levels of toxicity, it took increasingly extreme behavior from Paul before my situation registered once again as problematic. Albeit below any cause-and-effect level of awareness, his poisonous behavior wore me thin once again. I felt increasingly blue, struggling to make even the most basic decisions, felt unsure of my abilities (even in areas of great former expertise), snapped at the kids, felt like I was walking on eggshells around Paul, and asking "What just happened?" following interactions with my husband.

Ironically, I was complicit in allowing the weeds to invade my life again. Like so many other people sociopaths tend to target, I take great satisfaction in being helpful to others. Being empathetic, caring, and willing to invest in relationships are qualities that I like in myself. However, they are also characteristics of women who get trapped in long-term relationships with sociopaths, because we try so hard to make other people happy and to

CHAPTER 35

make our marriages work[39]! At first, when Paul was under so much pressure from the legal proceedings, I was happy to help out more, because Paul seemed so tired, stressed, and overworked. Harvard and Yale graduate or not, I never felt that doing the dishes, cleaning the house, raking the leaves, shoveling snow, or being a taxi for the kids was beneath me. It was just part of life. There was work to do, and I was glad to do it.

Judging from Paul's behavior, however, routine household work was beneath him. He consistently neglected to clear his own dishes from the table, toss away envelopes from letters he opened, put his dirty socks in the hamper, or remove a used glass from the family room.

If I asked that he take care of these things, he would suggest I was nagging and being petty. After all, *he* was working around the clock to provide for our family, and what was I really doing? Each plate I cleared for Paul and each envelope of his I tossed in the trash did not seem like a big deal at the time. Taken together though, it suffocated and corroded; especially because a "thank you" was rarely forthcoming. Inherent in his now chronic and consistent refusal to take accountability for his mess was a subtext of entitlement for himself and contempt for me—not a good recipe for a healthy relationship or a healthy "me."

During the lawsuit and while starting his consulting company, Paul's sizeable home office was quickly overrun with unfiled papers, boxes, office supplies, dirty coffee cups, and miscellaneous clutter. Instead of organizing the space, he simply abandoned it and took over an infrequently used but highly visible space in our house—the dining room. It only took a few weeks for the dining room to become so congested with Paul's unfiled materials, papers, and correspondence that there was no place to set his laptop. Instead of cleaning up the dining room area or his office, he found another area of the house that suited him—the kitchen table.

Soon, Daniel, Jessica, Paul, and I had no place to eat our meals, and Paul conducted his business calls while sitting at the kitchen table or on the family room couch, where the kids played, did their homework, and watched TV. Paul's clutter and phone calls were so distracting that the rest of us could hardly function.

When the kids came home from school, Paul reprimanded them to be quiet, because the noise from their normal activity in the kitchen or family room bothered him. Paul was working in the highest traffic areas of any normal house—the kitchen and family room—and blaming the kids for distracting him. If scolding them into silence did not work, he commandeered my tiny office, often interfering with my ability to get my work done. He had a sizeable home office rendered useless by his refusal to clean up. It was all upside down and backwards, but from the perspective of sociopath math, it all made perfect sense. It was Paul's world; the rest of us were just in it to forward his goals—business independence and success as well as a façade of normalcy that, together, gave him the power, money, and a home base to do whatever he wanted. We should have been happy to be his janitors.

Consistent with sociopath math, Paul's refusal to help knew no bounds. One Sunday, I went down to our basement to do laundry, only to discover two inches of water on the floor. The water heater had broken and flooded our basement with over sixty gallons of water.

Grumbling about being distracted from watching a football game, Paul sized up the situation, went to another part of the basement, and returned a minute later with our *seventy-pint* dehumidifier. He placed it in a remote, dry part of the basement.

"That should do it," he said, and then turned it on and started back upstairs.

"Paul," I said, "a dehumidifier isn't going to help. There's too much water."

"Don't be ridiculous," he replied. "Of course, the dehumidifier will take care of it."

Paul is smart. He had to know that a dehumidifier was an absurd way to clean up sixty gallons of water in a cold, damp basement. But he neither wanted to be bothered with the cleanup effort nor distracted from watching the football game, so he pretended to do his part. He suggested that if I did not think a dehumidifier was a great way to clean up a flood, that I was clearly misinformed. If I suggested that my knowledge of the behavior of water was correct, when he was saying it was not, that just indicated how unreasonable, stubborn, and—his favorite word for me—*controlling* I was. It wasn't worth arguing. The water had to be cleaned up immediately to avoid more damage. I did it myself.

Only years later did I realize that this was one of his "go to" manipulation and erosion techniques. To begin, he devalued the need to do a task. If I went ahead and did the job, he showed no appreciation. Instead, he ridiculed me, because the task was clearly unnecessary. This technique not only got him off the hook, it had the added bonus of devaluing much of what I did. Help mop up the basement? Just turn on a dehumidifier. Help shovel snow? *His* car could easily plow through it. Why do I need to leave the house? Help clean up the house before guests came over? It looked clean enough. Pick up cough drops for the kids? They didn't seem all that sick. I was just an over-protective parent. It was a win-win for Paul and a lose-lose for me.

If Paul had done this to me early in our relationship, I probably would have left. But I had grown used to being dismissed and minimized, so I could no longer see the forest for the trees. It was as if I was clinging to a branch that was so small I couldn't even see the tree in which I was trapped. Lacking a big picture perspective, was I going to divorce my husband just because he would not clear his plate or put his socks in the hamper when he was (apparently) working past midnight every night and throughout the weekends to provide for our family?

Once sociopaths have you hooked, they invest as little as possible in maintaining the pretense of normalcy, and their true, uncaring, selfish selves become more apparent. Given all the manipulative techniques the sociopath has unleashed over the years, his victim is well trained to accept her toxic life, too exhausted to resist and all too practiced at rationalizing her partner's behavior without even knowing she is doing it.

Attending a teacher conference, helping with Daniel's physical therapy, and taking Jessica to a sports practice or music rehearsal were all way too pedestrian for Paul. Yet, while playing less and less of a role with Daniel and Jessica, devaluing my volunteering efforts in any arena ("They'll never appreciate your effort—why are you bothering?"), scolding me for helping the kids with homework ("You're too involved. Let them figure it out themselves."), spending too much time with them ("I can't believe you guys are watching those stupid science shows again. Oh, just kidding!"), or getting after me about my work ("Why are you bothering to work anymore? I'm making enough money."), if we were in front of Paul's family or my family, he treated me like a princess.

When his family came to visit, Paul made amazing dinners, cleared the table, washed and put away the dishes, put out the trash, and was affectionate to me as if we were giddy teenage heartthrobs. Early in our relationship, I was thrilled to have a break from being the one accountable for everything around the house and gladly relaxed as I chatted with his family, especially his mother, while Paul cooked. Paul gently rebuffed all of my offers to help, creating the impression he was a caring, accommodating, and truly wonderful husband.

Warning! Dr. Jekyll/Mr. Hyde behavior is characteristic of sociopaths. The reason is obvious now that I know who and what Paul is. The nice behavior was *all* show, and he didn't bother with the show when alone with the kids and me. He already had me in his pocket and so eroded that I no longer trusted my ability to perceive accurately and to have feelings that made sense. However, he had to maintain the charade of being a great guy in front of the other people he needed in his life.

For someone who was brought up to be helpful and to please other people, the contrast between Paul's private and public behavior did not trigger the question, "I wonder if Paul is a sociopath?" Instead, it kept triggering the very self-destructive thought, *Paul is so nice to other people and can be so nice and considerate and loving to me some of the time. So what*

CHAPTER 35

am I doing wrong most of the time? It would take me several more years to understand that I was being played. It was that simple. The "nice" Paul was not real and never had been.

One Big, Happy Extended Family

Two years after starting A-M-P Consulting Solutions, we were stable enough financially to do something we had not done in years—go on a family vacation.

I was excited about getting away, just Paul, Jessica, Daniel, and me. My enthusiasm was short-lived, however. Paul and Anne-Marie realized if they conducted business while on "vacation," they could write off part of the vacation as a business expense. From then on, Anne-Marie, her husband, their two girls, Paul, Daniel, Jessica, and I vacationed together. Paul's soft, velvety voice was back when he spoke to Anne-Marie. The rest of his behavior seemed to dance along the line of professional versus personal. I could not get a good read on the situation. Maybe I could but was afraid to see what was right in front of me. They were now 50-50 business partners. My financial life depended on the success of their partnership. It was complicated. I begged Paul to have a vacation with just our family, but he would not hear of it. It wasn't financially prudent, he argued. I was being unreasonable, illogical.

Often when on one of these shared vacations, if I planned an activity with just Paul and the kids, Anne-Marie would find out about it and ask if she and her eldest daughter, Rebecca, could join us. Rebecca was about six years younger than Daniel and almost nine years younger than Jessica—too big an age gap for the older children to regard Rebecca as anything but an annoyance, but Paul always said, "Yes." Increasingly, I tried not to mention such plans to Anne-Marie, but Paul always let her know about our daily schedule. Once, I garnered the strength to suggest as kindly as I could to Anne-Marie that we had been looking forward to doing the activity just as a family, and that I was sure she would understand. (We never inserted ourselves into the activities she planned with her family.) Paul was horrified and told Anne-Marie in front of me, that, of course, she and Rebecca were *always* welcome to join us.

I pulled Paul aside and expressed how much I felt we needed family time together, and for the sake of our family to please back me up and ask Anne-Marie and Rebecca not to come along this time. I felt strong for standing my ground and expressing my needs and sure that, because I was so flexible and accommodating of Paul 99.9 percent of the time, he would

CHAPTER 36

be more than happy to take my very reasonable request into account. Paul refused to back me up. I felt humiliated. Anne-Marie and Rebecca joined us that time and consistently in the future, sometimes even sitting next to Paul on a boat trip, lunch, or other activity before Daniel, Jessica, and I could find places to sit. I rationalized it as Paul bending over backwards to be nice to his business partner. After all, he was such a kind, considerate, thoughtful man, wasn't he?

Over the years, I developed a closer relationship with Anne-Marie's husband than with Anne-Marie. She never seemed at all interested in what I did or in my opinion. Her husband was the main caregiver to their children, so I talked to him more parent-to-parent than I did to her. I suspect Paul told her little about me. In his mind I was so unaccomplished and irrelevant, what was there to say? Although I had been one of the best squash players in the country during college, and Anne-Marie was getting Rebecca involved in squash at an unusually young age (which seemed odd to me), Anne-Marie registered surprise that I had even played the game, especially at such a high level. Paul seemed very interested in Rebecca's evolving skill at the game, even though he refused to allow our kids to play squash. It was too elitist, he argued. The whole situation seemed beyond bizarre.

"It's Like Déjà Vu All Over Again."[V]

After the first seven years of my doomed marriage, Paul and I had "bottomed out," and I almost left. Seven years later, our marriage was back on life support. By then, Jessica was twelve and Daniel almost nine. I was miserable. Nothing I did was ever right. If I made breakfast for Paul, he said he was too busy to eat breakfast together. "Can't you see how busy I am? Why are you trying to slow me down?" If the next morning I made breakfast for only the kids and me, he rolled his eyes and suggested I was inconsiderate for not including him—that of course he had planned to have breakfast with the family, but now he was so hurt because I had excluded him that he just wanted to get to work.

If Daniel had trouble in a class and I mentioned that I was going to talk to his teacher, Paul accused me of meddling. When Daniel had trouble with a class four months later and I said I was going to let him work it out, Paul chided me for not demanding a conference with the teacher. "Why didn't you meet with the teacher months ago?" I know life is complicated and no two people will ever see a situation exactly the same way, but I felt that if I said "black," Paul would say "white." If I said "white," he would say "black" as a matter of principle. As in a formal debate, there were always good reasons for his "black" to my "white" or his "white" to my "black," but it was unrelenting, depressing, and exhausting. Was I really that incompetent and unkind that nothing I did was right, well intentioned, or reasonable?

Contradicting me was always so well couched in sincerity, subtle character assassination, or the almighty backwards "Paul logic" that no battle seemed worth fighting or, if waged, was winnable.

Even though his office was just a town away, Paul rarely came home before 8:00 p.m. and often did not return home until 10:00, ostensibly due to oppressive work demands. Once home, he would make something to eat and then crash in front of the television. He rarely ate the food I had prepared earlier for the kids and me. If I suggested he come home to join us for dinner and then work at home, he told me that was impossible, because he needed to be available to his clients constantly. This made no sense, because with cell phones and laptop computers, Paul was available to his

---
[V] Yogi Berra

CHAPTER 37

clients twenty-four hours a day, seven days a week no matter where he was. With his "work schedule" filling all of Paul's waking hours once again, his involvement with the children hovered at zero. I accepted his excuses and got used to functioning on my own as a virtually single parent. It hurt too much to expect Paul to be an involved father and husband and to have those expectations dashed continually or to be chided for having them at all. So, both consciously and unconsciously, I got used to his lack of emotional connection with Jessica, Daniel, and me as well as his minimal participation in our lives. But, like building a pyramid, once I accepted certain excuses as normal, this laid the foundation for the next level of excuses, and those for the next and the next. Still, there were occasions when Paul's behavior was so selfish and callous that it cracked the walls of my defenses, shining a small spotlight onto his dark heart.

When Jessica was thirteen years old, she developed an unusual medical condition. Extensive, invasive tests were required to confirm the diagnosis. If the diagnosis was correct, several years of medical treatment lay ahead. She was scared.

Although the final multi-hour test was scheduled a month ahead of time, Paul made it clear he would not accompany us. I could handle it, right? Again, his demanding clients and his work were his reason for his absence. It seemed absurd that he could not plan around an important medical procedure for his daughter more than a month in advance, but there was no reasoning with Paul. He always had the "clients above everything/ *someone* needs to support the family" trump card to play.

Jessica sobbed throughout the lengthy procedure, her fear almost giving way to panic several times. I stayed by her side for hours, holding her hand and comforting and consoling her. At the end of the test, we were both spent, but I pushed through my fatigue to stay strong for her. A week later, the results came back. Years of ongoing medical treatment lay ahead. I dealt with the doctors, the daily treatments, and the required monitoring. Paul never got involved. In Jessica's greatest moment of weakness and need, Paul walked away (there was always work to do!) or told her to "just get over it."

Soon after, I required minor surgery. As I had with Jessica's testing, I involved Paul when setting a date for the procedure to ensure he would be available to help the kids and me. I was forced to reschedule my procedure two times, because Paul's work demands kept trumping my health needs. Two days before the surgery, he called me from Chicago.

"Something's come up," he said. "A huge account's at stake, and I can't get back. You can handle this, right? This client's worth lots of money. I need to stay."

I hung up the phone and cried. Nothing had changed. If my health

CHAPTER 37

and medical needs and those of the kids could not come first, not even for a single day, not even for something important, not even for something known about in advance, it just punctuated how little we mattered to Paul.

Friends helped me out, gave me rides to and from the hospital, and checked in on the kids and me in the days that followed. Paul remained missing in action in Chicago. I think I knew then, without realizing it consciously, that no need of mine or the children, no matter how big, could ever trump any need of Paul's, no matter how small. What I did not know at any level, conscious or subconscious, was that I was describing sociopath math perfectly.

Although the reality of my doomed marriage should have been inescapable at that moment, I had a problem that I did not have when I hit bottom years earlier. I had stayed in an increasingly hostile environment for far too long, and I was drained. Because I felt trapped, I was trapped. I was like the frog that had not detected the slowly rising water temperature. Finally, when the danger was clear, my body and my will were too weak to flee or fight.

If I hear one more talk show host ask a victim of domestic abuse, "Why did you stay?" and not really listen to the answer or try to understand the psychology of how emotional, psychological, financial, and/or physical abuse can rewire your brain and murder your soul, I will scream, because I do not think the interviewer is really looking for an answer. Instead, it is as if the questioner is seeking to label the victim as "weak" and "not like us." This creates a sense that the victim is different, and that perceived difference creates the comforting illusion that it could never happen to us or someone like us. They were weak; we are strong. They were naïve; we are savvy. They were stupid; we are smart. They have no self-respect; we are self-assured. But this is wrong, false, naïve, and downright irresponsible. It can happen to almost anyone, and our only defense against it is accepting this inconvenient reality and being alert to the signs that someone with whom we are emotionally involved might be a sociopath—a sociopath who will blind us with love and the fulfillment of our dreams while leading us down the road toward self-destruction.

Almost anyone can become the target of a sociopath, and someone like I was, like most of us, who does not understand this is at even greater risk of being targeted. We need to understand and defend ourselves from this brutal reality. Evil exists in the world. Sociopaths are real and frighteningly common. They will present themselves as Prince Charming, poison us slowly, transform into the devil, and then feed on our souls, all the while making us feel so emotionally weak and confused that we stay on the "What am I doing wrong?" treadmill, unknowingly sowing the seeds of our own destruction. We need to know this and to watch for those fleeting

CHAPTER 37

moments when the disguise falters and the truth is revealed.

If you have not experienced the emotional and psychological erosion at the hands of a master puppeteer, it is probably hard to comprehend how profoundly your life can be altered by living with such subtle but chronic toxicity. Your strength is sapped, your confidence in your ability to perceive, decide, or "be" is all but gone. You cannot will it back to life with overused clichés to "Buck up," "Get back on the horse," "Get on with your life," "Don't give him power over you," or "Just think—GIRL POWER." Your strength is not hidden in a box that you simply have to discover and reopen. Even if you find the box and pull back the lid, it will be all but empty. Confidence and strength have to be remade, rebuilt, and coaxed back to life from all that is left—dust. There is no quick fix once you are so depleted. The road back is long and hard.

Over the years of consistent and discretely worded criticism that devalued my role as a mother and wife and being gaslighted, I was no longer "me." Not only was I spent emotionally and altered psychologically, through a series of decisions that seemed to make sense at the time, I felt compromised financially as well. As the money started flowing from Paul and Anne-Marie's consulting business, I let my own business die. The kids' medical issues, the need to fill in the all too frequent gaps in education even at the best public schools, as well as the after-school lives of both children, became my priority. It was too exhausting to try to keep my business alive when it was not necessary to pay the bills. Daniel and Jessica needed me. I loved being their mother, coaching their teams, volunteering at their schools, applauding their victories, and wiping the occasional tear. And if not me, who? I had no family within 200 miles, and Paul was rarely available to help with homework, life, or even with transportation to and from an occasional after school event. He was just too important, too unpredictable, and too busy with work—or, if not work, too deserving of much needed recreation and relaxation, right?

Liar

I always considered Paul honorable and honest, so it took me an embarrassingly long time for inconsistencies in his version of events to register as what they were—lies. I knew my husband had faults and, in all likelihood, had had an affair with Anne-Marie, but it never occurred to me that he was fundamentally dishonest and a chronic liar. But I could not escape the observation that Paul lied seamlessly about even the smallest things.

One night, I asked Paul if he had locked up the house. That task typically fell to me, but I was not feeling well and had already gone to bed. "Of course," Paul replied. The next morning, I was up before Paul and noticed that the front door was unlocked and a window in the kitchen was wide open. From then on, when Paul told me he had locked up, I found an excuse to get a glass of milk or leave a note for myself in the kitchen, only to discover that Paul had lied about locking the house for the night. Perhaps it was just too beneath him or too much effort, and it was easier to lie than take the extra minute to check if the doors were secure and his family was safe.

Sociopaths lie for the sake of lying. They lie about little things. They lie about big things. Some people have observed that sociopaths will even lie when telling the truth would be more advantageous. Others have observed that sociopaths lie not only to cover up questionable and even nefarious activities but also to feel in control and to manipulate others for the sheer fun of it. Why lie about locking the house for the night or taking the dog for a walk or forwarding a phone message? That's just what sociopaths do. Dishonesty and chronic lying are their hallmarks.

One summer evening, on Daniel's twelfth birthday, we planned for Paul to pick up a pizza and be home no later than 6:30. I called in the pizza order. Paul knew the timing was important, because I had to leave by 7:00 to get both children to their sports practices forty minutes away. Daniel wanted a special mushroom and pepperoni pizza from his favorite pizza place, which happened to be close to Paul's office.

Daniel, Jessica, and I waited and waited. Six-thirty came and went. No Paul, no pizza, and no phone call. At 6:50, I called Paul's cell phone. No answer. At 6:55, there was still no sign of or word from Paul. Just as we were about to get in the car to leave, Paul pulled into the driveway. He got

CHAPTER 38

out of his car holding a pizza. It was 7:02.

"Where are you going?" he asked, his voice laced with annoyance.

"Practice. We'll just heat up the pizza when we get back," I said.

If you are a reasonably normal person and you did not get home on time with a pizza requested by your pre-teen son on his birthday, what would you do? Wouldn't you apologize and try to do your best to make it right. Not if you are a sociopath.

First, a sociopath does not care that his son is disappointed or hurt. With no empathy, a sociopath does not have even a flicker of concern for another human being's feelings, even those of his own child.

Second, a sociopath cares only about himself. The only true emotions he can experience are anger and frustration. (A sociopath can experience pleasure and pain, but those are sensations, not emotions.) Paul felt frustrated and angry that he took time to stop whatever he was doing to get a pizza and to get home before he really wanted to be there. Now his family was leaving, and he would be alone (something he detested, because sociopaths dislike being bored), and it was not even the kind of pizza he liked. The fact that he knew his family had to leave at 7:00 did not mitigate the fact that he was the one who had been inconvenienced and *he* was the one who felt abandoned.

Third, a sociopath never thinks he does anything wrong, because he is an inherently superior being. If something has gone awry, it must be someone else's fault. As always, I was a convenient target of Paul's blame. I had grown accustomed to being held responsible for everything from misplaced credit card invoices (I had not figured out yet that Paul took them on purpose and hid or destroyed them so I would not notice his spending on "extracurricular activities") to having no socks to wear (the fact he never put them in the laundry hamper was my fault somehow) that I hardly noticed.

By now, I hope you are catching on to sociopath math and can predict Paul's reaction to arriving late with Daniel's birthday pizza.

"But I just got here, and I cut my day short to get the pizza," Paul said.

"Paul," I replied, "we have to leave or the kids will be late to practice. We'll heat it up when we get back."

"I never said I'd be able to get here earlier," Paul said. (He did, but he just made things up. Or maybe he never uttered those exact words. Regardless—he lied.)

"Paul, we have to go. We'll have the pizza when we get back. The kids are always hungry then."

"But that'll be ten-thirty or eleven!"

"I know, but we have to leave. The kids don't like being late."

"I can't believe I killed myself to get this pizza and you guys are desert-

CHAPTER 38

ing me," Paul continued. "This is ridiculous! The kids can be late."

"Dad, I don't want to be late for practice," Daniel said. "I'll get in trouble with the coach."

"Me too," Jessica said.

"I can't believe this!" Paul exclaimed.

"It's no big deal. I know you get busy," I said.

"I tried to get the pizza, but parking was crazy. I couldn't find a place; I kept circling but had to park really far away."

"Oh, were you away from the office this afternoon?" I asked instinctively. The pizza place was no more than a minute's walk from Paul's office, so getting the car from the public lot in which he parked normally and then driving to the pizza place made absolutely no sense, especially at that time of day when street parking could be challenging. The only thing that made sense was to walk to get the pizza and then carry it back to the car. If he had to find a place to park, it was logical to conclude that he had *not* been at his office.

"What makes you think that?" (Notice that since he did not answer "No" to my question, it was not technically a lie. And he tried to put me on the defensive for even posing the question to distract from the fact that he had probably not been at the office but did not want to admit to this for some reason.)

"Paul, we have to go. Come on, Daniel and Jessica, get in the car," I said.

As I pulled out of the driveway, the silence in the car was thick with disappointment.

"All I wanted was for Dad to bring home a pizza for my birthday," Daniel said softly, choking on the last few words.

"I know," I said. "I'm so sorry."

I glimpsed Daniel in my rearview mirror. A tear slipped down his cheek.

As I drove, I was so focused on the emotional hurt Paul had inflicted on Daniel that it distracted me from my interaction with Paul. But soon Paul's story replayed in my head. It made no sense. There was no way he would have driven the car to find a parking place when odds are that he could not have found one closer than his original parking spot. Why had he lied? Where had he been? More importantly, did I even care anymore? I wasn't sure I did. I was miserable, emotionally spent. I knew I wanted our marriage to end. But, sadly, I also knew something else—I no longer had the strength to end it.

Husband Liar Sociopath

Past The Point Of Rescue[VI]

Secretly, I hoped that Paul would just pick up and leave or be killed in a plane crash or in a car accident on one of those dark nights he came home late from a business trip or "working at the office."

I had never been able to shake my concerns that Paul had been and perhaps still was sexually involved with Anne-Marie. He always treated her like a princess. He had even paid for her half of the massive litigation expenses years earlier, told me she would pay us back, and then never asked to be reimbursed (even though I brought it up several times). He had handed her half of a now successful company on a silver platter. Once, when I'd met Anne-Marie's mother, she fawned over Paul, saying "Thank you for fulfilling every one of my daughter's dreams." I would have respected Paul for being a great mentor to Anne-Marie had it not been for concerns about the true nature of their relationship and for the fact that Paul treated me like a scullery maid. An image of Paul and Anne-Marie living happily ever after drifted into my mind. Good luck!

I felt dead inside—pathetic that I lacked the energy or will to escape from my pitiful life. But I wasn't pathetic. I had been poisoned emotionally. Sociopaths are brilliant at what they do. Disguised as Prince Charming, they are emotional vampires who rob people of their souls.

I reached out to my parents for help. Their response was that I was always welcome at their house if I needed a place to go. That was not enough. They did not understand that I did not have the confidence, self-esteem, or strength to get there on my own. Perhaps my cries for help did not resonate as being "real." Perhaps they could not comprehend how totally depleted I was, that I was flirting with serious depression. Perhaps I still looked like "me," the strong, independent woman who had excelled as an undergraduate at Harvard and a business student at Yale, who had been a fierce national squash competitor, and who was once a respected business professional. Perhaps it was too much of a disconnect to believe the words I was saying were true—that I was almost gone. Most people do not want to interfere. I get that, but there are times when they should.

Being involved with a sociopath is like being trapped in a cult. With reality elusive, fear of reprisal (emotional or physical) palpable, and your

---
VI Hal Ketchum

strength sapped, you need help. That doesn't make you weak; it makes you human. But no one reached out to help me. I would have to do it on my own, but I was not strong enough to do that. Not yet.

One reason victims of abusive relationships find it so challenging to leave is that in traumatic situations—whether a ten-day hostage event or a twenty-year emotionally abusive marriage—victims develop strong bonds with other people present during their trauma. As documented in the book *The Betrayal Bond—Breaking Free of Exploitive Relationships* by Patrick J. Carnes[40], although it sounds counterintuitive and even repugnant, if the main person present during the trauma is the abuser, then the victim is prone to developing a strong bond and great loyalty to the very person perpetuating his or her abuse. Consequently, it is challenging for a victim to exit an abusive relationship, because it violates the strong bond and loyalty she has developed, albeit unwittingly, with the very person she must escape. People do not choose for this to happen. They do not want it to happen. It just does. I knew Paul was the source of my pain and unhappiness, yet I felt totally loyal to him and dependent upon him. I certainly did not want to feel that way, but I did.

Clarity Is Hard

Whether I was alone or on the phone with a friend or my mother, tears flowed daily. I felt worthless, entombed in quiet despair. Hardly anyone would argue that, with Daniel twelve and Jessica going on fifteen, parenting would be a breeze. Yet, my parenting unraveled far more than can be attributed to dealing with two young teenagers or preteens. I grew increasingly short-tempered with Daniel and Jessica and nagged them constantly.

As a testament to how far I had fallen and how much I had become Paul's emotional captive, I felt that trying to regain my sense of self, my life, and my independence would be a profound betrayal of Paul, for which I would be punished through his anger, annoyance, contempt, or—ironically, what felt worse—total withdrawal of any human connection with him. Inside, I was dying. On the outside, life went on. There were meals to make, homework to help with, kids to get to practice, and other things to do.

To keep our overly rambunctious dog, Mr. Wrinkles, company, Daniel urged us to get a second pug. Daniel and Jessica named her Ella, after the protagonist in *Ella Enchanted*, one of Jessica's favorite books. Daniel adored Ella just as much as he loved Mr. Wrinkles. Daniel's challenges, which required years of therapy, had isolated him socially from other kids his age and made him the consistent target of bullies. His best friends were Mr. Wrinkles and Ella. They were a source of much needed emotional support.

One Saturday, as I was taking Mr. Wrinkles for a walk, I passed Paul and Ella in our small yard. Ella was still not fully housetrained, and she was not a fast learner, so getting her to do her "business" outside had been a struggle.

"Thanks a lot!" Paul snapped at me.

I had no idea why Paul was "thanking" me with such a caustic tone. What had I done that had been wrong, hurtful, or inconsiderate? I was simply walking down the driveway with Mr. Wrinkles. Something in me shifted. Why then? Who knows? Perhaps it was the unmistakable absurdity of the situation—that something as innocuous and well intentioned as taking Mr. Wrinkles for a walk could trigger this reaction from Paul. In that moment, the invisible gorilla became not just visible but sharply in focus.

CHAPTER 40

"You're welcome," I said, pasting a smile on my face. Then I turned back up the driveway and continued my walk with Mr. Wrinkles.

When I returned home fifteen minutes later, Paul was waiting for me in the front yard. He was smoldering, every muscle in his body and face strained.

"What did you say 'you're welcome' for?" he snarled.

"You said 'thanks a lot,' so I simply said 'you're welcome'."

I had been pounded into submission for far too long, requiring little effort on Paul's part to keep me embracing the Cinderella role, content to be mistreated, unappreciated, and to co-mingle with the crumbs and spiders in the corner. A new game had begun, one that Paul clearly did not like.

"Do you even know why I was thanking you?" Paul asked.

"No," I said, as cheerfully as I could, though my tone was obviously fake. I was determined not to cower. I would not be intimidated this time.

"I was *thanking* you, because Ella was about to pee, and you distracted her. So she didn't! Now she might pee in the house. It's your fault. *You* shouldn't have taken Mr. Wrinkles for a walk until *I* came in with Ella."

"So, you're mad because I took Mr. Wrinkles for a walk, and as a result Ella did not pee?" I asked. "And you think that because our dog didn't pee it's my fault and okay to yell at me?"

"I can't believe you're talking to me this way. The neighbors might hear," Paul raged.

"Really, that's what you care about, the dog's bladder and the neighbors? I'm not even being loud."

"You're shouting!" Paul yelled. "You're embarrassing me. You should've known what would happen."

My focus sharpened. It was as if a long-forbidden door was unlatched and opened just a sliver, supplying desperately needed oxygen to a hearth full of dying embers. In that moment, the coals burst into flame. Questions bolted into my consciousness. Would I ever have married this man—a man who treated me like this? If a friend had such a husband, wouldn't I be aghast? How long had it been since Paul had not treated me this way? Why did I tolerate it? Why did I try to make things right with someone so obviously wrong? Why was every misstep and inconvenience in Paul's life my fault? Why was nothing I did ever right? There was no love, no compassion, no honesty, and worst of all, not an iota of respect underlying this interaction or our relationship. None!

I turned and walked back down the driveway. Mr. Wrinkles and I did not come back for an hour.

In the past, I would have taken it upon myself to eliminate the tension and apologized to Paul for doing something that upset him. Not this time. Would Paul accept *any* responsibility for his role in the absurd encounter?

CHAPTER 40

I had to find out.

"Paul, I was hurt when you yelled at me about the dog," I said when I returned.

"You were the one yelling!"

"I would really appreciate an apology," I said, standing my ground.

"If there was something for *me* to apologize about, I would. But there isn't. *You* lost it in the driveway and embarrassed me and then took off for an hour without telling me where you were going."

"Paul, I don't recall yelling."

"You have this backwards," Paul said.

"So I owe you an apology?"

"Yes!"

I turned away from Paul and went to my small office, closed the door, and turned on my computer.

This had to end. I had to get stronger. I researched psychologists in the area. I left messages for three of them. Over the next few weeks, I interviewed each of them on the phone and then picked one, a woman considered to be one of the best in the area. The three-week wait for her first available appointment was unbearable. But with my new clarity, not going was not an option.

Week after week, I poured my heart out to Dr. Davis and listened to her prompts that encouraged self-reflection and new understanding. Paul's behavior continued to be "crazy making," dismissive, selfish, toxic, and controlling in ways I still did not fully understand. No matter how preposterous my story about Paul was, my therapy stayed focused on me and getting me emotionally stronger as well as understanding how someone like me had abdicated so much control over my life and had become so weak and beholden to another person. Getting out of this negative vortex and feeling that I deserved joy and respect in my life were a tall order, but with Dr. Davis's help, I started to make progress. Just having someone who listened to me and did not dismiss my reality was a huge leap forward.

Still, looking back, I am incredulous that Dr. Davis, one of the most respected clinical psychologists in the New Haven area, never said, "You know, your husband may be a sociopath, and if he is a sociopath, it is all about control and manipulation. You may feel emotionally depleted and worthless, because he has engaged in behaviors to make you feel that way. This gives him more control over you and the twisted satisfaction of destroying you. Not only does he not love and respect you now, he has never loved or respected you, because sociopaths are incapable of such emotions. His insensitive behavior may not be due to sleep deprivation, stress at work, his childhood, your own imperfections, or even possible depression. Such things can be 'fixed,' but being a sociopath is forever.

CHAPTER 40

"Sociopaths lack the capacity to care about other people. They only use people for their own purposes and discard them when they're done. Sociopaths have no moral compass. They lie, cheat, and steal as easily as they breathe. They also take ridiculous risks and typically have an insatiable appetite for sex. This ongoing affair with Anne-Marie you have been worried about is probably just the tip of the iceberg. His sex drive is probably being satisfied in ways to which you are completely oblivious and cannot even imagine. In fact, you should get yourself tested for sexually transmitted diseases and *always* have protected sex with him.

"Moreover, getting away from and divorcing a sociopath can be very complicated and even emotionally and physically risky for you and the children, because it threatens the things that motivate him the most—power and control. He has complete power and control now. He will not relinquish them easily. You will need to take precautions financially, because he will never be fair to you in a divorce. Once you are no longer any use to him, he will just toss you aside and try to minimize the financial damage. Be prepared for him to use your children as pawns to hurt you emotionally as well as financially. What's 'right' and what's 'legal' will mean nothing to him."

I would have liked to know that there was at least a strong possibility that Paul was a sociopath, because if I did, once I got stronger, the *only* logical decision would have been to leave.

Stronger

Over the next year, with Dr. Davis's help, I changed, but Paul did not. As my emotional strength and awareness grew, albeit slowly, I started to understand one of Paul's key manipulation tactics, and I refused to be sucked in.

Paul had a habit of entangling me in things someone else had done to disappoint or upset him. To show support for my chronically busy and overworked husband, he encouraged me to feel that I should take care of these issues for him. Not understanding this dynamic, I often did his dirty work for him, casting myself as demanding and unreasonable to help solve Paul's problems for him, all the while allowing Paul to maintain his coveted good guy image. Paul enjoyed playing golf, for example, and wanted Jessica and Daniel to learn to play as well. When neither child wanted to learn, Paul expressed to me how disappointed he was in the children. Through subtle and not so subtle cues, he encouraged me to pressure them into taking lessons so they could play with him. (This is the same man who refused to allow our children to play a sport I loved and at which I excelled—squash—because it was too elitist.) As I began to understand this unhealthy dynamic—that I was supposed to demand things that Paul wanted from other people—I refused to be a part of it.

"If you're disappointed Daniel doesn't want to play golf or you think a 3.9 grade point average is too low for Jessica, then tell them yourself. I don't agree, and I won't deliver your message for you."

Surprise! Surprise! While Paul continued to pressure me to be his enforcer, if I held fast and refused, he rarely delivered the unpopular message himself.

Realizing that, in my desire to please Paul, I had allowed myself to be overly demanding with my children—who deserved my love, guidance, and support rather than more manipulation—I was consumed with guilt. I wanted a cosmic do-over, but I would not get one. Staying mired in a brackish bog of regret would only tie me to the past and make change even harder though, so I fought against the resulting self-loathing, apologized profusely to my children for not being the mother they deserved, and started to eke out a modicum of forgiveness for myself.

This was only the tip of the iceberg though. The patient, kind, loving

CHAPTER 41

mother I had been initially remained elusive. Sure, I was compassionate, supportive, and helpful most of the time, but I still snapped at Jessica and Daniel and continued to nag them, especially when reasonable request after reasonable request (e.g., "please put your dishes in the dishwasher" or "we need to be on time for your dentist appointment") fell on deaf ears. Some of my bad parenting was part of the human condition; none of us are perfect, but I have to own much of it. The fact that I was emotionally frayed and fatigued due to incessant emotional and psychological erosion by Paul, which consistently slipped under the defenses of my conscious mind, explains how I morphed from such a great mom into being verbally harsh with my children far too often. Still, the behavior and the responsibility was mine. It is one of my deepest regrets.

Just as one of the Joker's goals in the Batman movie, *The Dark Knight*, was to make the embodiment of goodness and justice, District Attorney Harvey Dent, embrace evil and injustice, it was as if Paul delighted in seeing his formerly sweet, nice, empathetic wife turn angry and impatient with her children. Moments when I was not the mother my children deserved added to the backdrop of feeling awful. Only looking back now do I understand that some of the dynamics with Jessica and Daniel resulted not only from my flawed parenting but also from them modeling the behavior of the person in power—Paul—and the role in which I had allowed myself to be cast—doormat. Why should they listen to me? Why should they respect me? Jessica and Daniel were absorbing what they witnessed—their father constantly undermining me, the subtle and not so subtle communication that all my requests and opinions were stupid or unreasonable and to be dismissed with thinly veiled and always denied contempt. Brush their teeth? Are you kidding? Put on suntan lotion? Mom, you are sooooo controlling. Be ready to leave on time? Dad's always late. Sit down to eat for dinner? But Dad's watching TV. Honor your commitments? Dad always cancels at the last minute. It was endless.

The mountain I had chosen to climb—that of my own emotional recovery in the context of an emotionally and psychologically abusive relationship that I recognized as complicated and imperfect but not as "abusive"—was steep and high. Not only did I not have a cheerleader, I had the opposite—"crazy making," deceitful unraveling of any attempt to regain emotional strength. Still, day-by-day and week-by-week, I elevated myself in my mind as someone who deserved happiness and had independent needs that deserved to be met. After a year of weekly sessions with Dr. Davis, I felt ready to lay the foundation for a different future. I needed a life that was not defined totally by being Paul's wife and Jessica and Daniel's mother.

I started looking into possible future career scenarios, such as getting the necessary credentials to teach at a private school or getting my resume together to work at a public relations and advertising company in the area. Not surprisingly, in private or at home, Paul was less than enthusiastic about my moves toward strength and independence.

"Why are you even bothering? I make more than enough money. You'll never get a teaching position; it's too competitive. And besides, the pay's horrible. Why are you volunteering at the local arts council? You'll never be appreciated."

A metaphor broke into my conscious mind. Life with Paul was like an ongoing game of "Whack-A-Mole." I had become accustomed to living in the darkness. On those rare occasions when I needed to come up for air, Paul was waiting to whack me back down into my hole before I could feel the sun on my skin or fill my lungs with fresh air. This is a technique many controlling, abusive men use to keep their partners so eroded that it is all but impossible for them to escape the abuser's control. Paul wielded the technique with skill, constantly making me attribute my negative feelings to a character flaw of mine, such as being too sensitive, competitive, controlling, or impatient, because *he* was just being honest and respectfully realistic.

Keeping me off-balance and depleted was key, for if I regained my life, I would be less dependent on Paul. His power over me would wane, and I might have less time to be the stagehand for his show. I might even attempt to leave, and for him that would be both inconvenient and expensive.

This time, however, I would not allow Paul's putdowns and lack of support to derail me. They were all the more reason to get back into a world that, prior to Paul, had been a source of happiness, positive feedback, and purpose. It was time to do something nice for myself, something I had not done for ten years—get a new car. My old reliable minivan had more than 110,000 miles on it and had outlived its role in our family. I wanted something smaller, more reliable, and with better gas mileage—a small Toyota. Paul tried to talk me out of it. He wanted me to want a BMW.

We test-drove a Toyota. Paul did not like it. He convinced me to go with him to the BMW dealership, to stay open-minded. *That* was the car Paul wanted me to get. He was unrelenting, selling me on how incredibly reliable it was, how maintenance-free it would be, how much safer. The list went on and on. Even if I did not care about buying such an expensive car, I did care about reliability, because I was in the car with the kids constantly. I had checked out the literature. The BMW was not among the top picks on the criteria I valued, and the Toyota was. I wanted the Toyota. With my heart pounding, my voice tight, and both Paul and the BMW salesperson trying to convince me that they knew best what car I wanted to drive for the next ten years, I stood my ground and did not buy

CHAPTER 41

the BMW. Paul was incredulous.

It was the first time in years I had known what I wanted, had gone about the decision the way I wanted, and had not let Paul convince me of what I should want. Knowing that I had not caved in to what Paul told me I should do was satisfying.

Yet, pride in myself soon gave way to another feeling—an unsettling mixture of anger and confusion. Why should I be so proud of myself for fighting to have my needs met? If I was going to use the car 99.9 percent of the time, why was I being pressured to buy a vehicle that fell short of meeting my needs? Why was I even arguing with Paul that maintenance record, reliability, and gas mileage were more important to me than styling and status? This was absurd. Why did I have to explain to Paul that my needs and values were legitimate? It was as if I believed that if I just illuminated my perspective more thoroughly or in a somewhat different way, he would understand and support me.

The absurdity of the situation penetrated me. Paul pressuring me to get the car he wanted was really no different than Paul trying to convince me that my favorite color was red when it is, and always has been, blue. It was crazy! Why didn't I get to have a favorite color? Why didn't my needs count as valid? If you love someone, shouldn't you want what's best for him or her? Shouldn't you want to help the person you love have his or her needs and goals met? Not if you are a sociopath! Any need of mine multiplied by my value to Paul (zero) was and always would be zero. Paul had married me to fulfill *his* needs—period. There was no *quid pro quo*. To him, my needs were an inconvenience to be molded, extinguished, or adapted to his own ends.

Over years of Paul delegitimizing my needs, perceptions, and values, I hardly knew who I was, what I valued, or what I wanted. This made it easier for Paul to manipulate me. How could I possibly make a meaningful decision when my identity was all but gone? As one of my all-time favorite books, *How We Decide*[41], highlights, decisions are based on emotions. Emotions derive from a combination of who we were when we were born (we are all hard-wired a bit differently), past experiences, current situations, and how we think. There is no right or wrong emotion, because we are all individuals. For some, playing golf will make them feel good and become their life's passion, while others will feel bored and frustrated by the game and have no interest. Some will spark to the excitement of city life, others to the tranquility of the mountains. There is no right or wrong to such decisions, just what feels right to each of us.

But what if you have lost a sense of who you are and what you value? How do you make decisions when what you care about and value has been trampled and you are functioning on life support? Once Paul had dam-

CHAPTER 41

aged my internal gyroscope, decision-making became virtually impossible. As a result, I would defer decisions to Paul, because he always seemed to have a stronger, almost instantly formed opinion or valued something more highly than I did. By design, Paul created a void where a strong person had once stood, and then he filled the void exclusively with his needs, values, and priorities. *He* decided where we would vacation and with whom we would share our vacations. *He* decided that much of our furniture was too old and that we should redo our once warm and inviting house with a new man-cave decor filled with black, brown, and tan as well as lots of leather and faux fur. (Yuck!) *He* decided that we could never visit my family for Thanksgiving. No wonder Paul expected to dictate what car I should buy. When I did not agree to buy the BMW, Paul must have detected a significant shift in me. Action was required.

It started with mind games, couched in a loving, "I only want what's best for you" and "you deserve to have nice things" tone. Then, when I did not make the instant decision Paul wanted me to make, he indicated that I took too long to make decisions, overthought everything, didn't know what I really wanted, and didn't know what I *should* want. Wouldn't it be easier to just get the car Paul was so confident would be right for me? Shouldn't the speed of his decision-making and the voracity of his conviction be evidence of the rightness of his conclusion, compared to the lumbering quality of my decision-making?

But my labored, deliberate way of making the decision about my new car was not the problem. The problem was that I had regained some of my former self and strength. Paul wanted me to want what he wanted me to want, but for the first time in a long, long time, I wanted what I wanted, and I knew what that was—a Toyota. I was not going to be convinced otherwise.

Writer's Block

For a month, my work on this book stalled at this juncture. Yes, I had been distracted by the upcoming holidays, "life," and Paul's continual efforts to hurt me emotionally and drain my remaining assets through ongoing post-divorce litigation. I could also use the excuse that a seemingly inconsequential event that was a metaphor for my years with Paul (trying hard yet set up to fail miserably) triggered weeks of fighting back depression, anxiety, sleepless nights, a sense of helplessness, wanting to do nothing but watch TV, just doing the minimum of driving Daniel to and from school, preparing meals, and taking Mr. Wrinkles on walks. But I am guessing that the real reason for my writer's block was that I wanted to be able to time travel and send my "now" self back to my "then" self, who was growing stronger and starting to formulate an exit strategy. I wanted to scream out to her across time to "Stay on the path no matter what and no matter who Paul pretends to be." But I could not time travel. My still weak "then" self would have to make the best decisions she could, still unaware of Paul's true character and motivation. She would have to make even more mistakes, including some very big ones.

This is why I regret that my well-regarded therapist never focused on who or what Paul might really be. Unfortunately, most psychologists are not trained to even posit the question. Was he emotionally abusive? Clearly, he was, but I had been the puppet to a master puppeteer for so long that I did not see it or frame it that way. I never even asked the question. *I wasn't a battered wife.* That happened to other people, not me. I wish my therapist had broached that topic. Was I feeling so depressed, devoid of self-confidence, and emotionally and physically drained because I was in a long-term relationship with a sociopath who was constantly undermining me and trying to control me? Yes, but my therapist did not even pose the question. No one in my life did, including me. We didn't even know to ask. Most people don't.

Even so, I am grateful to my therapist for helping me regain some of my former self and strength, but without asking the above questions, I was likely to make bad decisions once I got stronger. If I was feeling so weak and depleted due to some unresolved issues in my past or flaws in my character (not because Paul was an abusive, controlling, manipulative sociopath), once I started getting stronger, perhaps developing a happier and healthier life with Paul would be possible. If, however, Paul was truly abusive and/or a sociopath, traits that often go together, then, even if I regained some strength, the only logical way to channel that strength would be to leave Paul as soon as possible. It made a difference who and what Paul really was and is, not just who I was and am and want to be.

At the point I decided I wanted a Toyota and was researching how to get one for the best price, a few data points must have been worrying Paul. I had been in therapy for over a year and was getting stronger emotionally. I had started thinking about my career and financial future, and I was starting to explore options by interviewing with companies. No longer was I Paul's pit bull with the kids. I was starting to be "me" again. I had even met with a divorce lawyer to gain information on the divorce laws in Connecticut so I would not be immobilized by fear and ignorance. Paul did not know about that last part—at least I did not think he did.

No Way Out

At the end of the summer, before Jessica's first year of high school and Daniel's first year of middle school, I took them with me to spend four days in Vermont with my parents. I needed the weekend away from Paul to try to know my own mind. I did not tell Paul this, only that I wanted to take the kids to see my parents. When I had done this in the past, there was always never-acknowledged, emotional hell to pay for "abandoning" Paul. I didn't care.

Over the weekend, with my mind getting clearer with every mile that distanced me from Paul, I decided to separate from him. I would not leave right away, but I would start gathering information and taking the necessary steps, such as getting a job and interviewing more divorce lawyers so that I could take an intelligent approach to the process of separating and then ending my marriage.

In the past, whenever I left for a weekend, I always returned to a messy house—letters and papers left where Paul had last worked with them, dirty clothes draped on the bed and cluttering the bedroom floor, bed unmade, dishes in the sink and on the counter, crumbs still on the table, snow in the driveway during winter, leaves littering the lawn in the fall. This time when I returned, the house was spotless—not a crumb on the counter, not a dish in the sink, not a piece of paper out of place or a sock on the floor, and the bed perfectly made. It felt terribly wrong. I was filled with dread and suspicion. Paul had *never* done this before. Why now?

While my mind raced, trying to decide if I should be amazed or alarmed, Paul asked me to come outside. He had something to show me. He opened the garage door. There in my garage bay was a brand new Toyota—the exact color and model I wanted. On the driver's seat was a gift bag filled with books. I love to read, but Paul had often teased me about being "geeky." Now he had actually bought me books that I was likely to enjoy. That had never happened before.

"Let's take your new car for a ride, just you and me," he said. There was no way I could refuse.

"Onna, I've been thinking," Paul said as we pulled out of the driveway. "You seem to be getting happier and stronger. It's made me realize that I haven't been happy for years. I've been a workaholic, and I haven't given

CHAPTER 43

you and the kids the attention you deserve."

I nodded, forcing myself to swallow. My mouth felt dry. What was going on?

"I want to start seeing a therapist, too. Things have felt wrong and broken inside me for a long time. I've been obsessed with my company and feel that you and the kids are strangers. I don't want to live like this. I want you back; I want our relationship back. I want to be a better father to the kids. I want to be a better husband. Our marriage is on life support. I want a do-over. I don't know if I deserve your help, but I hope you'll support me. I want us both to be happy, and the kids, too. Maybe your therapist could give me some recommendations. Would you ask her?"

I realize now that this was all an act. If Paul sensed I was going to leave him (and our marriage was going to dissolve on my terms, not his), he needed to do something drastic—appear to care, to accept some responsibility for our relationship, and to be committed to change. He needed to tap my empathy.

Paul's request felt surreal, partly because it was so out of character and partly because a piece of me must have been holding onto the foolish hope that the Paul with whom I had fallen in love was still there and would return someday.

"Of course," I said, not knowing how else to respond. "Therapy is a great idea. I'll ask her for some names the next time I see her."

When we got back home, Paul hugged me. "Thanks so much," he said. "I love you. I know I don't tell you that often enough, but I really do."

My head was spinning. What was going on? I needed air. I needed to think, to get out of the house and be alone. I took Mr. Wrinkles and Ella for a long walk. After fifteen minutes, I sat down near a tree in a quiet cul-de-sac where no one could see me. Sobs erupted from some deep place, shaking my body uncontrollably. Blood pounded inside my forehead with such force that I feared a blood vessel could burst. *I am too young, in too good of physical shape, and my blood pressure is too low,* I reasoned. *I can't have a heart attack or stroke.* Still the powerful, out-of-control unrelenting pressure in my head scared me. My spine, neck, and gut felt like they were on fire. My stomach convulsed, and I suppressed the urge to vomit. Never have I experienced something so primal, my body raging out of control. I tried to breathe, to focus my thoughts. My instincts were screaming RUN! But Paul had pulled out the ultimate weapon once again—he had tapped my empathy. Damn him! Damn him! Damn him!

Why now? What should I do? Just a day earlier, I had decided I wanted out of this marriage. Now Paul was saying he felt broken, that he wanted to change, that he wanted to start seeing a therapist, that he wanted my support. Was this real or should I stay on the path of independence and plan

CHAPTER 43

my exit? Should I give him a chance? How could I know? What the hell had just happened?

I suppressed the strong, animalistic urge to run and decided to wait and see. After all, I was not planning on walking out the door that night. I was planning on using whatever time I needed to get stronger emotionally and to make changes that could create a foundation for a new life—like getting a job, continuing with my therapist, and researching divorce lawyers and places to live. I could still do those things while seeing if Paul was genuine in his desire to change, couldn't I?

A Second Honeymoon

As the next school year unfolded, it was as if Paul and I were on a second honeymoon. He started seeing a therapist weekly, and his dedication to change was apparent immediately. When an old college friend contacted me to let me know she would be in the area and wanted to know if I wanted to get away for a girl's weekend together, Paul assured me he would look after the kids so I could go. And he did. Prior to that, he had never watched the kids for more than a few hours, always saying that his work commitments were too great or cancelling at the last minute. Books I would enjoy continued to show up at the house, ordered by Paul. He even planned dinners together and time to go to shows—just the two of us. He started arriving home earlier, allowing him to invest time in Jessica, Daniel, and me.

At first, I did not know whether to trust if the new Paul was real or not. After six months though, Paul's change seemed so profound and consistent that I became certain I was one of the "lucky ones," someone whose marriage had been rescued from disaster. As in a novel, I was the long-suffering wife whose selflessness and faith that the man she married was still there, albeit buried for over a decade, were rewarded by her husband finally seeing the light and realizing how much he loved and appreciated her.

I continued to build my strength, to see my therapist weekly, and to take steps to reenter the workplace. I networked to find potential jobs in the area and chipped away at the lengthy process of becoming certified as a teacher. I felt a new life and a new happiness unfolding. I felt lucky. Jessica was now a freshman in high school and excelling academically as well as in her favorite sport—lacrosse. She played on a high-level competitive team. Daniel was in seventh grade. As a result of being labeled and ostracized by his earlier difficulties in life, making friends had always been challenging for him. Daniel poured his energy into school and karate, achieving great success at both, but he still had a sad air about him, because he wanted greater social acceptance than he was able to achieve. Ella and Mr. Wrinkles remained Daniel's constant companions at home, his emotional anchors.

Paul was transformed, and I was regaining self-respect and independence. At last, life was heading in the right direction. That February, we vacationed in Utah *without* Anne-Marie and her family. It was a place where I could enjoy cross-country skiing and we could all go downhill skiing,

CHAPTER 44

Paul's favorite sport and one that Daniel and Jessica also enjoyed. It was a magical time. I cross-country skied high in the Wasatch Range, and Paul hardly worked at all—a rarity. For the first time in a very long time, it felt like we were a family.

On the flight home, Paul reached for my hand, leaned over, and whispered in my ear. "Let's move to the mountains," he said. "Let's start fresh, in a place we'll all enjoy. Let's get away from the suburbs. You've always wanted this. Let's move to Utah."

I looked at him. "Are you serious?"

"You've talked several times about moving to give Daniel a fresh start. Let's do it. We'll have to do it fast. We need to make sure we sell the house and have the kids there by the summer so they can meet people and be ready to start the school year. I know it sounds crazy, but how about it? Let's give us the second chance we really deserve. Let's give the kids the life you've always wanted for them."

"What about your business? My parents?" I asked. "They're getting old, and I don't want to be thousands of miles away when they need me."

"My business is doing so well now that I can manage it remotely. Jessica will be driving soon, the kids are older and more independent, and I'll make sure you can get back to see your parents four times a year, more if you want. And just think, now you can cross-country ski every day all winter."

My first response was "NOOOOOO!" I had done so much good work to get my life back on track in Connecticut that it would be crazy to derail my efforts now. I had friends, and my family was only a half-day's drive away. I had developed connections to try to get a teaching job. All the work I had done to start my life over was in Connecticut. But Paul was persuasive, using my affinity for a simpler life, our newfound connection, a more wholesome life for the kids, and a life in the mountains where I could enjoy my favorite sport and activities to convince me to go.

I agreed to think about it. While I did, Paul continued to be attentive, respectful, caring. The ice that, out of self-preservation, had encased my heart, continued to melt. Defenses built up below conscious awareness and reinforced through necessity over more than fifteen years did not dissolve instantly. Yet, as the months passed, I had started to fall in love with Paul again. Not only that, I felt hopeful and confident in the future, something I had not felt for a long time. Sociopaths can be very convincing.

To help make the decision about moving, I agreed to another trip to Utah in April. Paul planned it all. It was early spring; with snow still in the mountains yet an embracing warmth to the mountain air by midday. The tall peaks and snow tugged at my heart. For years, I had wanted desperately to give Daniel a fresh start. We spent our mornings skiing or hiking, our afternoons looking at houses, and our evenings at charming restaurants.

CHAPTER 44

The mood while we were there was magical, warm, even loving and exciting at times. We found a house nestled in the woods with just enough of a break in the trees to offer a spectacular view. The house resonated with me, reminding me of my childhood home in Vermont. It felt so right. At the end of the trip, I said, "Yes."

We would need to move at lightning speed to orchestrate the move by summer. (This is consistent with a sociopath's tendency to make quick, risky decisions and to convince others to come along for the ride.) Seeing as Paul would not be able to take time off from his business—our only source of income now—it was only logical that my life would have to come to a screeching halt once again to organize the move, but it seemed like a worthwhile tradeoff.

Finally, I had Paul back. More importantly, I was getting "me" back. Plus, I was going to be able to escape the suburbs and live in the mountains. I had scheduled a few interviews for teaching positions at schools in Connecticut. I cancelled them. My brother was skeptical and downright worried. He thought it was all happening too fast and that Paul had a hidden agenda. But I argued that Paul was different now. Once again, he was the man with whom I had fallen in love and married. We were closer than ever before. Finally, we would have the more grounded, simpler life that I had always wanted, and we were going to do it in a beautiful place. His business was thriving, which would allow me to travel back East to see my parents any time, and Paul would stay with the kids while I did. It would also be a great fresh start for Daniel.

To make the move happen in less than three months, I went into superwoman mode. I purged our family's belongings, built up over almost two decades together, repaired, staged, and put our house up for sale, and I worked hard to keep the house and yard in pristine condition to help it sell fast. In Utah, I researched schools, teams, karate studios, doctors, and so on. It was overwhelming, but feeling that Paul and I were part of a team once again, I put in eighteen-hour days as logistics coordinator for the move. Paul's mother came for a week to help. Although, over the years of family visits, Ruth was always more focused on getting things done than on being a doting grandmother, I had always appreciated her help and companionship, especially because my own mother was considerably older and unable to visit frequently due to her and my father's health issues.

By the end of June, the wheels touched down on our flight to Utah, and we closed on our new house in the mountains. Every item we owned had been given away, thrown away, or packed, and our house in Connecticut was under contract. It had been a Herculean effort, but I had done it. I felt strong and empowered.

The second day we were in town, Jessica met her new travel lacrosse team. I had prearranged her spot on the team while in Connecticut. After looking at her stats and talking to her Connecticut coach, the Utah coach had given her a place, sight unseen. I chatted with another mom, Melinda, about being new in town and noted the different style of play in this team versus the team on which Jessica had played for years back in Connecticut. Paul joined the conversation.

"No one cares what you think about the team's attack strategy," Paul said to me in front of Melinda. My breath caught. Melinda's eyes widened. The conversation screeched to a halt. What?

"We're just really happy to be here," I said, trying to ease the tension that had resulted from Paul's insulting comment.

Determined not to make a mountain out of a molehill, I did not even bring up the comment when Paul and I were in private. I just let it go. Moving out here had been like sprinting a marathon. We were all excited but also stressed and tired from the effort. It was a lot of change, and change is unsettling. That had to be the reason for Paul's behavior.

Two days later, Paul left for several days on business. I was alone at the house when the movers arrived with all our belongings and our cars were delivered. Still, with the new energy I felt, I treated the work of setting up the new house as a fun challenge. Waking up in the mountains was exhilarating, cleansing, and soul-affirming.

Yes, life was good—for about a week.

Whack-A-Mole Returns

In spite of my exhaustion from managing a cross-country move for our entire family in such a compressed time—with almost no help from Paul—within a week of our arrival in Utah, Paul wanted to go on a midsummer vacation with Anne-Marie and her family. I told him the timing was horrible for me, because I was spent. Also, the two weekends Paul wanted to be away would coincide with an opportunity for Jessica to join her new lacrosse team for back-to-back summer tournaments. She wanted desperately to go so she could get to know her new teammates, many of whom would be her high school classmates in the fall. Paul was relentless, insisting on how much he wanted to spend some quality time with the kids and me in a beautiful place. Could I please do it for him?

We compromised. Paul would not pressure me to do anything but rest and relax if I joined him and Anne-Marie's family for vacation, and Jessica and I would only come for part of the vacation so Jessica could attend both tournaments. That meant Jessica and I would travel together for a four-day vacation while Paul and Daniel would travel together for an eight-day vacation.

As I feared, the extra travel with Jessica, so soon after relocating to Utah and sandwiched in between the two lacrosse tournaments, was draining. I tried to rally, but I was dead on my feet.

Upon returning to Utah, I sorted through the mail and noticed an invitation to a wedding from someone with whom Paul had worked years earlier, someone with whom we hardly even kept in contact. It had been forwarded from our Connecticut address, so by the time I opened the invitation the wedding was only weeks away.

When Paul returned, I told him about the wedding, almost certain he would not want to attend, but I was wrong. I told him that I could not make the trip but that it was totally fine if he went without me. I was just too worn-out.

"You never do anything fun," Paul snapped.

"Paul," I said, "I'm exhausted from moving in such a short period of time. I haven't had time to catch my breath. There are still boxes to unpack."

"You never do anything I want to do!"

CHAPTER 45

"I just put my whole life on hold and moved us to Utah—something *you* wanted to do." I was hurt and incredulous. "We hardly know these people anymore. If you want to go, that's fine. I just can't come. We don't even know anyone here who could stay with the kids. The timing's all wrong for me."

"It's always about *you*, isn't it?" Paul said.

"What are you talking about?" I asked, feeling back in an all too familiar nightmare. Paul had not mentioned these people in years. Why did he suddenly want to go to their wedding? If he had been so close to them, why did he not even know about the wedding until I dug the invitation out of a pile of forwarded mail?

"Don't you realize what I've been doing the last few months?"

"Like you really did all that much!" Paul said. "You're mean and controlling, and you complain about everything."

"What?"

"You heard me."

"If I'm so mean and controlling, give me an example," I retorted.

"Your towel!" Paul said.

"What?"

"The one you use for the shower. It's ugly and doesn't even match the bathroom. The only reason you use it is because you know how much I hate it, and you're doing it just to upset me."

"What are you talking about?" I said, shocked at Paul's comment. "Did it occur to you that I don't use the ones you picked out because they're so big and heavy that they hurt my neck when I dry my hair? And it's my body and my hair. I can use whatever towel I want!"

"And I planned this great vacation, and you didn't even go on half of it. You stayed here to make sure Jessica could go to those worthless tournaments. You didn't care how *I* felt. They didn't even win! What a waste of time! You gave up time on the vacation *I* planned to do *that*!"

"I told you I never wanted to go on that vacation so soon after the move," I replied. "I'm exhausted. I jumped through hoops to do it at all. Does that matter?"

Paul glared at me as if I were the most evil, self-centered, hateful person in the world.

"I guess not!" I said, fighting back tears and trying to control my fear and anger. I couldn't believe it. I got in my car, drove a few miles to a secluded spot, and, with the beautiful mountains that had lured me away from Connecticut in the background, stopped the car and cried. Evil Paul was back. Had he ever really gone away?

In retrospect, I wish I had had the energy and foresight to move back East immediately, but I was too tired and too ashamed that I had made such a disruptive change in my life, maybe for nothing. Also, both kids seemed to be enjoying life in the mountains, and I did not want to uproot them again in such a short time span. That would hardly be fair to them. There would be time to move back East, just not now.

The game of Whack-A-Mole had returned, but now it was occurring in a place of great social isolation for me. I had no friends or family in the area, no job or volunteer activities to fall back on for validation, no outside human interaction. In that context, the game was desperately eroding, hacking away at my newfound strength and hopefulness. To create a life of my own, I started making new friends, tutoring, and sending out resumes.

Still, in case Paul was reacting to the upheaval from moving—a stressful life event—as well as to managing his company remotely (which I had always been concerned about), I tried to give him the benefit of the doubt and "invest in my marriage" once again. I woke up every morning determined to show interest in Paul and express my love to him, to share my enthusiasm for our family's new life in the mountains. But it was useless. Each interaction I initiated merely provided an opportunity for Paul to play Whack-A-Mole once more.

For the first time, in a flash of insight, it became clear to me how Whack-A-Mole really worked and what role I played in the abusive game. Although this was not necessarily happening at a conscious, purposeful level, throughout my marriage, to prove to myself as well as to Paul what a good person I was, I tried to engage Paul daily in some way, to share my life, my concerns, to learn more about his life, celebrate his successes, and to be supportive when he needed it (which he almost never did, because that would validate me and imply weakness for him). It was this active engaging of Paul that gave him the ability to play Whack-A-Mole with me. The mole (me) was constantly venturing out of its hole to interact with Paul, and by doing so I was (excuse me for mixing metaphors) a sitting duck. It occurred to me that Paul might never engage the mole in a positive, healthy interaction, nor let the mole run away. It was quite possible that Paul simply wanted the mole to keep poking its head out of its hole so he could feel the power, superiority, and satisfaction of whacking it back in. All the while, he encouraged the mole to blame itself for its miserable existence and to come out and play again, to try to show what a good wife I was by trying to have a meaningful interaction with my husband.

Finally understanding my role in the game, I stopped the insanity of doing the same thing over and over and expecting a different result. After years of trying to figure out some way to interact with Paul that would help us connect or reconnect, I simply stopped. I decided not to interact with Paul at all unless he initiated a positive conversation or interaction with me. I decided to not even say "good morning" to him unless he said "good morning" to me first. If he interacted with me in a respectful way, I would respond in kind. But if he ignored me or was harsh with me, I ignored him. No negative reaction, no reaction at all.

I did not know it at the time, but I had stumbled upon a strategy other victims of sociopaths have used to get a sociopath out of their life when having absolutely no contact with the sociopath is not an option. It is referred to as the "grey rock method."[42] It involves turning yourself into such a boring, nonreactive person around the sociopath (psychopath, narcissist) that the sociopath loses interest and leaves you alone, because you are no fun to manipulate and control. Like a cat toying with a mouse, once the mouse stops squeaking, struggling, and running about, the cat is likely to find more exciting things to do.

The one exception to my new strategy was that I was upfront with Paul about my perception that our marriage was spiraling down again and that the situation had become unacceptable. We needed to either fix the problem or end our marriage. We had been married long enough to know that this was not going to fix itself, and that the change of venue I had worked so hard to bring about had had no impact on our relationship. I loved our relationship for the year prior to moving to Utah and was willing to work on our marriage to bring it back to that point, but I could not do it alone. I wanted to know which direction he wanted to go—to work on our marriage with professional help or to end it. Months passed without Paul answering the question or engaging in a conversation about our broken marriage and what he wanted to do about it.

Privately, I consulted two divorce lawyers, and to my horror learned that once I had lived in Utah three months, the State of Utah and its laws had jurisdiction over my children and their fate in a divorce. I was past the three-month mark. I was stuck. Without Paul's endorsement or that of a judge (which I was told I was unlikely to get, because it is so important to keep families together in Mormon Utah), I could not relocate Jessica and Daniel to another state—even one in which we had lived for years up to a few months ago.

One night soon after that, without warning or any obvious trigger, Paul stomped into our bedroom at midnight and awakened me. "So this is it!" he screamed.

"Paul, I am happy to talk to you, but not by you waking me up and yelling at me in the middle of the night."

The next morning, the next day, the next week, and the next month, Paul was silent on the issue. I felt the ball was in his court. I had made my position clear. I waited.

The only topics Paul broached repeatedly were his company and our finances. Magically, as soon as we rang in the New Year, only six months

CHAPTER 45

after being assured of the financial success and viability of his company that would allow for this move and enable trips back East to see my aging parents multiple times a year—not to mention rebuilding our depleted assets—Paul informed me that his company was in trouble. In March, he stopped all payments to himself. Skeptical, I asked if Anne-Marie was doing the same. He danced around the answer in typical Paul fashion.

For the first fifteen years of our marriage, I had taken care of all the household finances—mortgage payments, credit cards, utility bills, and so on. However, a few years earlier, after I had searched the house in vain for a credit card statement so I could pay it, Paul offered to take care of all the credit card payments and bills via online banking. He also had to comment on how disorganized I had become. I trusted him—he was my husband—and I was happy to have that off my plate and to have Paul share in the household financial responsibilities, which had been up to me for so long. As a result of that transition, I had not seen a credit card statement for about two years.

The day after Paul told me of his company's sudden financial difficulty, I tried to take an inventory of our assets, because I knew how quickly money could be depleted in a zero-cash-flow situation. I could not access our bank account online, because Paul had changed the password. I went to a local branch. There, I confirmed our balance and noted something odd. In the first week of January, Paul had transferred $30,000 from our personal accounts back to his company.

Now I was kicking myself for letting Paul talk me out of renting when we had moved to Utah barely six months earlier. With no money coming in, our savings and checking account would be depleted rapidly by the mortgage alone.

Another month passed. Paul hardly spoke to me, and unless he addressed me in a kind, civil manner, I did not initiate any conversations with him that were not absolutely necessary. He bristled whenever I brought up the subject of money, bills, or our finances, often using anger to avoid answering any relevant questions. He was gone on business a lot, almost always to Chicago.

Then, early in April, UPS called our home regarding an unexpected package delivery, leaving a tracking number on the answering machine and an estimated time of arrival—apparently a signature would be required. When no package arrived, I went to the website to check on the package. The item was not slated to be delivered to our house; it was scheduled for delivery in Chicago to someone named Linda Peters. I Googled her name and discovered she worked for one of Paul's clients in Chicago. However, the package addressed to her was not being delivered to the company address but to a residential address. It struck me as odd. I kept the informa-

CHAPTER 45

tion about the package and put it someplace safe.

Paul returned from Chicago several days later. "I've put a deposit down on a condo," he said. "I'm leaving. I'm done with this marriage. I'm going to Chicago for a week on business. We'll tell the kids when I get back."

It was exactly a year after Paul had convinced me to move to Utah, and nine months since our arrival in the beehive state. I was both relieved and panicked. This marriage had turned toxic again so quickly that it needed to end. But to accommodate Paul's illusion of a second chance and a new life, I had put my plans to resurrect my professional life on hold. If we had stayed in Connecticut, I would probably have had a job and my own source of income already. I would certainly be surrounded by old friends and be near my family. Having moved to Utah only months earlier, and investing many of those months in getting the house set up and the kids settled, I was dead in the water. Now I was almost a continent away from much-needed emotional and financial support. Getting divorced in Utah would be hard, but as of that moment, I still thought of Paul as an honorable man. I assumed that divorce laws must be fair and reasonable and that Paul's integrity, and the fact that we had two children together, would make for a reasonable dissolution of the marriage.

But disparate pieces of the puzzle kept rattling in my brain, clamoring for attention or an epiphany that would make sense of everything. I could not escape an increasingly unsettling, fearful feeling that now—when I could most use the support of my family and friends, a free place to stay, the comfort of familiarity, and a job or job prospects with some income or benefits—I was farther away from a port in a storm than I had been in my entire marriage.

Not only was I far away from any safe harbor, a hurricane was on the horizon. This couldn't be an accident. Paul's behavior had changed too quickly from romancing, loving husband, doing everything right to ensure his wife would give him another chance and move the family to a remote place he wanted to be, to expert Whack-A-Mole player, screaming at me about my choice of a towel. As if lightning had struck, providing energy to fuel neural connections waiting patiently for years to be made, my whole mental framework recalibrated. A new clarity emerged, and with that clarity came an overwhelming sense of despair and disbelief. Paul had isolated me on purpose. It had all been a setup. If the past year had been a setup, what else had been a fabricated manipulation? All of it? Oh my God! Had *any* of it been real? The thought drained air from my lungs and strength from my body. I collapsed to the floor.

The next morning, I wrote furiously in a journal that I had started to keep only recently at the recommendation of a friend. More pieces of the puzzle fell into place, my hand barely able to keep pace with my thoughts.

CHAPTER 45

What kind of person would manipulate his spouse as Paul had done over the past two years and probably even before that, perhaps even from the beginning? Moment of weirdness, vignettes from my life with Paul, flashed through my mind. Paul's anger on our first New Year's Eve when I was too tired to stay up until midnight. His behavior on the eve of Daniel's birth. His refusal to help with Daniel's ongoing therapy. Paul's absence when Jessica went through her invasive medical testing. His refusal to help me when I had my surgery. What kind of person would disregard even the medical needs of his children and spouse?

"No empathy! He has no empathy. THAT explains it all," I wrote, underlining the words repeatedly and with such force that the paper nearly ripped. That alone accounted for everything. My head was spinning. The ramifications were profound. Pieces from my past that had never made sense before became clear with meaning. If Paul had no empathy, that meant he had never had empathy. It meant he had never cared about me. It meant the past twenty years of my life had been a sham, a massive investment of my life, my emotions, and my compassion into a black hole, consuming everything and paying nothing in return.

Nausea rose within me, and despair crashed down upon me. Fear sparked somewhere deep inside. My head slumped forward and rested on my arms, which lay crossed on the table. My hair slipped over my face but was unable to shield me even temporarily from the blackness of my realization. Sobs wracked my body. Who was this man?

Drowning in a sea of confusion and blackness, I called my mother, seeking both emotional comfort and a second opinion. She could not bring herself to believe my conclusion was true.

"It can't be," she said. "How can someone totally lack empathy?"

She could not understand it, because she was so filled with empathy for others that fulfilling her needs is often challenging. It was the only way she could perceive the world, and I had inherited my vast capacity for empathy from her. It had kept me blind to what was right in front of me for almost twenty years. I had been played. It was that simple. Damn it! Damn it! Damn it!

What no one in my family, including me, understood was that some people are simply abusive, and it does not matter what their victim or target does, they will still be abused, because that is what abusers do. Abusive people, like sociopaths, cannot be healed by unconditional love, understanding, flexibility, or any once-in-a-millennium alignment of the planets. They are different, not even damaged, just different. They are devoid of something the rest of us value beyond measure but also take for granted— the ability to care for other human beings, to empathize. Searching for validation of my chilling conclusion, I thought of the one person who could

CHAPTER 45

help me—Sally. I still had her number. I had not spoken to her in years. Would she even talk to me after we had been out of touch for this long? Of course she would; she was one of the nicest people I had ever met. I dialed her number, hoping it still worked. She picked up.

"Onna," Sally said, "every Christmas I hope to get a card from you saying you've left Paul. I don't use this word lightly, but, Onna, he's evil. I'm so sorry it's taken you this long to see it."

I cried, and Sally stayed silent on the phone as I did. Crying yielded to sobbing, my body convulsing uncontrollably. Betrayal is an intense emotion. I sobbed for the charade that was my life, for the wasted twenty years, for my children's and my uncertain future, for the emotional investment of a lifetime that had left me with nothing. I had devoted more than half of my adult life to a man who had never cared about me or our children. The despair was physical, as if a large part of my insides, my heart and guts, had been ripped from my body. This happens to people in movies, not to real people, not to people I knew—not to me!

"Onna," Sally said after waiting patiently like the good friend that she was, picking up right where we had left off over a decade before, "there's a book you should read. It'll help you understand who and what I think Paul really is."

"What?" I asked, hungry to understand the mess I had made of my life and the lives of my children.

"*The Sociopath Next Door*. I think Paul's a sociopath. They have no empathy. None."

I was silent. A sociopath? Could Paul be a sociopath? It wasn't a question I had ever known to ask. It certainly did not fit my flawed preconceptions about sociopaths.

"I could send you my copy," Sally offered.

"No, I'll get one," I said, skeptical but willing to entertain anything that would bring clarity and understanding.

Sally and I agreed to stay in touch, and we have. Her nonjudgmental, "How can I support you?" approach was and continues to be incredibly comforting.

I got the book the next day and read it that afternoon. I underlined paragraph after paragraph, each perfectly describing Paul. Once done with the book, I poured through relevant websites about sociopaths, or psychopaths, as they are called sometimes. (Sociopath and psychopath are laymen's terms, not medical terms. Narcissistic personality disorder or antisocial personality disorder are the closest official diagnoses.) It was all there; the book and the websites described Paul perfectly. If only I had known that "Could he be a sociopath?" was a relevant question. If only I had known that the moments of weirdness were not signs of sleep depriva-

148   Husband Liar Sociopath

tion, stress, childhood hurts, or depression. They were signs of something dark and sinister—of a soulless human being devoid of compassion.

Not only are sociopaths characterized by a complete lack of empathy for other human beings, another equally key characteristic is their complete disregard for the rules of society. They lie easily and proficiently, often engage in illegal or unethical behavior, and never feel what they have done is wrong. I thought back to the countless times I felt odd about Paul's explanations. They were too numerous to count. If there was validity in my concern even half the times I sensed something was off, it suggested incessant lying, not to mention multiple affairs. I tried to recall a time in the past when Paul had apologized to the kids or me. There were only a few, and they had occurred in extreme situations—to keep me from walking out on him. I shuddered at what this mean for my future.

Divorcing a Sociopath—Round I

As we discussed dissolving our marriage, Paul's initial strategy was to act kind and generous. He urged me to follow his lead, and everything would be all right. I asked him if he was involved with another woman—not that it made a difference. I just wanted to know. He assured me he wasn't dating anyone and laughed at the absurdity of the idea.

A few weeks after he left, we met at a coffee shop for him to review his proposal for our divorce. Paul suggested that neither of us hire a lawyer so as to preserve our assets, which were dwindling quickly due to his financial situation at work and the fact we were now supporting two household locations. I should purchase the house from him, keep physical custody of the kids and, per the laws of the Utah, I would be required to stay in Utah with Daniel and Jessica. Paul, if he chose, would be able to relocate anywhere in the country and pay me minimal alimony and child support (not even enough to cover the current mortgage). This was more than generous, he believed, because he was currently making *no* money. Seeing as I had an MBA from Yale, I should be able to get a job immediately, pulling in a $100,000+ salary. Also, even though I was legally entitled to half of his portion of his company, A-M-P Consulting Solutions had no actual value aside from Paul and Anne-Marie's personal brilliance (which, by law, belonged to them alone).

"If you're a good mother and really care about the kids," he said with his hypnotic, velvety voice, "you'll get this over with quickly—for their sake. Don't get a lawyer or do anything to deplete our assets. Anyway, you'll need that money to live on until you get a job. Onna, it's the right thing to do. And you've wanted to work again for a long time. It'll be great."

Paul's gentle, lyrical voice, concerned countenance, and deep, loving eyes were like a siren's song, drawing me ever closer to my demise. "It's what's best for Daniel and Jessica. Don't you love your children? Don't you want to be a good mother? Don't put yourself and the children through a messy, painful divorce. I've heard of even very wealthy people draining all of their assets arguing over the value of a business. And we're not starting out with that much. Onna, you are over fifty now. Don't do anything stupid."

"Paul, I haven't worked full-time since Jessica was born. I've invested

CHAPTER 46

most of the last fifteen years of my life in the kids, *their* health, *their* future, and in *you*—to give you no distractions while you built your company. Finding meaningful work again now, at my age, out here—it's not going to be easy. Everyone knows that. This doesn't make any sense."

"Of course it does, Onna. I haven't hired a lawyer yet, but I've talked to several, and they *all* think this is beyond generous, especially with your education. Assuming you can make six-figures right away is *conservative*. Most judges would hold you accountable for more. In fact, the lawyers I spoke with said I was giving away way too much and that I was foolish to be so generous. But I want to do the right thing. And, Onna, we both know you had absolutely nothing to do with my success. Since you are such an ethical person, it would be wrong to claim any right to it. Someone as honest and ethical as *you* would never do that."

Locking me in his enchanting, seductive gaze, his voice now almost poetic, calming, soothing, Paul continued, "I've drawn up the papers. Just sign right here, and we'll be done. I'll file them. I'll take care of everything. We'll be divorced in a few weeks. Simple, painless, easy. We'll both be so much happier, and the kids, too."

"At least agree that I can leave Utah with the kids," I said. "It'll be a lot easier for me to restart a career back East."

"No. The law's clear. To take the kids out of Utah you need the other parent's agreement or a judge. Judges here almost never agree to that, and I'll fight to have the kids stay here. Even though I'll be traveling a lot, I'll make it clear that Utah is my permanent home. You'll just spend a lot of money, and you'll lose. It'll be fine. It's so beautiful here. It'll be fine."

The quiet, even quality of Paul's speech was so hypnotic that I had to shake free from the voice beckoning me to the crags, a voice trying to distract me from the absurdity of what Paul was proposing. Interestingly, a 1998 study found that, compared to male nonpsychopaths, male psychopaths speak more quietly and with less variation in emphasis between neutral and potentially emotional words.[43] Perhaps this is some of what contributed to Paul's spellbinding vocal delivery.

"Paul, I am going to work with a lawyer," I said. "I don't want this to get adversarial or take a long time, but it's a very important decision at this point in my life."

"Onna, that's not necessary," Paul said, his face still soft, his tone gentle. "It's a *great* offer, *really* generous. If you get a lawyer and we start spending lots of money ... " Paul tilted his head down, sighed, and shook his head, then looked up at me as if to say, *Come on, sign the papers, Onna. You can do it. Just sign the papers.*

"Yes, I'm sure," I said. "Getting a lawyer is what people do."

The sweet, reassuring smile left Paul's face. "You fucking bitch!" Paul

CHAPTER 46

shouted.

People in the coffee shop turned in our direction.

"You'll regret this. I'll go after the kids. I'll make sure you never see Jessica. I'll hire someone to prove you should be making six figures, and the only reason you haven't worked full-time is that you're a lazy bitch. I owe you nothing! A lawyer told me it would look bad that I've moved out. I'm moving back in *tonight*. Either take this deal or you'll be sorry—really sorry!"

My breath caught. My chest tightened. Fear welled inside me. I swallowed, trying to coax moisture back to my mouth so that I could speak and conceal how scared I was of Paul in that moment and of what might happen in the future.

"Don't move back in," I said. "It won't be good for the kids. It's already hard enough. And I saw the check you wrote for $15,000 for three months' rent on the condo. That's crazy, but it's even crazier to waste that money. We both need our space. I've also talked to a lawyer. She said neither of us is supposed to spend money that isn't necessary until this all gets sorted out. That rent's ridiculous, but if it's already spent, stay there. Don't come back."

"It's *my* house. They're *my* children. It's *my* stuff. I'm moving back! Sign this, or I'll be back tonight after I have dinner with the kids. You better have them at *my* place on time! Anyway, I didn't spend $15,000 on rent—a third's a security deposit. I'm getting it back."

"Paul, please ..."

"Fuck you!"

"Paul, don't move back in."

"I'll do whatever I want!"

"I've changed the locks." I wasn't bluffing—both my lawyer and friends had advised me to do it.

"You bitch!"

"I'm not going to sit here and listen to this," I said, the dryness of my mouth and my raging pulse making speech difficult. Avoiding eye contact with Paul, as well as that of any stunned onlookers, I fumbled for my wallet, slapped down enough cash to cover my bill, and walked out. *This* was the real Paul, and he was a monster.

As I drove the fifteen minutes back to the house, my phone signaled multiple incoming text messages. When I arrived home at about 10:00 a.m., I read them. All were from Paul.

You can't change the locks. MY house. What YOU did is ILLEGAL. Be there at 11:00 to give me keys. If not, I'll have you ARRESTED.

Shaking, I called my lawyer. She told me I should not give him a key. She also stressed that I should not be at the house when Paul arrived.

CHAPTER 46

Will not be here at 11:00, I texted Paul back.
I insist! Paul said. *What could you possibly have to do?*
Again, I did not respond.
I expect you to give me keys @ 11:00. Called my lawyer. This is illegal! Another text followed. *You MUST give me a key. Leave it under mat!*
Once again, I ignored him. I had never seen him like this before, cursing at me in public, demanding total control.

Racing around the house, I threw every financial and other document I thought I might need—old credit card statements, bank statements, tax returns, the title to the car, my passport, the kids' passports, our social security cards, mortgage documents—into a box. As I did, I recalled that during a friend's divorce, her husband had gained entrance to her house and destroyed family pictures and other sentimental items. I grabbed several picture albums of the kids and put them into the car as well. Others I secreted away, along with a few irreplaceable items inherited from my grandmother. Any extra keys to my car and the house that I could find I threw into my purse. My heart pounded, and my body dripped with sweat. It was 10:45 a.m. when I loaded the last item.

Taking a deep breath, I went to every door to make sure they were locked. A tightness rose from my abdomen to my throat as I looked at my watch—10:50. Would Paul be early? Had he bluffed about coming at 11:00?

My eyes scanned the driveway for his car. Nothing. If I did not get out before he arrived, he could block my exit from our narrow driveway, which was carved out of the side of a steep hill. There was no other safe way out with a car. I did not know who this man was anymore—had I ever? Our house was nestled in the trees and quite isolated. Would he hurt me? Would they find my lifeless body in a ditch?

My breathing quick and shallow, I drove out of the driveway at 10:52. I was so glad it was a school day and that Daniel and Jessica would not be home for hours. If Paul came the most direct way to the house, I would pass him if I exited the driveway by turning right, so I turned left, took a deep breath, and drove down the road.

The windows! I slammed on the brakes. I had forgotten about the windows! Were any of them unlocked? If so, with no alarm system in our house, all Paul had to do was slide a window open and he would be inside.

My pulse raging, my hands trembling, I turned the car around. Would I make it? I had to try. I stopped at the top of the driveway and peered down. Paul's car was not there. I parked on the side of the road so Paul could not block my exit, locked the car, and then ran down the driveway to the house. From the outside, I checked every ground-level window, hoping they would all be locked. Two were unlatched and opened easily. Damn

CHAPTER 46

it! I hurried to the front door, raced inside to the problem windows, and secured them. Then I ran out and sprinted to my car.

I felt transported, as if I were above my body watching the scene unfold below me like a movie. But this wasn't a movie. It was *my* life. It was real. It was now.

Halfway up the driveway, seconds away from the safety of my car, a thought flashed through my mind—had I locked the front door? I tried to replay my exit from the house in my mind, but with adrenaline coursing through my veins, I had no memory of whether or not I had secured the front door. I had to be sure. I ran back. At least if Paul drove in now, I could scramble up the rocky embankment that separated our driveway from the road above.

I reached the front door and turned the handle. I *had* locked it. Sweat pouring from my brow, I hurried back up the driveway, looked around for Paul's car, and then jumped into mine. It was 10:56 when I drove away.

Divorcing a Sociopath—Round II

As I turned the corner and the house slipped from view, I took a deep breath and tried to calm myself. Five minutes later, text messages and calls flooded my phone. I ignored them and kept driving. A few minutes later, I pulled into my bank's parking lot and tried to breathe normally. I checked my phone. All the texts and calls were from Paul. I neither read them nor responded to them. I turned off my phone. To get my mind off the unfolding drama, I went into the bank to apply for my own credit card, something I would need for my new life. Recently, I had discovered, to my horror, that while married to Paul, only one of my credit cards was joint with him. The other two were Paul's credit cards, on which I was only an authorized user with no actual authority to get records of previous spending or to even cancel the card. I had always assumed that all of our cards were joint credit cards. Nope! When and why had I stopped having my own credit card? I could not even remember.

I probably looked more nervous than a first-time bank robber when I applied for the credit card. My confidence was nonexistent, thanks to constant battering from Paul. Even the smallest effort on my behalf seemed overwhelming. I fought back tears at the bank, and my hands shook as I completed the credit card application. *I can't! I just can't!* my mind screamed. A Harvard graduate with an MBA from Yale lacking the confidence to apply for her own credit card? It seemed unimaginable that I could have fallen so far.

After years of Paul's constant criticism, my fear of making a mistake was so palpable it immobilized me. Compounding the certainty of my incompetence was the conditioned fear of taking any action that would give me independence from Paul. For over a decade, he had subtly but consistently punished me for autonomous thoughts or actions, as if being my own person was a profound betrayal of Paul. Now, frozen with fear of making an error on the application and of Paul's wrath for taking even a baby step away from him toward personal liberation, it took all the strength I could muster to hand the banker the completed form. *What if I'm not approved? What then?*

Wimp! Fool! an inner voice taunted. *You gave Paul everything, and look how he repays you! Not even enough confidence to apply for a credit card.*

CHAPTER 47

How pathetic! You're pathetic!

I pushed past my self-defeating thoughts and continued with the task at hand.

As I left the bank twenty minutes later, I turned my phone back on. A multitude of new texts and voicemails from Paul registered. Without reading or listening to them, I called him back on impulse.

"What do you want?" I said. "I'm *not* giving you a key."

"I don't need one," he said.

"Good," I replied. "It's better if you have your own space and I have mine."

"Don't you want to know where I am right now?" Paul asked.

"I don't care."

"Well, you should care," Paul said. "I'm sitting in *our* living room. I like the way you rearranged the furniture. Nice touch."

My heart sank.

"Don't you want to know how I got in?"

My mind raced. Mentally, I visualized every room. I had locked every door and checked and locked every window. Oh my God! As I pictured the area near one of the doors, I "saw" my laptop on the desk. I had meant to take it but had forgotten. Would he notice it? Would he harm it? Would he take it? My whole life was on that computer. God only knew when it had been backed up last or where the backup drive was. Paul had always taken care of the family's computer needs. He always had full access to my computer. There was no password protecting it and nothing I could do now but stay silent.

Idiot, an inner voice taunted. *Left your computer. Don't even know how to back up your computer.*

Paul's voice distracted me from my self-deprecating thoughts.

"Well, you should want to know how I got in," Paul continued. "It was soooo easy. I just called a locksmith. My license shows that this is my legal address. This is *my* house. The locksmith was more than happy to help. It might even have been the same guy you used to change the locks. Ironic, don't you think?"

The deep breath I took was probably audible to Paul.

"Onna, I can get into this house whenever I want! Anytime ... day, night ... anytime."

A wave of despair broke over me. I tried not to signal my terror. The threats to my privacy and my dignity were real. Was he threatening me physically as well?

This is how ex-wives get killed, I thought. These men who appear so normal, so successful to the outside world, mask their need for total control. Experts say it's always about control. Paul wanted control, to win—to drain our assets so there was less to divide, all while probably squirreling away tons of money in his company that would be his, and his alone, after the divorce. Unethical people who own their own businesses can do almost anything they want to hide money in a divorce, and finding out what they have done can be virtually impossible and cost a fortune.

I thought about the wire transfer of $30,000 to his company back in January and the "I'm suddenly unable to pay myself, so sorry, honey" story that followed soon after. I could only conclude that Paul had been planning this for some time.

Now he wants to get the kids away from me, to drive a stake through my heart and to avoid paying any financial support. And he wants me to agree to virtually no alimony. If I don't capitulate on that point, he will shred me emotionally and financially. If I thwart him, will I end up dead?

My body trembled.

In that moment, I understood why, throughout our marriage, Paul had criticized me so often for being controlling. It had always seemed odd, and I had stupidly responded by bending over backwards to make sure he would not view me that way. I caved in to what he wanted to prove that I did not need to be in control. Fool! Most people consider me flexible. One of the most common criticisms of me at work was that I was too nice, never that I was too controlling. But Paul is not a normal person. He is a sociopath. Not being in *total* control was so anathema to him that even having ninety-nine percent control must have felt out of control. Nothing but 100 percent would do. Sociopath math, remember?

It was clear to me now. The give and take of any normal relationship would be stifling to a sociopath like Paul. The only give-and-take equation that feels right to a sociopath is take-take-take-take-take. Sociopaths are the black holes of the human universe—they suck in all surrounding matter and energy and give nothing back.

Snapping back to the here and now, I knew I needed to push through the self-doubt and fear and regain some control, and I needed to do it fast. But how? I had always been an honest, nonmanipulative, "cards-on-the-table" type of person. I was brand-new at this game. Paul had decades of experience. This was hardly a fair fight, but that was the point.

"Paul," I said, "go ahead and move back in. In fact, the house is huge and a lot of work. We both know *you* will be able to afford it, and I will not."

I truly did not want to be stuck with the house, because I knew we would need to sell it if Paul did not want it, and I knew how much work selling the house would be. I had just gone through that grueling process not even a year earlier, and that was not how I wanted to spend my time again.

"So, that's fine. But before you take the time to move back, I want you to know that I will move out as soon as possible. There are tons of rentals

CHAPTER 47

available, even some that allow dogs. I've already checked. So go ahead, but the kids and I will be gone within a week. Then we'll have a mortgage and *two* rents to drain our assets."

"I'll be back tonight after dinner with the kids," he said, his voice calm and steady, not a hint of anger or agitation. "And I expect you to have Daniel and Jessica at my place this afternoon, as *you agreed* yesterday. Four-thirty sharp!"

This was another one of Paul's manipulation techniques. Knowing that I took honoring my commitments seriously (as do many nonsociopaths), he tried to hold me accountable for something to which I had agreed previously, even when the commitment I had made was based on a foundation of falsehoods, partial information, and invalid assumptions. Who had poured that false foundation? Paul, of course.

In his rulebook, no promise he made was ever worth keeping the moment it became inconvenient. ("I never agreed to that." "You must have misunderstood." "That no longer works for me." "I didn't understand correctly." "*That* is not how I meant it.") Yet, he tried to make me feel irresponsible, guilty, or dishonest for not honoring a commitment of any kind or size no matter the outright deceit involved on his part when obtaining the commitment from me in the first place or the radical change in circumstances after the commitment was made. For example, after we divorced, Paul got Jessica an expensive car. He sent me a bill for half of it—involving his lawyer and mine. Paul insisted that because, when we were married and living in Connecticut, we had promised to get Jessica a car when she got her license, I was legally obligated to reimburse Paul for half of the cost of the high-end car that he unilaterally selected for her. Sociopath math! When I learned not to feel obligated by surreptitiously obtained promises, Paul's shifted tactics to assault my character, accusing me of being dishonest, a liar, or irresponsible. By doing so, he hoped that, to prove I was none of those things, I would live up to the original obligation.

Because I was not yet aware of this manipulative technique, I foolishly agreed to honor my commitment to get the kids to Paul's condo later that afternoon, all the while trying not to show how deflated I felt by Paul calling my bluff.

"Fine," I said. "Just let me know when you're out of the house so I can come back and you won't be there."

"I'll be gone in five minutes," he said.

I let a half-hour pass. When I got there, the front door was unlocked. I opened it and stepped inside. My laptop was still at my desk, and it looked undisturbed. Flooded with relief, mixed with a sense of profound personal violation, I slumped to the floor and wept. When the tears finally stopped and I thought I could talk without crying, I called my lawyer.

CHAPTER 47

In all her days practicing divorce law, she had never known someone to do what Paul had just done.

Afterwards, I continued to look around the house. Why had he broken in? Simply to scare me and prove he could do it? Was there another reason? Only one thing looked disturbed. A picture had been tipped over that was normally on a desk in front of a drawer where we kept small, expensive things, like season passes to the theater and concerts that we had bought for the upcoming year. Combined, they were worth over $500. I opened the drawer. They were gone.

Toxic Emails

I spent the rest of the afternoon making phone calls to find someone who would let me store my financial files and sentimental items at their house. Melinda, a mom whose daughter was on the lacrosse team with Jessica, offered the use of her house. I only knew her casually, but I knew she had been through a physically abusive marriage. Was I putting her in danger? Was I in danger? What about the kids? I could not believe I had to ask myself these questions, but anyone in my situation would have been foolish not to. I drove my files and other prized possessions, like the kids' baby albums, to her house.

As a result of all the scrambling, I did not get back until well after Daniel and Jessica arrived home from school. I did not tell them what had happened. I just reminded them that their father was expecting them at his place for dinner that night.

Paul's new condo was about fifteen minutes away. I pulled out of the driveway with Daniel and Jessica at 4:25 to take them there. I asked Daniel to text his father that we were running a few minutes late but that we were on our way. We arrived at 4:40, ten minutes after the time upon which we had agreed the previous day. I avoided any eye contact with Paul when he opened the door to greet them.

Once I returned to the house, I opened my computer and checked my email. A message from Paul was waiting:

In spite of you clearly being distracted today, I would greatly appreciate your respecting my time and how much I value my time with Jessica and Daniel. My relationship with my children has always been very important to me. We had both agreed to a mutually convenient time of 4:30 p.m. for you to bring the kids to see me. You were late, and this impacted my ability to share quality time with my children. Please make every effort to be sure this never happens again.

Kindest regards,
Paul

As if to expel a toxin, my abdominal muscles spasmed. I ran to the bathroom, dropped to my knees in front of the toilet, and vomited.

The mixture of manipulation, dishonesty, condescension, and control woven into less than 100 words was sickening. Paul had broken into the house, taken joint property without agreement, been verbally abusive in public, and threatened me, yet because none of this was actually illegal (legally, it was also his house, and he did not threaten *explicitly* to harm me), he wanted *his* email to be the official record of the day—that I was irresponsible, inconsiderate, and interfering with his ability to have quality time with Daniel and Jessica, that he was the aggrieved party. It also implied that he had a close and caring relationship with both kids—something that was not true.

This is who Paul really is, an inner voice taunted as I suffocated in despair. *You wasted twenty years on a man who battered you with criticism, lies, deceit, and distortion. This is the man you married! The father of your children! This is the person to whom you dedicated your life!*

I willed the negative thoughts out of my head, took a deep breath, and sat at my computer to document what had really happened that day while the events were still fresh in my mind. This was the first of hundreds of toxic emails and text messages from Paul. He used a few minutes of each day to create a misleading record of events. Each email or text (which left a permanent record that could be used in court) crafted an impression that was 180 degrees opposite of what had actually transpired, often making it look like I was guilty of "custodial interference," "parental alienation," hiding income or assets (e.g., "I can't find any record of where you deposited our tax refund," which is because we did not have a tax refund), or similar offenses.

It was a brilliant sociopathic strategy. Paul's daily onslaught forced me to spend time documenting the truth. This documentation forced me to relive each manipulative incident. This reliving kept me mired in negativity, draining my time, strength, and emotional resolve. Sharing the documentation with my lawyer caused my legal bills to soar. To Paul, this was war, and our children and our legally required communication about them was a Trojan horse that provided an entry point for an unending emotional and financial assault.

Clarity And Its Consequences

A few weeks later, when we needed to inventory all of our physical assets, at my lawyers' recommendation I invited Paul back to the house. Room by room, we agreed on the list of what we owned: furniture, outdoor grill, prints, appliances, jewelry, and so on.

"Paul," I said, "we need to add the items you already took or that you have at your office that belong to us, as well as at your condo and other places."

"I just took my clothes and some sports equipment, and we're not counting that stuff, right?" (Notice that he did not answer the question.) The fact that Paul had three bikes and I had one that was fifteen years old, and that he had four pairs of skis and I only one, should have mattered, but I did not want to be petty. I still did not understand the full implications of Paul being a sociopath. I wrongly assumed that, if I was reasonable and not petty about things (such as tolerating the big disparity in the value of the sports equipment each of us had), Paul would reciprocate and be reasonable. That was and is a bad assumption when dealing with a sociopath. There is no give and take, no *quid pro quo*. None! That's not how sociopath math works.

"Paul, my lawyer said we need to list *anything* valuable. Like we left some prints in your office back East when we moved. I listed them here."

"No we didn't," Paul said in a matter-of-fact tone. "We moved everything. I think the *movers* stole some pictures. That's why they're not here."

"Paul, they didn't. We left them at your office in Connecticut. We even drove them there together."

"No, I clearly recall several large paintings and prints that never made it off the moving truck," Paul said with no hint of tension or any other "tell." (Think about it: Of course the prints and paintings never made it off the truck, because they were never on the truck. Nice touch, Paul.)

"Paul, if you're so sure they were stolen, why are you only bringing it up a year after we moved? It's too late to file a claim. Besides, they're at your office."

"It was a hectic time, and I think I would know what's in my office." (Not an outright lie, but a clear mistruth.) I knew it was futile.

"Okay then, there's nothing else of value that you have? Remember, we have to include gifts to each other, jewelry, anything."

He shook his head. "I can't think of anything else."

CHAPTER 49

I probed Paul, giving him every opportunity to mention items I remembered, such as the Rolex watch that he bought for himself when he made partner years before as well as the concert tickets I was sure he had taken a few weeks earlier. I had just started to realize how profoundly dishonest Paul was, and I wanted this to be a test. Finally, when Paul had been given every opportunity to 'fess up, I asked him directly.

"What about your Rolex watch?"

"Oh yeah, I *may* have that. But it's probably worth only a few dollars, right?"

"I still have the receipt. I'll use that number. What about the concert tickets?"

"Aren't they still here?" Paul asked. (Note the deception but not an outright lie.)

"No, they aren't."

"You sure? You can be really disorganized, and you've been pretty stressed lately."

"Come on, Paul. You took them when you got the locksmith to let you in. I checked. They were gone *then*."

"Do I have them? I'll check." (Notice how Paul never admitted to *taking* them, just that he might have them. He's good.)

"I'm going to assume you have them and add them to the list."

"Why? You don't really want them, right?" he said. (Attempt at diversion.)

"That's not the point. I'm adding them to the list, Paul."

Lies, lies, nothing but lies. If I wanted a foolproof test of Paul's integrity and honesty, one had just unfolded right in front of me. He was a liar and a thief. It was no more complicated than that. That realization left me eerily cold. Even more disturbing than the lies themselves was how seamlessly, easily, and calmly Paul had spun them. Like other sociopaths, he did it without a hint of apology, culpability, guilt, or remorse, even when caught red-handed. He just glossed over the lie and the theft, as if each were no more remarkable than someone noting that the sun was shining on a sunny day. As I realized he must have been lying every day I had known him, I felt a rift tear through my sense of the universe's inherent harmony. I had been living in the presence of something—someone—very evil.

Later that day, an email arrived from Paul.

> *Please be advised that you are never to set foot in my company's building or talk to any of my employees. I will consider it trespassing and take necessary legal action.*

In other words, "Yes, the prints we bought together are indeed in my office in Connecticut, but you'll never prove it. Screw you, Onna."

CHAPTER 49

With each interaction with Paul, each toxic email, each review of my scary financial situation, each new piece of evidence confirming who and what Paul really was and how much my soul and strength had been sapped in his presence over nearly two decades, depression loomed and increasingly would not be denied. It was as if the earth opened up and swallowed me, dragging me down into a cold, damp inescapable void. I could not will myself out. This is what my marriage and the past twenty years of my life had really been. This is who Paul really was. This is what had been going on all along—manipulation, deceit, and exploitation. Processing it all was overwhelming, exhausting, excruciating.

Fool! Fool! Fool! depression taunted, draining my physical strength and emotional resolve. I could see why so many turn to alcohol, pain killers or other "substances" to numb the pain. My outer and inner life had exploded. My assumptions about the inherent goodness of people, and my faith in myself and, therefore, in my future, were mere dust. I turned to TV to self-medicate. I was drawn almost obsessively to shows about people who were not who others thought they were—people who were probably sociopaths. It was as if I needed to know everything possible about these masked vultures. Perhaps I also sought reassurance that I was not the only smart, capable, loving person whose life had been derailed by a master puppeteer.

Sometimes a new day brought temporary relief before the next communication from Paul reminded me of the blackness of his soul, the charade of my marriage, and the uncertainty of my future. I felt I was in a fight I could never win. He had probably hidden sources of money. I had not. He accepted no moral, ethical, or legal bounds on his actions. I had always honored all three, and I would stay true to that no matter how underhanded Paul chose to be. Fighting seemed futile, but capitulation was not an option.

Increasingly, a night of sleep did not erase the darkness of my mood. Soon, sleep itself proved elusive. Sometimes I slept only a few hours, at other times, not at all. Fighting exhaustion, I stumbled through the days, struggling to focus, to will myself into not being short-tempered with Jessica and Daniel, driving as little as possible for fear of my fatigue causing an accident, and doing only the minimum required for fear that anything I did would be marred by mistakes and misjudgments.

My lawyer, friends, and family all said things like, "Don't let him get to you!" "Why do you give him so much power over you?" "You have to grow a thicker skin." "Maybe ask your doctor for some medication." "Just think about it differently." I could not help but feel that the unstated premise was that *they* would not be bothered by any of it, and I should just snap out of it. Such attempts to help backfired, leaving me feeling like a weakling for

CHAPTER 49

being so shaken by Paul's carefully crafted, unremitting emotional assault.

But I wasn't a weakling. His communication was designed to drain my resolve, confidence, and feelings of self-worth, and it was being done by a person who knew my sensitivities better than anyone. With the emails ostensibly regarding the children, I had to read them, because the courts required that I do my best to co-parent, even with a man who viewed his children as mere pawns.

The cumulative effect of this unending barrage from Paul—most of it couched in respectful, polite language and carefully veiled threats to divert a potential third party, such as a judge, from the true intent of the communication—was poisonous. Some days, I fought just to breathe. Other days I simply surrendered to the searing emotional pain that was now my life.

With my computer serving as the conduit for most of Paul's venom, I developed an anxiety response to checking my email and eventually to even turning on my computer for any reason. As a result, sometimes I went days without checking email. I refused to configure my phone to receive emails. I did not want to fear my cell phone as well.

At first, when I read Paul's toxic emails, I wanted to scream. *How could someone I was married to for eighteen years do this? How could the father of my children say that? How could someone I loved and supported want to hurt me so much?* These are exactly the kinds of questions people ask when interviewed on television after someone they thought they knew did something unforgivable. Most newscasts and talk shows miss the mark on this crucially important teachable moment. The answer is often frighteningly simple. Paul was and is a sociopath—he lacks empathy and ethics, and he is an amazing actor, masterful at using language to deceive and manipulate. Just as lions are beautiful but deadly, sociopaths may appear to be pillars of the community when they are actually vengeful, manipulative, sabotaging, chronic liars who thrive on power and manipulation.

Oh My GOD!

On my lawyer's advice, I called all the locksmiths in the area, and they agreed to refuse Paul entry to the house without my consent. Fortunately, the threat of me moving out with the kids and incurring the rent of an additional apartment big enough for two kids, two dogs, and me had worked. Paul never moved back into the house.

At one of my early meetings with my divorce lawyer, she handed me a standard form and told me I needed to document all of our financial assets to prepare for the separation and the divorce. In addition, I would need to show how much my life with the children cost. I was not working, so this would be used to determine financial support from Paul during our separation as well as during the legally mandated divorce mediation. I did not have any electronic or paper copies of credit card statements for the past several years, but I recalled a year-end summary we had received for a prior year. I had never reviewed it, but I had filed it away.

Line by line, I poured through the annual summary from two years earlier, categorizing each item on a spreadsheet I had created with line items like, "food at home," "food at restaurants," "education expenses for the kids," "Jessica's lacrosse," "Daniel's karate," and so on. As I looked at each expenditure, a memory of the event flashed to mind. I looked at many of them so differently now that I knew my life at the time had been a sham. The expense for an evening with Paul at a dinner theater in New Haven now had a completely different hue. Should I put it under "food at restaurants" or "Onna gets set up?" Tough call.

When I got to the section labeled "entertainment," I was shocked by how large the total was for the year. How could we have spent that much money on entertainment—ever? My eyes widened as I looked at expense after expense for $1,000, $750, $2,200, totaling over $6,000 for a *two-day* period from a place I had never heard of. I did a web search for the name on the page. As the website materialized on my computer, my heart sank. It was a high-end "gentlemen's club" in Chicago. Repelled and shocked, I dug through the website. To end up with bills that large, Paul was paying for "private sessions." Feeling sick, I checked our bank statements. Significant cash withdrawals from ATMs in Chicago coincided with the same time period. I scanned down the page. There were other clusters of such ex-

CHAPTER 50

penses a month later, and then two months later. The bills were enormous. The dates were familiar. I flipped through my old calendars to find the date of the surgery that I had to keep rescheduling, and which Paul could not attend due to a "critical client situation." It overlapped perfectly with the obscene spending sprees on strippers. Nausea rose in me. I fought it back. Instead of attending to his wife while she was having surgery, he had been pawing and probably screwing a stripper, maybe multiple strippers. Fueled by adrenaline, I kept going.

Under the "travel" section of the credit card were hotel bills—bills for a hotel *one town away* from our home in Connecticut. They appeared religiously for five months almost exactly one month apart. What else could it be but evidence of an affair? I kept looking. A $600 expenditure in the "services" section of the credit card summary popped up. It was a name I did not recognize, accompanied by a telephone number. A few strokes of my keyboard later, a website for a Chicago escort service appeared on my screen. Incredulous, I rechecked the name on the credit card statement and rechecked the phone number. It was no mistake. Everything matched. Paul had hired a prostitute.

Her "stats" were featured prominently alongside her nearly naked, provocatively positioned body, with her legs splayed apart exposing her barely covered crotch. She was brunette, buxom, and 5'2". Paul liked his women petite—Jenny had been tiny, I am only 5'1", and this prostitute was small as well. I guess petite women helped Paul feel like a big, powerful man. How disgusting!

Hoping against hope that Paul had only used her for phone sex, I checked our bank statements. What were the odds? On the exact same day as the escort charge on our credit card, Paul had made a withdrawal at an ATM in Chicago. From deep inside, my body released a primal, guttural scream. My knees buckled. I dropped to the floor in a heap of disbelief and tears. I held down the vomit. I had only scanned a few months of the credit card, and there it was, a triumvirate of betrayal—prostitutes, sex clubs, and affairs. The bastard! And the amount of money Paul spent on his extracurricular activities in just the three-month period was staggering.

Every suspicion I had ever had resurfaced, framed with new meaning. I ran to my filing cabinet and found the old credit card receipts from before Paul had teased me for being so disorganized and then graciously offered to take care of our bills online. I knew what I would find. The sex expenses first appeared on the credit card the same month that Paul took over paying our credit card online. It was all lies and deceit, and he had the audacity to put it on our joint credit card.

Fool! Fool! Fool! depression screamed in my ear.

I raced to his home office, where a jumble of discarded receipts lay scat-

CHAPTER 50

tered on his desk. Pouring through them, I found evidence of a credit card I did not even know existed, including some receipts for high-ticket items. One was for a pair of $2,000 earrings from a Neiman Marcus in Florida, near where Paul had a client. They certainly had not been for me.

Any remaining fragment of the foundation of my life crumbled beneath me, but adrenaline continued to fuel me. I went to every closet and emptied every pocket of every article of clothing that Paul had left behind. I ripped apart drawers in which he still had lots of clothes. In a winter coat was his new lease. He had lied about the security deposit. He *was* spending about $5,000 a month on some luxury place, all the while saying he wasn't making any money and that it was "all he could find."

I picked up the phone. Paul had not yet discontinued the two credit cards for which I had just found out I was only an "authorized user." I knew they would not honor a request to send me the past year's statements. However, I pieced together enough information to use the automatic system that would list past transactions. It went back six months. I put the phone on speaker and took notes.

Two months earlier, there had been thousands of dollars of expenditures in California—hotels, restaurants, and over $3,000 in women's shoe stores. I poured through our bank statements, looking at every line and finding sizeable cash withdrawals made through our credit card that appeared in a place on our statement where, ordinarily, I would not look. The magnitude of the deceit was staggering. A day later, Paul cancelled these two credit cards, ostensibly to simplify our joint finances to set the stage for our divorce. Was this a coincidence? How had he known? Had an automated service called him back to confirm all of his questions had been answered satisfactorily?

Who was Paul? How long had he been doing this? I thought back to every woman with whom things seemed off when they were around Paul or when Paul spoke of them. The consequences were mind numbing. Surrounded by credit card statements, bank records, receipts, and piles of paper, I cried until I was numb and exhausted, my sides aching from the violence.

Sociopaths do not rein in their sexual appetites. It is that simple. And since they hide who they really are, they put at risk anyone who becomes their sexual partner, especially a faithful wife of almost two decades. It's all about them and gaining power and pleasure. In their mind, the rest of us are just here to help serve that end. Who cares if they infect us with a disease in the process? Not them. No ethics. No empathy.

An hour later, my tears spent, I called my doctor. As I dialed her number, I steeled myself to face the humiliating words I was about to utter. "Hello, I just found out my husband has been cheating on me. I need to be tested for sexually transmitted diseases."

The Earthquake Strikes

The devastation of the sham that was my life—of the betrayal, of my naivety, my weakness, my precarious financial predicament, of some of the qualities that I like most about myself being turned against me (my empathy, love of the country, mountains, and a simpler life) was overpowering. I did not want to kill myself, but I wanted to die to escape the searing pain of the treachery and of the wasted investment of the past twenty years. I see now why so many women do not fight for what is legally and financially theirs in a divorce. Even more than the hope of financial solvency, they need the emotional pain to stop. They need to avoid drowning. Only the need to be there for my children kept me going.

Legal wheels turn slowly. Lawyers have many clients, and courts are overbooked. Before my lawyer could file the paperwork to freeze our assets, "cash-strapped" Paul bought a $1.1 million house. He used some of our assets as part of the down payment, and he used our brokerage account as collateral for a loan to cover the remainder. It was profoundly unethical but not illegal. In making the financial arrangements, he scrambled our finances and misrepresented the loan to the point that I was unwittingly paying for part of his mortgage until months later when our divorce became final and our accounts were divided. Our financial advisor, a close friend of Paul's, had to know exactly what was happening, but he never told me. When I started digging into the details of the transaction, the advisor was evasive and confusing. He knew who would have money and who would not when the dust settled.

On Jessica and Daniel's first weekend visit to their father's new palatial home, Paul encouraged Daniel to bring Ella along "for the weekend." Ella had always been Paul's favorite of the two dogs.

On Sunday evening, when Paul dropped Jessica and Daniel back at my house, I got to the front door just in time to catch the end of a conversation between Daniel and Paul. Paul's car was idling in the driveway, and Paul was leaning out the window as he spoke with Daniel. Jessica looked emotionless as she approached the front door, leaving Daniel alone with his father. Something was wrong, but what? Then it hit me. Where was Ella?

Jessica pushed passed me, barely nodding hello, perhaps thinking that if she kept herself from witnessing what was transpiring it would not be real.

CHAPTER 51

Maybe it was her seventeen-year-old way of controlling cognitive dissonance and allowing her to maintain the belief that her father was a great guy.

"Don't you care about *me*?" Paul said to Daniel. *"I'll* be all alone in that big house. *I* need Ella's company. Don't you care that I need companionship?"

"Dad, I want my dog back!" Daniel sobbed. "I want Ella!"

Without another word, Paul's car pulled away, leaving Daniel alone in the driveway.

I ran to him.

"He's keeping Ella! He's keeping Ella! He won't let her come back." Daniel gasped for air between words. His chest heaved, and tears cascaded down his cheeks. I drew Daniel to me in a deep hug. In seconds, my shirt was soaked with tears.

I called Paul. There was no answer. I left a message and then texted him, saying that Daniel was beyond distraught and that Ella needed to come back to be with him. Daniel needed both dogs to stay with him, because they were his best friends and his emotional anchors. With our family in chaos, the dogs were even more important to Daniel than ever before. I emailed Paul. Hours later, there was still no reply.

That night at 2:00 a.m., I heard Daniel rummaging around the kitchen, and I went down to investigate. His eyes were red and puffy. He looked exhausted.

"Have you slept at all?" I asked.

Daniel shook his head.

We both had a mug of hot milk and put on a mindless television program to distract us from the day. An hour later, I went to my bedroom to try to sleep. Daniel stayed on the couch. By the look of his face the next morning, a Monday morning, a school day, he had not slept at all.

I got my lawyer involved in trying to get Ella returned to Daniel. She proposed to Paul's lawyer that Ella move back and forth from Paul's house to my house with Daniel. Paul's lawyer even tried to convince Paul to return Ella to Daniel, but Paul would not budge. I did not know what else to do. Daniel was devastated.

Two weeks later, as Paul dropped Daniel and Jessica off at school after a mid-week overnight, Paul told them he had a girlfriend and that she was moving in. The moving van arrived from Chicago the next day, as did Linda Peters (the name from the UPS package), and her cat, Freedom. The cat's name struck me as ironic, because anyone involved with Paul was doomed to anything but freedom. Paul told the kids he had started dating Linda *after* he left me. Did he really think they were that naïve? It was less than six months since Paul had left, and this woman had sold her house in Chicago and moved halfway across the country to be with him. I never told

CHAPTER 51

Jessica and Daniel about the UPS package with Linda's name on it that had been delivered before Paul and I separated. What was the point?

Daniel did not like the idea of his father having a live-in girlfriend so suddenly, but he naively hoped that, now that Dad had some companionship, Ella could come back and live with us at our house, or at least travel back and forth with him. While sitting in the family room one day, he called his dad to make that request. From the adjoining kitchen, I heard Daniel's side of the conversation.

"Dad," Daniel started, "now that your girlfriend's here, can Ella come back here and live with me? I really miss her ... Please, you're out of town a lot. I'll bring her with me when I visit ... Please ... Dad, pleeeease ... Ella was the *family* dog, not *your* dog ... Of course she's the family dog. We got her to keep Mr. Wrinkles company. He's been so sad since she left ... That's not what happened ... No, I'm not calling you a liar ... I didn't say that ... That doesn't mean I called you a liar ... Of course Mom took good care of Ella ... That's not true! ... Mom takes great care of her. She walks her, feeds her, brushes her, takes her to the vet when she eats stupid stuff. Please give Ella back ... I can't do this anymore."

Tears slipped from Daniel's eyes.

Even from hearing just one side of the conversation, I could tell that Paul was using manipulation and deceitful techniques against Daniel, unleashing a tapestry of lies, including that Ella was Paul's dog, not the family dog, and that we had mistreated her. He also got Daniel on the defensive by accusing Daniel of calling him a liar, which Daniel never did. I knew Daniel did not stand a chance against Paul. I held up a sign that read, "HANG UP! This is not going to end well!"

Daniel shook his head and continued amidst his tears. "Dad, I can't do this anymore. I can't do this anymore. I want Ella back!"

I held up the sign again and put the most pleading expression my face to communicate, "STOP! GET OFF THE PHONE!" It did not work. I knew if I actually spoke to Daniel and Paul heard me, it would only inflame the situation, because Paul would accuse me of meddling or coaching Daniel. Their "conversation" continued.

"No way! No one here spurns Ella. Ella was *always* happy here. I want my dog back! ... She's the family dog. The *family* dog!"

Finally, something inside Daniel snapped. Tears poured down his cheeks as he screamed into the phone. "You stole *my* dog! You piece of shit!"

Daniel threw his cell phone onto the couch and ran out of the house and up the driveway. I let him go. My heart sank.

Minutes later, my phone chirped, indicating an incoming text. It was a message from Paul to check my email. I did. Paul's email read:

Husband Liar Sociopath 171

CHAPTER 51

Because of Daniels disrespectful behavior, I won't allow him to do karate anymore. No more lessons or tournaments. Nothing! He needs to spend more time studying. His grades this semester are unacceptable. Please tell him. While he's been living with you, he has become disrespectful, withdrawn, and argumentative. You have done a horrible job as his mother and obviously don't care about him. What else should I have expected from you? Jessica wants to live with me and Linda. She says you are bitter and nasty and that you have shunned her and kicked her out of the house several times.

Daniel acts as if I've done something that I should apologize about. I haven't done anything wrong or hurtful to anyone. If I didn't spend much time with him before, it's because you drove me away, making me feel unwelcome with my own children. You are obviously planting hostile ideas in him and turning him against me. You are a hateful, vindictive, horrible person and mother. If you persist in this illegal and amoral behavior, I'll take you to court for parental alienation. You'll lose! I no longer agree that you can have primary physical custody of him. He needs to live with me at least half of the time, hopefully more. You cannot provide a stable environment. I am the one who has a stable home with both a mother and father. You need to sell the house. You need to move. You may not even be able to afford to stay in town. This is likely to be very disruptive to Daniel, who is clearly already emotionally fragile due to you.

Paul
P.S. FUCK YOU!

I knew I should not let it get to me, but those words on the screen in front of me from Daniel's father, from someone I had loved and supported were crushing. As if pinned by a rockslide, I fought to breathe. The accusation that I had shunned my own daughter and thrown her out of the house ripped out my insides. I had done no such thing, but would Paul try to make that case against me? I had heard of horrible things like this happening in contentious divorces. Would Jessica betray me and lie that I had kicked her out? I knew Jessica was falling under Paul's spell. At her age, there might be little I could do, but I had to protect Daniel.

How perfectly, sociopathically ironic—Paul had manipulated me into moving to Utah while he was having an affair. Then he had run off with his girlfriend, introduced her prematurely into the lives of our children, stopped paying himself, drained our savings to pay everyday bills and to fund his even more expensive lifestyle, and scrambled our finances to buy

CHAPTER 51

a massive house, leaving me with a house that was too big and expensive and that I would have to sell. Now he had kidnapped Daniel's dog and was trying to keep Daniel from the only activity he enjoyed, and he was bribing and manipulating Jessica with expensive gifts—jewelry and a credit card with no restrictions. And now Paul was accusing *me* of manipulating our children and creating chaos in their lives?

I tried to fight the wave of despair cresting above me. I could not. Gravity won—it always does. Anguish and hopelessness pounded down, expelling the air from my lungs and the tone from my body. Yet, driven by the instincts of a mother bear protecting her cub, I pushed through the emotional train wreck and crafted a response to Paul's email.

> *As before, the inaccuracies and untruths in your email are too numerous to list, so I will not attempt to do so. Suffice it to say, I agree with nothing you wrote. I also disagree 100% with your taking away your support from Daniel's karate. It is all he has and lives for. Especially at a tumultuous time in his life, he needs anchors and stability and sources of self-esteem and pride. He needs Ella back and he needs karate. As for school, I believe his 3.5 GPA while taking honors and Advanced Placement classes is amazing, given his inability to sleep and focus due to our family's upheaval and actions you have taken. I do not agree with your message to Daniel. I will not deliver it.*

Before I could hit "send," I received another email from Paul. He had copied me on an email to the karate studio where Daniel trained. In Connecticut, Daniel had been working hard, with the goal of becoming one of the best in the state. Now, in less populated Utah, he was already among the top five in his age bracket and was a clear contender for state karate teams that would be sent to compete nationally. Karate was a source of great accomplishment and pride for Daniel, his main source of exercise, and a venue for interacting with his peers, something Daniel found difficult. In my view, it was critical for Daniel to continue in karate. Paul's email read:

> *I am sending this letter to officially withdraw my son, Daniel, from your program. Please no longer use my credit card for monthly payments. Also, Daniel will not be traveling to any tournaments, so please give his spot away to a more deserving student. If Daniel's mother makes any attempt to re-enroll him, please contact me immediately, as she does not have the legal authority to do so.*
>
> *Kindest regards*

CHAPTER 51

I sent my email to Paul and then called my lawyer for clarification. I had the legal authority to enroll Daniel in any program as long as it was not harmful to him. Like so many sociopaths, when the truth was not convenient, Paul offered an alternative reality, and he did so with such calm confidence and conviction that he was rarely questioned. His version of events typically sounded plausible but often was neither accurate nor true. I called the confused karate studio and ask them to put everything on hold and not give away Daniel's hard-earned spot on their competitive team until I could figure out the finances. They agreed to work with me so that Daniel would not have to withdraw.

When Daniel returned to the house an hour later, he went into his room and slammed the door so hard that a picture fell off the wall and crashed to the floor. Glass shattered; I cleaned it up. An hour later, he emerged, tears welling in his eyes and his cell phone in hand.

"Daniel, what's wrong?" I asked.

"Dad sent a text that I owe him an apology and that he withdrew me from karate. Mom, what am I going to do? I love karate. The only reason I didn't hang up when you held up the sign is that Dad said if I hung up he would take karate away from me. And he did anyway." Daniel's voice choked, and tears overflowed his eyes. "I just couldn't take it any longer. Mom, I hate him."

Hours later, when Daniel calmed down, I urged him to send a text to apologize for calling his father a "shit," but I did not see anything else he had done that was disrespectful. In fact, I had been amazed at his poise and maturity in such a difficult situation.

Daniel did as I suggested. Here is what his father texted back.

Apology accepted. I will still not allow you to participate in karate. Since you will not be doing karate anymore, I want a list of new activities to keep you busy and in shape, and I expect your grades to improve. I love you very much and only want what is best for you.

Your loving father

Daniel was crushed by his father's choices—his betrayal of our family, his instant girlfriend, the disrespectful way Daniel had learned that Linda even existed and was moving in, the kidnapping of Ella, the mounting lies, and his father's attempt to keep him from participating in karate. Although I needed every bit of money I had, I promised Daniel that he could attend karate and that I would support his karate as long as he kept working hard in school. It was clear to me that Paul was not only trying to hurt Daniel for not buying into the "Paul as saint" view of the world but also to avoid the expense of paying for Daniel's karate training and pricy tournament travel—something we had supported for years. Paul was also hurting Daniel to weaken and distract me, because there is no better way to hurt a mother than by harming her child.

Jessica was unfazed by her father's behavior and choices. Over the summer, Paul had given her a credit card with no spending limit. Without my knowledge, he had even rented a condo for her and her friends to use as she wished—no questions asked. When I found out, I put my foot down, forbidding her to use it. I had to get my lawyer involved. The horror stories of what teenagers across the country had gotten into when left without supervision were all too common. For establishing normal parental limits, Jessica painted me as a controlling witch. Dad was the good guy. Even though Paul asserted in court documents that his income was approaching zero for the year, he always had plenty of money to spend on himself, his new house, his girlfriend, and Jessica. And, unlike me, Paul "trusted" Jessica and let her do whatever she wanted, including buying over $2,000 in jewelry in just two months. She still wanted more, surfing the Internet for hours to plan her next purchase. The manipulation horrified me.

Even worse, as the jewelry purchases mounted, I worried that Jessica was developing a dangerous shopping addiction, linking buying expensive jewelry with affection from her father. I expressed my concern to Paul, but he would not stop the purchases. I involved my lawyer. When she got the purchases to stop, Jessica had already spent $3,000 in four months. I could not compete. I would not compete. Paul offered confidence, a huge house, money, status, and no behavioral limits. I was shattered by recent events, my eyes red from lack of sleep. I needed to sell the house, move, and downsize radically, and who knew if I would even have any income? I had applied for several jobs, but no offers were forthcoming. My spent appearance, red eyes, lack of recent work experience, and age were not strong selling points.

I stood by what I thought were reasonable limits for a teenager, knowing it might jeopardize my relationship with Jessica if Paul did not do the same. The fact that Jessica and Paul had never been close left her hungry for a relationship with her father and vulnerable to his love being used as bait. He offered her a relationship now. All she had to do to get unbridled independence, status, money, and her father's long-desired love was to embrace being *his* daughter and reject me. Pretty easy decision.

Jessica was spending a lot of time at Paul's but had not officially moved in with him and Linda. One day, prior to Paul and I going to court for the first time to work out our pre-divorce separation agreement, I noticed a light on in our basement. Paul's home office was on that level, but with him

CHAPTER 51

gone, Jessica, Daniel, and I rarely, if ever, went down to that part of the house. It struck me as odd. Tension rose within me.

As I reached the bottom of the stairs to turn off the light, I noticed that the door to Paul's office was ajar and a closet light was on. My body tensed even more. I took a deep breath to clear my thoughts and to manage my mounting anxiety. I had not left Paul's office like that. Seeing as it was unused, all the lights were kept off and the doors closed. Paul had always been above everyday menial tasks like shutting off lights or closing doors. My blood pressure surged. Paul had been there. How had he gotten in?

I asked Daniel if he knew anything about his father being at the house. He didn't. I believed him. Then I asked Jessica if she had let her father in. She denied it, but when I confronted her with evidence that I knew Paul had been inside, her story changed.

"So what if I let Dad in?" she said defiantly. Parroting what Paul must have told her, she continued, "It's his house, too, and you have no legal right to keep him out. He just needed to get some of his stuff."

"Jessica," I replied, horrified, "I was clear with you that your father can never be in this house."

"It's no big deal, Mom!"

"It *is* a big deal!" I said, trying to control the mixture of fear and anger welling up inside me. "We both need our privacy during the divorce. I don't have access to where he's living now. He's not supposed to have access to where I'm living. I have to prepare documents for my lawyers. So does he. We both need privacy to do it."

The issues were much bigger than those I expressed to Jessica, but I tried to couch her father's ban from the house in as neutral terms as possible.

"I can't believe you think Dad would *ever* do anything wrong," Jessica said. "He never would. You're just paranoid. He says what you're doing is illegal and that he's being so nice and reasonable to respect *your* stupid, controlling wishes."

"Your father broke into this house before and took things!" I said, against all the advice I had been given to not say anything bad about Paul to Jessica and Daniel. I did it to buy some credibility with Jessica. It was a mistake.

"He'd never do that! You're making it up!" Jessica cried.

"Jessica, have I *ever* lied to you?"

Jessica glared at me without answering.

"You can *never* let you father in this house. NEVER! You have to trust me. I have good reasons."

Jessica shot me a look of pure hatred and contempt and then stomped off to her room, slammed the door, and did not come out for hours. Paul's

CHAPTER 51

credit cards and promises of total independence went a long way.

A week later, I felt eerie when I got back to the house. I had been volunteering at a lacrosse tournament for hours, someplace Paul knew I would be. I found a receipt of Paul's from a purchase months ago near my desk that I was ninety-nine percent sure had not been there hours earlier. But was I 100 percent sure? Sometimes when I was locking up for the night, I discovered a window unlatched that I could not remember unlatching during the day. Had Jessica left it unsecured so Paul could gain access? I would never know.

One day when I walked into the house after being away for hours, I noticed a curtain askew that I typically left pulled over a glass door to keep sunlight from overheating the house. It was positioned as if someone had exited via the door and, therefore, was unable to pull the curtain back into place. I walked around the house, but nothing jumped out at me as looking wrong or missing.

Later that evening, I went to use the toilet in my bathroom before going to bed. I lifted the seat cover. The toilet was filled with excrement. Blood drained from my face. My pulse quickened. Could Paul have gotten in and done that? Could the toilet have backed up? Could Jessica and Daniel have used my bathroom and forgotten to flush it? When I asked, they said they hadn't used my bathroom. What were the odds that any of us had used my bathroom and not flushed it? Almost zero.

Thoughts flooded my mind. How was Paul getting into the house? Was I safe? Were the kids safe? I waited until Daniel and Jessica were asleep, and then I barricaded all the doors after checking the locks on all the doors and windows. I slept with my cell phone and home phone in my bed. I set the alarm clock unusually early so I could remove my safety precautions before Daniel and Jessica awoke, so as not to alarm them. Sleep eluded me. My mind overflowed with fear, and adrenalin coursed through my body.

The next morning, I called a home alarm company. I did not want to spend the money alarming a house I knew I had to sell soon, but I had no choice.

The Tsunami Pounds Ashore

My lawyer forwarded Paul's official court documents to me, documents we needed to legalize our temporary financial agreement pending our divorce. I waited until I felt strong enough to read them, but I would never be prepared for what I was about to see. In those documents, submitted to the court for a judge to read, Paul accused me of being a horrible mother, of purposely being underemployed and leaching off him, and of never contributing meaningfully to the marriage in any way—emotionally, physically, or financially. He also detailed that I had thrown Jessica out of the house on several occasions and that Jessica hated me now and did not want to live with me. According to these documents, I had decided to be underemployed for years as a ploy to lead a life of leisure at the expense of my hard-working husband. Hence, despite the fact I had not worked full time in years, child support should be based on assigning me a $100,000 salary that I could easily command if I simply got off my butt, so to speak. Apparently, the fact that my skills were now out of date in an era of profound technological change was irrelevant.

In the documents were quotes from discussions Paul claimed to have had with me about how much money I could earn. My jaw dropped, and my heart sank. He was quoting conversations I had had with people as I discussed how I might resurrect my freelance career and how much money I should charge if I was able to get assignments. But they were not conversations I had ever had with Paul. The references were so detailed, sometimes referencing my tone of voice or a particular turn of phrase, that it could not be a coincidence. My heart raced as my brain came to the only possible conclusion—either my house was wired or my phone was tapped or both.

Strength drained from my body. Feeling as if I were living in some surreal dream, I walked out of the house and called my lawyer on my cell phone. I thought of the two credit cards that Paul had cancelled within hours of my phone inquiry. Was my cell phone tapped, too? Was any place safe? My house? My car? Me?

I hired a private investigator to sweep my house, computer, and phones for listening devices. Something on my laptop seemed suspicious but inconclusive. The investigator purged anything irregular from my computer and cell phone, but he told me to buy new cell phones for the kids and me.

CHAPTER 52

(Buying a new cell phone for Jessica was irrelevant, given her alliance with Paul.) He went through the house room-by-room and then called me over to show me what he had found. In the utility room, located off Paul's home office, the investigator pointed out where a phone line had been spliced into the existing line. Compared to the existing line, it was clearly new and virtually dust and dirt free. Paul had tapped my home phone. No wonder he had convinced Jessica to let him sneak back into the house. He needed to remove the recording device before I read the court documents and suspected it even existed. Thanks to Jessica, he had succeeded.

"This is where it was," the investigator said. "Once this line was added, all he had to do was snap on a recording device. It's actually pretty simple to do. But it's obviously gone now. Unfortunately, without the recording device, we cannot prove he tapped your phone. It's a federal offense, you know. They take this kind of thing pretty seriously. People go to prison over this."

I remembered Jessica telling me that Paul went to his home office when she let him in the house. His story was that he wanted to take a picture that was on the wall there but then decided against it and left empty-handed. Paul's threat, "I'll do whatever I want!" rang in my head. He respected no boundaries, legal or otherwise. Who was this man?

My lawyer and a psychologist I consulted pressed upon me the importance of not telling the children anything bad about their father, because it was likely to backfire. So, I did not tell Jessica about the wiretap. That did not stop her from expressing her contempt to me about "not letting things go," "being paranoid," and "being controlling." She stood up for her father at every turn because, "Dad would never do anything wrong."

The hypocrisy and irony were more than I could take. I needed to understand how much she was under Paul's spell and likely to betray me again. Paul had not been a very attentive father to Jessica and was often harsh and demanding with her. Had she forgotten that so quickly?

"Jessica," I said after dinner that night, "do you remember your father ever doing anything hurtful to you, Daniel, or me?"

"No," she replied quickly. "I don't."

"Jessica," I said, concerned that I was treading on thin ice but unable to stop myself, "you don't recall when you got a B on a Spanish test and your dad got so mad at you for not studying hard enough that he unraveled a scarf you were knitting? It took you a week to redo it. I had to stop him from undoing the whole thing."

"I have no idea what you're talking about, Mom," Jessica said with a straight face. "Dad would *never* do anything like that!"

I continued, "It happened only a year before we moved out here. You were sobbing. I came running upstairs when I heard you screaming for

Husband Liar Sociopath 179

Dad to stop."

"I hate it when you say bad things about Dad," Jessica said. Then she turned and went to her room.

Feeling that Jessica was lost to me, another searing wave of despair crashed down upon me, dragging me under, leaving me gasping for air. The world I knew had ceased to exist. Nothing made sense. Paul and his big house, his credit card, and the unbridled independence he bestowed upon Jessica were too powerful for me to fight. He was a sociopathic, lying, scheming, disgusting, and vile human being who was turning my own daughter against me. To get his love and all the financial goodies he offered, she was throwing me under the bus at one of the direst times in my life. The pain of losing her was excruciating.

More sleepless nights and more days during which I could hardly function followed. But that was the point. The more Paul could weaken me and make me want it to end, the better he would make out financially after the divorce. The more he could prevail, the more my life was in shambles, the more he could wound me, the higher his black sociopath's heart would soar.

It did not matter that I had dedicated years of my life to help him pursue his career and build his current business. It did not matter that I had orchestrated relocating our household on average every four years to help bring his goals to fruition. It did not matter that I was the mother of his children and had invested so much of my time and life so that they would have options for the future. It did not matter that I had genuinely loved Paul once and tried my best to make him happy for so long, as I had promised years ago, "for better or for worse." It did not matter that I was a good, honest person who valued her morality and ethics.

All that mattered was that Paul wanted me as emotionally and financially depleted as possible, as soon as possible. If I lacked emotional strength and financial resources, I would be less likely to engage in an expensive, multi-year battle involving hiring a forensic accountant to investigate years of inappropriate spending and to investigate his company to determine its value. By depleting me emotionally, he would also gain the moral high ground by saying to his friends and family, "Look how depressed and unstable Onna is. Can you believe what a saint I am to have endured her for so long? Even Jessica doesn't want to live with her mother. Onna is such a damaged, bitter person."

In spite of the adultery and Paul's clear manipulation in getting me to move to Utah, which was clear to anyone who had two eyes and a brain, Paul's family rallied around him. I'm sure the money he lavished on them did not hurt, and he likely reframed everything, finally revealing the "truth" about me. He had endured me long enough. Surely, they wanted him to *fi-*

nally be happy.

I had always enjoyed the time I spent with Paul's mother, and she consistently presented herself as deeply religious and moral, so when Paul took Ella, I reached out to Ruth for help. I was not prepared for her response. She said she was sure Paul was doing what was best for the kids, that he would never do anything wrong or hurtful, and that I was just being melodramatic and would be laughing about this in no time. Knowing Daniel was distressed about Ella, Ruth sent Daniel a letter quoting advice from a famous sports coach that said he should never allow himself to be upset about anything for more than twenty-four hours. Ruth added that Daniel needed to show more respect for his father and his father's decisions. She was sure Daniel was only angry with Paul because I was encouraging Daniel to feel that way. Worse, she told Daniel that, obviously, I did not value family the way Paul and Linda did.

Ruth's behavior is another example of "cognitive dissonance" at work. How does a woman who takes great pride in her strong religious beliefs, goes to church every Sunday, and admonishes others for any lack of ethics or morality not even blink an eye at the amoral and hurtful behavior of her own son? How did she rationalize the inconsistency between her religious beliefs and Paul's adultery and other hurtful behavior? Paul really deserves to be happy? Onna probably drove Paul away—what else was he supposed to do?

Daniel was hurt and incredulous. He wrote unrepeatable words on his grandmother's letter. Paul sent me an email with a not so veiled threat that he would take me to court for slandering him to his family. Ruth and I never spoke again. Given Ruth's choice to blind herself to her son's behavior and to be insensitive and hurtful towards Daniel, I had no interest in continuing a relationship with her even without Paul's threat.

I was furious at Jessica for her betrayal and for abandoning our relationship at a time when I desperately needed to maintain the close relationships in my life. Some nights my anger at her kept me awake. In a pique of frustration at 3:00 a.m. one sleepless night, I pounded my pillows, sobbing, and then threw each of them against the wall. It did not help. It just made me feel stupid, because I knew my fury was misplaced. I tried to view Jessica as the victim of a brilliant and well-funded sociopath. I had been fooled and manipulated by Paul for almost twenty years. It would be unfair to hold my teenage daughter to a higher standard.

Even though I knew Jessica was slipping away, I refused to compromise my morality or my parental obligations to win her favor. So I lost her. She was seventeen. The courts would allow her to pick with whom she wanted to live. My lawyer explained, to my shock and dismay, that the mockery Paul had made of our marriage vows, the alleged financial dishonesty and manipulation (which would take considerable time and money to prove), the verbal abuse toward me, and his loose sexual ethics did not matter to the court in determining whether or not Jessica could live with her father. She moved in with Paul and Linda.

The day she packed her belongings to make the transition official, I felt dead inside. I could hardly breathe. Tears flowed, ignoring any attempt to slow or halt them. I had lost my daughter.

With Jessica no longer living at my house and indicating little, if any, interest in returning for an overnight, I changed the locks yet again and voided Jessica's code for the alarm system. Given her lies about allowing Paul into the house, and fearful that Paul might escalate his emotional and financial attack on me to physical abuse, I could not allow Jessica unsupervised access to my house. It was horrible to not be able to trust my own daughter, but I couldn't.

The Puzzle Pieces Finally Fit

Knowing my fear of financial ruin—I was now over fifty years old and had not worked full-time in almost two decades—Paul pushed every financial button he could. He sent me frequent emails about the dire financial situation his firm was in and made sure I was aware of our ever declining bank balance. Even if my lawyer and I were sure he was withholding paying himself and even asking his clients to not pay the firm until after his divorce was finalized, proving this would be a time-consuming and expensive gamble. If he was good enough at hiding the money, there was no guarantee that even an excellent forensic accountant would find it. Even if an accountant did find it, it might take years and hundreds of thousands of dollars to do it. In Utah, legal fees are rarely recoverable, even when you prevail. It was a huge gamble when my own personal cash flow was zero.

To maintain my fear about our finances, and to build the case that his company was doing so poorly that he could not pay himself, Paul even missed estimated tax payments on his income and sent me the documentation about the fines incurred. He hounded me about any expenditure I made, because we still shared a checking account and one credit card. He got so mad about the fact that I started working with a therapist (an expert on abusive domestic relationships) that when I wrote a check to her for $100, he drained our bank account and cancelled our remaining joint credit card. I found out when my credit card was declined for a pizza.

When I refused another "generous settlement" from Paul, he sent me back-to-back emails. The first email was blank but contained an attachment. The second read, *Ignore the attachment in the first email. I sent it by accident.* Of course, I took the bait. The attachment was a recent photo of Rebecca, Anne-Marie's oldest daughter. She was smiling, proudly holding up a squash trophy. I had last seen Rebecca about a year ago during our shared family vacation shortly after moving to Utah.

Why did Paul want me to see this picture? Did he want me to be jealous about Rebecca's success at squash? As I wondered about his motive, I keep staring at the picture—Rebecca's smile, her eyes ... I gasped. The eyes looking back at me from the picture were eyes I had seen before—eyes I saw every day. I printed the picture and hastened to the shelves that held our photo albums. I searched for pictures of Jessica and Daniel when they were Rebecca's age. I found them and held them next to the picture. How could I have been so blind? How could I have been so stupid? The eyes were exactly the same, and the shape of the face, nose, and mouth were all remarkably similar. Oh my God!

All the pieces snapped together: the connection between Anne-Marie and Paul, the family vacations, the intrusion of Anne-Marie and Rebecca into our family time. Even strangers on our shared vacations had noted that Rebecca looked nothing like her "father," while her younger sister was clearly a patchwork of both Anne-Marie and her husband. The answer had been there all along. Rebecca was Paul's daughter! Bile rose in my throat. I choked it back. Another searing wave of despair pummeled me into submission, engulfing me in blackness and pain. Daniel, Jessica, and I had been nothing but a smokescreen of normalcy for Paul's true life of sex, lies, and deceit.

How could I have been married to this monster? And for so long? Who was he? He was disgusting, and I had shared a bed and a life with him for almost twenty years. Not only had he betrayed me for so long, he had put me in the humiliating position of spending countless vacations with his lover and their daughter. How disgusting. How vile. In case I was too blind and stupid to figure it out on my own, Paul wanted to be sure I knew that Rebecca was his child. Only then would he be sure to inflict maximum pain and humiliation.

I would not give him the satisfaction of being sure that I knew and resolved to never reply to or acknowledge the email. I raced to the shower, but the feeling of being debased and having my life defiled would not wash away.

With my mind solving puzzles that I should have pieced together years earlier, I fixated on two final pieces that had never made sense. If Paul had set me up to move to Utah not only to isolate me but also to get me to put in all the work so he could get divorced out where he wanted to be, why had we bought the house? Wouldn't it have been to his financial advantage to rent if he planned on disposing of me once we got here? The other thing that confused me was the degree of Paul's hatred for me since the separation. Now that Linda was out of hiding, it was clear that Paul was the one who had cheated and manipulated, not me, so why was he so angry with me? Why was he spending so much time trying to hurt me? Why not just move on with his new life?

Unbeknownst to me at the time, part of the answer is that sociopaths have a long history of going after ex-spouses, ex-girlfriends, and ex-boyfriends. They are vengeful, sadistic beings, even when they are the ones doing the betraying and hurting, and they thrive on inflicting maximum damage and pain on their victims. It is as if once their victim is no longer of use to them, the sociopath feels that person has no right to live. The now "useless" possession must be destroyed.

CHAPTER 53

Insight is an interesting thing. Why it comes at some times but not others is unclear. Maybe I had to be ready for the answer. Maybe I had to shed assumptions that were blocking a better understanding, but one day, the answer just happened. The house only made sense if Paul had been leading a double or triple life all along. He had wanted to continue the charade of our marriage, but in Utah. Perhaps his motive was to distance me from another ongoing relationship that would be too risky if we continued to live in Connecticut. Why not get me to relocate to a place where he'd rather be—where he could enjoy his favorite sport, skiing, and where he wanted to be when he retired? He could continue seeing Linda in Chicago and Anne-Marie in Connecticut, and I would keep up the legitimacy he craved by continuing to play his dutiful wife. Maybe his initial plan was to continue with his double or triple life in Utah, where I would be isolated once again and easier to control.

But I wrecked everything by disengaging and refusing to play Whack-A-Mole any more. That's why he was angry with me. I had ruined his perfect triple life, making it more complicated and potentially much more expensive. Even without ever being able to label what I had been experiencing as emotionally or psychologically abusive (and it was), I had stopped allowing Paul to abuse me by refusing to play Whack-A-Mole. When I refused to be cast as a puppet, Paul could no longer play abusive puppeteer. It wasn't fun anymore, because he was no longer able to feel the power and gain the satisfaction of putting me down and gaslighting me, and he had already extracted everything else from me that he could possibly want. Lacking the enjoyment of lording over me and hurting me, there was no reason to keep me around. It had to end.

I can only imagine what he told Linda—what a bitch I was (the usual story sociopaths give about their exes), how unloving and unsupportive I had been, and that he would have left me years ago if he was not such a great guy who was concerned about his children and the vows he had made. Paul would marry Linda *if* he could, but his conscience would not allow him to divorce me. He may even have told Linda that the move to Utah was my idea and that he had tried so hard to accommodate me, hoping against all odds that moving there would make me happy. Alas, I was still a shrew, and he could not go on like this any longer. He deserved happiness.

Just like years ago when I heard the story of Jenny's alleged betrayal of Paul, Linda probably felt that "Paul deserves so much better—he deserves me." Although Linda was probably an unwitting conspirator in providing a home that allowed Ella and Jessica to be taken from me and huge amounts of money to be squirreled away, I felt sorry for her, for I had a crystal ball into her future—a future that was cold, soulless, and black.

Our divorce was mediated at record pace, not even nine months after

CHAPTER 53

Paul left. To get the emotional abuse to stop and to get on with my life, I made huge financial tradeoffs. I left the mediation feeling broken, tears streaming down my face. Paul left the mediation downright giddy. As in many states, Utah assumes and requires joint legal custody of minor children in all but the most heinous situations. It also requires both parents to stay within 150 miles of each other "for the sake of the children." I offered that Paul reduce my already modest financial settlement (compared to what I was due legally) by one-third if he would allow me to relocate back East with Daniel, where I could be with my friends and family and have a much better chance of resurrecting my career. He refused, and Utah law backed him up.

Knowing that I had been conned into moving where Paul wanted to be for the rest of his life and that he could now bar me from returning to my family back East, the most likely place where I could craft a meaningful career, was more than I could take. If I could relocate at fifty-five years old, it felt "young" enough to start over. If I had to wait until Daniel was eighteen and a legal adult, I would be almost sixty when I would be free to move back East, it seemed much harder economically. Even worse, I would not be able to help my parents in their advanced age. They might both die while I was required by law to stay in Utah unless I was willing to leave Daniel behind with his father. I asked Paul if he would agree to send Daniel to private school somewhere, because he had become desperately unhappy in Utah due to our divorce. Paul refused.

In tears, I told my mother and father the next day that I would not be able to relocate back East for almost four years, because Paul would not give his consent. The only other option was to bring the case before a judge, but I would not likely win. My mother and I cried together on the phone. We agreed to call each other daily to help each other through this difficult time.

But the next day, I could not get in touch with my parents. I couldn't reach them the day after either. I called my brother. Unable to reach my parents, he called the State Police to see if they had been involved in an accident. We called local hospitals. Two days after my gut-wrenching divorce mediation, I discovered my mother was in the hospital fighting for her life. She had suffered a major heart attack hours after we spoke. The guilt was more than I could bear. Already on shaky ground, my faith in humanity, the future, and the world making any sense shattered. My will to keep going, to care enough about even seeing the next day dawn, slipped to nothing. But somehow I had to make myself care. My son needed me, my mother needed me, and my family back East needed me. If something happened to me, Daniel would have to live with his father. I could not let that happen. One breath at a time, I had to keep going.

Just Plain Mean

I flew back East to be with my family. My mother survived her heart attack but was altered permanently by the event—physically, emotionally, and cognitively. Due to my overwhelming guilt, profound sadness, and a complete loss of faith in people and in any belief in the triumph of good over evil or in justice and fairness, I was numb.

A few weeks later, back in Utah, I came in from an hour of cross-country skiing and made hot chocolate for Daniel and me. I still skied as often as I could, even though I neither experienced any joy nor appreciated the beauty of the mountains when I skied. I only did it because, intellectually, I knew it was better to ski than not to ski. Exercise and sunshine help ward off depression. Skiing was exercise. It was done outside. It was sunny today. Case closed. I needed to do anything I could to make each day less dark. It was that simple. As with all other facets of my life, I forced myself to go through the motions, to exist—doing what I needed to do, what I should do, but all of it was empty, artificial, joyless.

While sitting at the kitchen table and sipping hot chocolate, I checked my email. Daniel was next to me. An email from my lawyer read, *The judge signed the papers yesterday afternoon. You are now officially divorced. Congratulations!* I sighed. It was good to have it over. Paul's abusive behavior had been brutal. I hoped I had hit bottom and that I could start healing and rebuilding. Maybe Paul would be more reasonable now, and together we could co-parent our two children. (The fact I had this thought demonstrates that I still did not fully comprehend the consequences of Paul being a sociopath, because there was, and is, no possibility of constructive co-parenting with him.)

An email from Paul followed. With trepidation, I opened it. My eyes refocused several times to confirm that I was really seeing what was before me on the screen. My abdomen heaved. In front of me was a scanned copy of my journal from the first months following my separation from Paul. My most private thoughts, fears, and insecurities, my revelations about who and what Paul really was, my clarity about the sham of my marriage and about my wasted life with Paul were in those pages, those intensely personal pages. Even matters and strategies discussed with my lawyer were there. Paul must have gained access to my journal during one of his break-ins.

The pure, undiluted meanness of not only breaking into my home but

CHAPTER 54

also reading my journal, copying my journal, and—on the date our actual divorce—making sure I knew he had done so, drove a dagger through me. In just a few words, Paul's note reflected who this man was—who he is—evil, dark, and soulless.

Look what I have!

Strength left my body, and I crumpled to the floor, gasping for air. Primal sounds emanated from my body, though I was not aware of making them.

"Mom! Mom! What's wrong?" Daniel shouted, his face tight with concern. Daniel looked at my computer and then dropped to the floor and hugged me.

I drew him close, drinking in the love I felt for him, as if the inherent goodness of this child and my infinite affection for him could exorcise the demon to which we had both been exposed.

"I'm so sorry, Mom!" he said. "Dad's an ass. No, he's not an ass, he's evil."

Daniel was right. Sociopaths are the working definition of the devil—devoid of human compassion and willing to do anything no matter how heinous to experience pleasure, power, and the thrill of prevailing.

My cell phone buzzed, signaling an incoming text message.

"Do you want me to see if it's something important?" Daniel asked.

He looked at my phone. His eyes widened, and his face whitened.

"Daniel, what's wrong?"

"It's from Dad," he said. "I don't think you should see it right now."

"Please give me the phone," I said.

Daniel did not move.

"Daniel, give me the phone!"

Daniel handed me the phone. The text message from his father, my husband of almost twenty years, the father of my two children read, *FUCK you! You BITCH!*

Days later when Daniel told his father he had seen the text, Paul accused me of being an irresponsible parent because I clearly did not have needed security features activated on my phone that would have prevented Daniel from seeing a private communication that was clearly intended just for me. Sociopath math!

Paul's Way

Between his father's ongoing behavior, the loss of Ella when Daniel needed her most, his sister leaving to live with Paul and Linda, and my work to get our house staged and sold, Daniel's world had turned upside down. School provided a needed distraction and a semblance of normalcy, but it was not enough. Daniel became short tempered and found it increasingly hard to sleep, concentrate, and study.

Just two weeks after our divorce was official, Daniel came home from school shaking his head and laughing in an "I can't believe what just happened" way.

"Dad married her," Daniel said. "He didn't even invite me, Mom. Jessica was there, but he didn't even invite me to his own stupid wedding! Who does that?"

"I'm so sorry," I said. I had expected that Paul and Linda would marry quickly. However, it never occurred to me that they would do it in a way that would hurt Daniel so profoundly.

"Do you know how he told me?"

I shook my head.

"I had dinner there last night and spent the night," Daniel said. "He told me *one stupid minute* before he dropped me off at school this morning. 'By the way, Linda and I got married.' It was last week, after school. Jessica was there, but they didn't even tell me. He didn't even invite me!"

"I'm so sorry," I repeated.

"Who does that?" he yelled, tears rolling from his eyes. He stomped to his room, slammed the door, and did not come out for hours.

Money started flowing into Paul's life the moment the judge signed the divorce papers. New cars, vacations, expensive artwork. Paul made sure I knew about it, too. The tradeoff of money for my life would have been a good one if it had worked, but it didn't. Paul started dismantling our divorce settlement before the ink was dry. He even had the audacity to take me back to mediation just a few months after our divorce, accusing me of lying about my few premarital assets to which he said he was now entitled to 100 percent due to my deceit. I had not misrepresented them and, fortunately, I had the documentation to prove it, but Paul thought he could take advantage of some less than perfect wording in our divorce agreement.

CHAPTER 55

It was as if I had never been through mediation. My legal bills mounted higher than they had been before the judge signed our divorce decree. Paul used the low settlement to which I had agreed (in exchange for regaining my life and getting away from him) as a starting point to hack away even further at our divorce settlement.

One of Paul's "new" issues was that he had a greater tax liability than he had estimated (of course he did, because he claimed his income for the year approached zero), and he claimed that I owed him for half of the tax owed, because we had been married almost the entire year in question. The fact that the estimated taxes I paid as part of our settlement almost exceeded the income I enjoyed for the year and that, based on his self-reported nonexistent income, he should have received a tax refund after we were divorced, did not stop him from pressing the issue.

With that new piece of tax information in hand, I calculated Paul's income for the last year we were married, when he argued that his company was worthless and in such financial straits that he could not even pay himself. I had to check the calculation twice. A man claiming minimal income and a company devoid of value had made about $1,200,000, apparently in the few days remaining in the year after the judge made our divorce official! It was well beyond what he had ever made while we were married. Where had all the money come from? How long had it been there? Had he been squirreling away hundreds of thousands of dollars all along, preparing in advance for the divorce? I did not care. What is the price of regaining one's soul? Immeasurable. He could have his millions.

It's Not Over Until Paul Says It's Over

Three months after the divorce became official, Daniel was at one of his hated, required weekend visits with his father when he walked by Paul's home office. Apparently, Paul was on the phone telling a friend that Linda was more than four months pregnant. That meant she was pregnant before Paul and I had even finalized our speedy divorce. Daniel's pain from the news itself and the way he found out (by overhearing his father telling *someone else*) was incalculable, his respect for his father down to air.

Daniel started getting into arguments at school, almost coming to blows with classmates multiple times. Night after night, sleep proved elusive. He became reclusive, and his grades plummeted. Intermediate grade reports even showed D's. Paul thwarted my efforts to get Daniel help at every turn. No time off from required weekends with his father, no therapy, no antidepressants (of which I am only a believer as a last resort), no sleep-away summer camp for a struggling teenager. In Paul's self-serving, uncaring, sociopathic mind, nothing was wrong. In Paul's mind, the only problem was Daniel's lack of reverence for his father.

Daniel became so chronically angry and agitated that I tried to never leave him alone. I worried he would hurt himself. If things got any worse, I feared an attempted suicide. I had to get Daniel help. After I made an appointment with a psychologist, Paul cancelled Daniel's appointment and told the therapist I had no authority to take Daniel to see him. It wasn't true, but it scared off the therapist. Paul undermined efforts with a second therapist as well. Finally, I found a therapist who was not intimidated by Paul. Daniel liked him, and he started making immediate and significant progress. I was thrilled and hopeful.

Unable to stop the appointments, Paul called the therapist to insist that his relationship with Daniel be "off limits" during therapy. He also demanded that the therapist back him up in his view that Daniel should not be allowed to continue with karate. The therapist thought just the opposite. When Paul failed to bully the therapist into accepting his terms, he involved our lawyers in the debacle, costing me thousands. Meanwhile, Daniel was finding therapy helpful; he was starting to sleep better and feel less angry. He wanted to continue, because he was finding some resolution and peace about his relationship with his father.

CHAPTER 56

Our divorce decree specified Paul would pay for any therapy the kids needed. To try to undermine Daniel's therapy, Paul insisted Daniel did not need therapy and refused to pay. I paid for it. My son was hurting. He needed help. The cost was irrelevant. When that did not stop me, Paul took me to court to make me stop taking Daniel to the therapist. In addition, Paul trumped up charges and filed an official complaint against the therapist with the state licensing board. An investigation ensued.

The therapist was cleared easily and quickly, but Paul's actions, if successful, would have resulted in the therapist losing his livelihood and his license to practice therapy. The risk to the therapist who had been so helpful to Daniel (and, ironically, to Daniel's strained relationship with Paul) was now enormous. He called me and said that, regretfully, he could no longer work with Daniel. Having seen the monster Paul really is, he recommended that Daniel and I have no contact with Paul ever again. But that was impossible. Thanks to the laws of the state in which I was divorced, I did not have that choice. Quite the opposite, Paul was entitled to have my email, phone number, and address and to share in all decisions relevant to Daniel. To a sociopath, shared decision-making means having the power to blackmail, using the child as leverage. It was madness. I tried to find another therapist so Daniel could continue to deal with the considerable anger he still felt. In light of Paul's actions, no other therapist was willing to work with Daniel as long as he was a minor. He was sixteen at the time.

A month before Daniel's half-sister was born, and after a sleepless night at his dad's, Paul woke Daniel early and demanded he help Paul paint the baby's room. Daniel refused. Ruth, who was visiting at the time, called Daniel "lazy" for refusing to do so and splashed water in his face to get him out of bed. Daniel's conflicted feelings about his half-sister were irrelevant. That night, Linda made shrimp for dinner; despite knowing that Daniel is so allergic to shellfish that he could die if he ate even one piece of rice that it touched. Hysterical, Daniel called me to pick him up.

I raced to Paul's house and found Daniel crying on a bench outside his dad's front door. On top of everything else, because Daniel called me to come get him and swore at his father in a heated discussion about leaving, Paul confiscated all of Daniel's electronic games and hardware—Daniel's only escape, other than karate, from the toxic vortex that had become his world. When I drove down Paul's long driveway to get Daniel, Paul threatened me with trespassing charges. It was worth it. I had to rescue Daniel.

State laws required Daniel to see his father every other weekend and once during the week. Daniel refused to go back to his father's house or to see him. Paul called me, furious, demanding that Daniel come back the next weekend. My answer to Paul was simple. "It's up to Daniel. He says he doesn't want to see you." Paul cursed at me, threatening litigation for

CHAPTER 56

"parental alienation and custodial interference." Daniel's realization about who and what his father really was, as well as the verbally abusive treatment he had received from Paul, had Daniel flirting with serious depression. My child was teetering on a precarious emotional precipice. I needed to get him to safety, not set off a rockslide that might carry him over the edge. I did not care what it cost me; I was not going to be part of putting Daniel back in that poisonous household with Paul. Lawyers called lawyers. Paul took me to court. Legal bills mounted. Psychologists were called in, and when the first psychologist determined that Daniel's alienation from Paul was due exclusively to Paul's actions, Paul insisted the first psychologist was a quack and hired his own psychologist to offer a second opinion.

Every member of our family was interviewed multiple times, and the second psychologist reached the same conclusion—Daniel's anger with Paul and refusal to see him were due to Paul's decisions and actions. I had not alienated Daniel from Paul. Quite the contrary, I had exhibited considerable restraint under the circumstances. Like the previous psychologist, she recommended that Daniel be able to rebuild his relationship with Paul only if Daniel chose to do so and only on Daniel's timetable. Unable to get professionals to back up his view, Paul did the next best thing—he went after me. If Daniel would not see Paul, Jessica would not see me.

Paul and Linda gave Jessica an expensive car under the condition that she never use it to see me or to do anything to benefit me or Daniel. Paul sent me a bill for one-half the cost of the car, because, he argued, prior to moving to Utah *we* had promised Jessica a car when she got her driver's license. He even involved our lawyers in the absurd request. True to her word, Jessica ceased all communication with me, even on birthdays and holidays. This was particularly poignant, because in the preceding months our relationship had started to thaw. We had met several times for shopping or dinner. I was devastated to lose her all over again.

Night after night, I did not sleep, struggling to let go of wanting a relationship with my daughter and frightened that Paul was keeping me engaged in malicious and punitive legal actions designed to drain me financially and erode me further emotionally. This is what I had made a massive financial tradeoff to avoid, but I had not succeeded. The demands of defending myself legally approached that of a full-time job at times. Paul could not let go of wanting to hurt, of needing to get an almost daily fix of playing Whack-A-Mole with me. He is a sociopath—that is what they do. They are nonpeople, vampires, evil, void, dark. That is their true nature; anything else is just disguise and pretense. Paul was a millionaire now. I was unemployed. Hardly a fair fight, but that was the point. That had always been the point.

It was beyond my control. Finally accepting that, and forgiving myself for the mess that, despite my best intentions, my life had become, brought me a peace that had eluded me previously. Yes, I might end up poor, but I would survive. Yes, I might not have a relationship with my daughter for years, if ever. I could not control that. I had to accept it. Wanting something that would be thwarted while she lived with her dad and chose to be financially dependent on him could only bring me pain, so I let go.

There was some comfort when the psychologist asked for a final conference with just me. We talked about Jessica and Daniel and how best to help them and if I was getting the support and help I needed. Before I left, the psychologist assured me that he had talked to Jessica at length about me. "You two have a strong and loving foundation," he said. "In time she'll come back to you if you stay open and if you do your best to *never* say anything negative about her father. I know you've been very restrained, but you haven't been perfect. She has to come to her own conclusions about her dad and about you. She made it clear that you never threw her out of your house and you never abandoned her, as Paul has been telling people and as he told me. Give it time."

Tears slipped from my eyes as I listened. I refused to allow myself to hope the psychologist was right, for hope would keep the issue of wanting a relationship with my daughter alive, and keeping the issue alive would mean keeping the pain alive. I simply had to disengage—completely. If Jessica came back to me, I would be welcoming and loving. If not … well, I cannot control that. I am not a sociopath. I will not try to control my daughter, because the only relationship worth having with her is one that both of us choose freely.

No Fairy Tale Ending—Yet

I do not want to disappoint, but there is no fairy tale ending, not yet anyway. That is why my story and similar cautionary tales are so important and why it is critical not to dismiss me as inherently weak, naive or "not like you." My story could be your story or the story of someone you love. Don't let it be. There is no easy fix once your life has been entwined with evil, especially when children are involved. Children give sociopaths a conduit of contact and control over the other parent, one that is often codified in law and supported by the courts. Although hard to believe until you live it, too many family courts view children as mere possessions that must be divided evenly between parents. When one parent is a sociopath, the resulting custody arrangement can be caustic for both the children and the nonsociopathic parent.

Even when we hear about horrible custody battles and situations, it does not register that such a situation may be lurking in our future. Maybe part of the reason we do not worry is that we believe what we have been told: "There are always two sides to every story," "It takes two to tango," "Both sides share the blame." If that is true, and if we are reasonable people, then we will never be in a situation like this because of our inherent fairness and sensibleness. Nice story, but it is not true—not if the other person involved is a sociopath.

You will be accused of fueling the fire and told that you should just compromise, but agreeing to compromise when you have already compromised repeatedly is just agreeing to be exploited (especially when the other party refuses to compromise at all), and agreeing to be exploited only encourages more exploitation from the sociopath—no thanks! Not anymore, I've had enough! The reason sensible, responsible actions fuel the fire is because the sociopath keeps resetting it.

I get it now. I have made my peace with the effect Paul had (and has) on my life. I do not get a do over. Instead, I have inched forward one small step at a time. Working with a wonderful therapist who understands abusive relationships has helped immensely, as has keeping my focus on Daniel and fighting for him as a mother bear fights for her cub. Equally important is that a new spark was ignited in that tin of dying embers that was my battered soul. I have found new purpose by understanding what happened to

CHAPTER 57

me and why and then sharing my story to make sure it does not happen to you or someone you love.

It has been over two years since I finished the first draft of this memoir. Symptoms of post-traumatic stress—intrusive thoughts and memories, sleeplessness, heightened alertness, feelings of despair, lacking interest in things I once enjoyed—are waning. I am still involved in expensive litigation with Paul, because he has not yet transferred all of the assets I was awarded in our divorce. He is a sociopath. No promise made or contract signed means anything to him. It is just the starting point for further exploitation.

Daniel sees his father rarely. Paul continues to use his legal rights as Daniel's father to harass and extort (e.g., refusing to allow Daniel to attend karate practice on weekends Daniel is supposed to be with Paul unless I pay Paul off). I will not be Paul's victim anymore—I played that role long enough. I see Paul's manipulation now in every word he uses, in every fact he includes or omits. I see it so clearly that it is hard to believe others do not. But I didn't either, not for almost twenty years.

As my understanding has deepened and as my emotional fortitude has returned, I have become much more difficult prey, often derailing and sidestepping Paul's manipulation. I am not as much fun to pick on anymore. While still outgunned financially, I have the truth on my side, and I am willing to draw a line in the sand and stand my ground. The thought of being taken to court no longer terrifies me. With Paul, I pick between three strategies depending on the situation:

Strategy 1—The only way to win is not to play (in other words, no contact if at all possible, don't engage, never engage emotionally). When contact is required, just stick to the facts.

Strategy 2—I won't negotiate with terrorists.

Strategy 3—Let consequences flow to their rightful source. (e.g., If Paul wants to stop Daniel from doing karate every other weekend, go for it. Life will go on without karate, and Daniel can decide for himself how he feels about his father's actions.)

My mother never fully recovered from her heart attack and passed away about eighteen months later. I was with her the week she died. Daniel came to her memorial service with me. To my surprise, Jessica came as well. Since then, Jessica and I have begun rebuilding a relationship—one that is thin but positive. She attended college where Paul pressured her into going. She never liked it there, and after a year she transferred to a place of her own choosing. Paul was hardly supportive. Jessica turned to me for help with the logistics and to review her application. I felt like her mother for the first time in a very long time—I felt honored.

Daniel sleeps through the night now and has rebounded academically,

CHAPTER 57

ranking among the top students in his class. We never got Ella back, but Daniel volunteers at a local dog shelter, often bringing home dogs to foster while they await permanent adoption. The dogs adore him, and the feeling is mutual. Daniel hopes to attend college someplace far away from his father. He wants to be a psychologist.

I am still in Utah. Although I've had many offers, I don't date. I am not ready. Soon, Daniel turns eighteen and will be a legal adult. Then I will be free to move. The mountains of Vermont beckon. It is time to go home. There I can provide my aging father with needed support, reinvent my life, and finally start the business I have been working toward over the past year. After all, I do have an MBA from Yale.

Final Thoughts

Some women write to and fall in love with incarcerated serial killers, but most of us would never knowingly marry a sociopath. However, many wonderful, caring, intelligent, and confident women do. They don't realize that the Prince Charming who romanced them is a brilliant manipulator and is secretly recruiting them into a private cult, from which escape will be elusive at best. It happens far more often than we imagine, because sociopaths are far more common and far better disguised than we think.

Don't let a sociopath bring the destructive force of a tsunami into your life or into the life of someone you love. The best way out of a relationship with a sociopath is to never fall into one, or at least not to fall in too deeply. And the best way to never fall in is to recognize that sociopaths exist, camouflaged exquisitely as our soul mates, mentors, and best friends. Yet, there are imperfections in their disguises that, like water retreating from a beach before a tsunami, are warning signs of impending doom. Accept that these soulless manipulators exist and learn how to catch moments when their disguises falter and their true self is revealed. If you miss the subtle signs, you could easily have your own cautionary tale about a marriage to the devil and an unending battle for your soul and that of your children.

If you notice any parallels between my story and your life or the life of someone you love, I hope you will keep a journal or urge the other person to do so, get help from a professional who is knowledgeable about abusive relationships, and then plan an escape. For escape you must!

What I Found Most Helpful

Please keep in mind that I am not a doctor, lawyer, psychologist, or a licensed therapist. What follows are a few things I found helpful in my journey.

THERAPISTS AND LAWYERS

Find a therapist and a lawyer (if relevant) who are experts on abusive relationships and who have a track record of helping abuse survivors understand and leave these toxic partnerships and take the steps necessary to craft a new life. Sometimes these situations are referred to as "high-conflict" divorces. Also, keep in mind that "sociopath" is not a medical term or an official diagnosis. Others refer to such individuals as psychopaths, suffering from narcissistic personality disorder or antisocial personality disorder, high-conflict individuals, personality disordered, abusers, and, of course, "jerks."

JOURNALING

I started keeping a journal many months before Paul and I separated and continued to do so throughout our separation and in the months after we divorced. I highly recommend doing this. (Just make sure you keep it secure!) Journaling kept me grounded in reality (not Paul's distorted version of it), made it harder for him to gaslight me, and allowed my brain to make long-overdue connections. These new connections heralded insights that, brick by brick, helped build a new foundation for my life—a foundation based on the truth no matter how brutal that truth was.

SEEK OUT THOSE WHO "GET IT"

Often, I find that you get support from the most unlikely sources, while some people who you think will help you (such as family members and friends) fail miserably when called upon. Stop looking for support where there is none, or, even worse, where there is subtle (or not so subtle) blame, criticism, and judgment. There are many people and even online communities who have gone through similar experiences and who will be empathetic and helpful. Find those who resonate with you.

AVOID NEW IMPORTANT RELATIONSHIPS UNTIL YOU ARE STRONG

If a sociopath has targeted you, you may have characteristics such as empathy, persistence, and flexibility that sociopaths find particularly appealing. If you are recovering from a relationship with a sociopath, your emotional vulnerability may make you even more attractive to other sociopaths. Recovering from a relationship with a sociopath is like recovering from a general anesthetic—avoid all important personal and financial decisions until the impact has worn off completely.

EXPECT PAIN, BUT HAVE FAITH IT WILL LESSEN AND ULTIMATELY PASS

The pain of having your worldview, your family, and your future security explode is searing and seemingly unrelenting. You may experience a profound sense of betrayal, despair, grief, and self-blame. Get the professional and personal support you need. Don't expect to brush this experience under the rug and get on with your life in a nanosecond. I wish I had not married Paul and been forced to learn a hard lesson about sociopaths. I wish I did not experience day after day of immobilizing despair. But I don't get a do over. By accepting the pain, getting the support I needed, and coming to understand what happened, the pain finally subsided. I emerged scarred but wiser—with a more complete understanding of human nature, more insight into myself, a clearer sense of my boundaries, and a new sense of purpose I never could have anticipated.

QUESTIONS I WISH I HAD ASKED MYSELF (or been encouraged to ask)

1. If Paul treated me *before* we were married like he did *after* we were married, would I have continued to date him? Would I have married him? Would I have wanted to have children with him? (Answers: No! No! No!)

2. If a friend's husband/boyfriend treated her like Paul treated me, what would I think? (Answer: I would he horrified!)

3. What does a loving relationship really look like? Does my relationship resemble that image? What *meaningful* tradeoffs has Paul ever made for me? (Answers: Relationships are complicated and highly individual, but minimally, there should be no fear, and there should be mutual respect and honesty. As time progressed, I grew afraid of Paul, and he treated me with contempt. I cannot think of one meaningful tradeoff Paul ever made for me—not one.)

4. Do I like who I am in this relationship? (Answer: Not at all. After marrying Paul, I had a hard time making decisions, lacked confidence, and doubted myself and my recollections. I also felt I was walking on eggshells constantly, short-tempered, unattractive, incompetent, and trivialized. I felt

profoundly unhappy, weak, and worthless. This was *not* how I felt about myself prior to being married to Paul.)

5. Since children model what they see, do I want my children to have the same type of marriage I have with Paul? (Answer: No!)
6. What evidence do I have that this will ever change? If this is not going to change, is this the life I want? (Answers: None and no!)
7. Post Traumatic Stress (PTS) symptoms result primarily from two situations: war/physical violence and abusive relationships. How many PTS symptoms do I have and how did I get them? (Answer: Almost all of them! They resulted from being in an emotionally abusive relationship.)

Additional Resources

There are many informative and helpful books and websites about sociopaths and recovering from relationships with them. Below are some books I found particularly helpful. They are listed in alphabetical order according to title.

The Betrayal Bond: Breaking Free of Exploitive Relationships by Patrick Carnes, PhD

But He'll Change: End the Thinking That Keeps You in an Abusive Relationship by Joanna V. Hunter

Character Disturbance—The Phenomenon of Our Age by Dr. George Simon

Divorcing a Narcissist: Advice from the Battlefield by Tina Swithin

The Gift of Fear and Other Survival Signals That Protect Us From Violence by Gavin de Becker

In Sheep's Clothing: Understanding and Dealing with Manipulative People by Dr. George Simon

Liespotting: Proven Techniques to Detect Deception by Pamela Meyer

Life Code—The New Rules for Winning in The Real World by Dr. Phil McGraw

Psychopaths and Love by A.B. Admin

Psychopath Free: Recovering from Emotionally Abusive Relationships with Narcissists, Sociopaths, & Other Toxic People by Peace

Red Flags Of Love Fraud: 10 Signs You're Dating a Sociopath by Donna Andersen

Snakes in Suits: When Psychopaths Go to Work by Paul Babiak and Robert D. Hare

The Sociopath Next Door by Dr. Martha Stout

Trauma and Recovery: The Aftermath of Violence—From Domestic Abuse to Political Terror by Judith Herman, M.D.

The Verbally Abusive Relationship: How to Recognize It and How to Respond by Patricia Evans

Why Does He Do That? Inside the Minds of Angry and Controlling Men by Lundy Bancroft

Without Conscience: The Disturbing World of Psychopaths Among Us by Robert D. Hare, PhD

http://aftermath-surviving-psychopathy.org
www.lovefraud.com
www.onemomsbattle.com
www.psychopathfree.com
www.psychopathsandlove.com

ENDNOTES

1 Martha Stout, *The Sociopath Next Door*. New York, NY: Three Rivers Press, 2006.

2 Robert D. Hare, *Without Conscience: The Disturbing World of Psychopaths Among Us*. New York, NY: The Guilford Press, 1999.

3 George K. Simon, *Character Disturbance: The Phenomenon of Our Age*. Marion, MI: Parkhurst Brothers, Inc. Publishers, 2011.

4 Pathological lying is one of twenty behaviors on the now famous Hare PCL-R Checklist for assessing psychopaths.

5 Charles F. Bond, Jr. and Bella M. DePaulo, "Accuracy of deception judgments," *Personality and Social Psychology Review*, 10 (2006): 214-234.

6 Robert Hare, *Psychopathy: Theory and Research*. New York: Wiley, 1970. Gordon Trasler. "Relations between psychopathy and persistent criminality," in R.D. Hare & D. Schalling (eds.) *Psychopathic Behavior: Approaches to Research*. Chichester, England: Wiley, 1978.

7 An inflated, grandiose opinion of oneself is one of twenty behaviors on the now famous Hare PCL-R Checklist for assessing psychopaths.

8 Charm is one of twenty behaviors on the now famous Hare PCL-R Checklist for assessing psychopaths.

9 Jeff Bercovici, "Why (Some) Psychopaths Make Great CEOs," www.forbes.com/sites/jeffbercovici/2011/06/14.

10 Martha Stout, *The Sociopath Next Door*. New York, NY: Three Rivers Press, 2006.

11 Liane J. Leedom, "New Hope for the Children of Sociopaths," http://www.lovefraud.com/blog/2007/05/18/new-hope-for-the-children-of-sociopaths.

12 Donna Andersen, *Red Flags of Love Fraud: 10 Signs You're Dating a Sociopath*. Egg Harbor Township, NJ: Anderly Publishing, 2012.

13 Martha Stout, *The Sociopath Next Door*. New York, NY: Three Rivers Press, 2006.

14 Paul Babiak and Robert D. Hare, *Snakes In Suits: When Psychopaths Go to Work*. New York, NY: HarperCollins, 2006.

15 Donna Andersen, *Red Flags of Love Fraud: 10 Signs You're Dating a*

Sociopath. Egg Harbor Township, NJ: Anderly Publishing, 2012.

16 Tina Swithin, *Divorcing a Narcissist: Advice From the Battlefield*. CreateSpace, 2014.

17 Tina Swithin, *Divorcing a Narcissist: One Mom's Battle*. CreateSpace, 2012.

18 Gavin de Becker, *The Gift of Fear and Other Survival Signals That Protect Us From Violence*. New York, NY: Dell, 1999.

19 Donna Andersen, *Red Flags of Love Fraud: 10 Signs You're Dating a Sociopath*. Egg Harbor Township, NJ: Anderly Publishing, 2012.

20 Martha Stout, *The Sociopath Next Door*. New York, NY: Three Rivers Press, 2006.

21 Andreas Bartels and Semir Zeki, "The neural correlates of maternal and romantic love," *NeuroImage* 21 (2004): 1155– 1166.

22 Anthony Damásio, *Descartes' Error. Emotion, Reason, and the Human Brain*. New York: Penguin Books, 2005.

23 A review of research on the topic can be found in: Steven F. Maier and Martin E. Seligman, "Learned helplessness: Theory and evidence, *Journal of Experimental Psychology*: General, Vol 105(1), Mar 1976, 3-46.

24 Donna Andersen, *Red Flags of Love Fraud: 10 Signs You're Dating a Sociopath*. Egg Harbor Township, NJ: Anderly Publishing, 2012.

25 www.innocenceproject.org/causes-wrongful-conviction/eyewitness-misidentification.

26 Christopher Chabris and Daniel Simons, *The Invisible Gorilla: And Other Ways Our Intuitions Deceive Us*. New York, NY: Crown Publishers, 2010.

27 Gavin de Becker, *The Gift of Fear: Survival Signals That Protect Us From Violence*. New York, NY: Dell, 1999.

28 Jeff Thompson, "Is Nonverbal Communication a Numbers Game? Is Body Language Really Over 90% of How We Communicate?" www.psychologytoday.com/blog/beyond-words/201109.

29 An overview of relevant studies is covered in Dr. Stout's book *The Sociopath Next Door*. New York, NY: Three Rivers Press, 2005.

30 These qualities of psychopaths/sociopaths are discussed at length in Dr. Hare's book *Without Conscience: The Disturbing World of Psychopaths Among Us*. New York, NY: The Guilford Press, 1999.

31 psychopathyandlies.blogspot.com.

32 Gavin de Becker, *The Gift of Fear and Other Survival Signals That Protect Us From Violence*. New York, NY: Dell, 1999.

33 Robert D. Hare, *Without Conscience: The Disturbing World of Psychopaths Among Us*. New York, NY: The Guilford Press, 1999.

34 Tina Swithin, *Divorcing a Narcissist: Advice from the Battlefield*. Create Space, 2014.

35 Weak behavioral controls are one of twenty behaviors on the now famous Hare PCL-R Checklist for assessing psychopaths.

36 Coyle, Daniel, *The Talent Code: Greatness Isn't Born. It's Grown. Here's How*. New York, NY: Random House, 2009.

37 Asch, S., "Effects of Group Pressure on the Modification and Distortion," in *Readings in Social Psychology*, (Eds.) E. E. Maccoby, T. M. Newcomb, & E. L. Hartley, New York: Holt, Rinehart, & Winston, 1958.

38 Milgram, Stanley, "Behavioral Study of Obedience," *Journal of Abnormal and Social Psychology* 67 (4) (1963): 371-378.

39 Donna Andersen, *Red Flags of Love Fraud: 10 Signs You're Dating a Sociopath*. Egg Harbor Township, NJ: Anderly Publishing, 2012.

40 Patrick J. Carnes, *The Betrayal Bond—Breaking Free of Exploitive Relationships*. Deerfield Beach, FL: Health Communications, Inc., 1997.

41 Jonah Lehrer, *How We Decide*. New York, NY, Houghton Mifflin Harcourt, 2009.

42 http://180rule.com/the-gray-rock-method-of-dealing-with-psychopaths.

43 S.M. Louth, S. Williamson, M. Alpert, E.R. Pouget, and R.D. Hare, "Acoustic distinctions in the speech of male psychopaths," *Journal of Psycholinguistic Research* 27 (3) (1998): 375-384.

Printed in Great Britain
by Amazon